Andrew Fleming Hutchison

The Lake of Menteith

It's Islands and Vicinity

Andrew Fleming Hutchison

The Lake of Menteith
It's Islands and Vicinity

ISBN/EAN: 9783744717472

Printed in Europe, USA, Canada, Australia, Japan

Cover: Foto ©ninafisch / pixelio.de

More available books at **www.hansebooks.com**

The Lake of Menteith:
ITS ISLANDS AND VICINITY

WITH HISTORICAL ACCOUNTS OF

The Priory of Inchmahome

AND

THE EARLDOM OF MENTEITH

BY

A. F. HUTCHISON, M.A.

Illustrated with Pen and Ink Drawings
by Walter Bain.

STIRLING:
ENEAS MACKAY, 43 MURRAY PLACE.
MDCCCXCIX.

The Sentinel Press, Stirling.

LIST OF SUBSCRIBERS.

ADAMS, Wm., West Kilbride.
AITKEN, Mrs. Isabella T., Philadelphia.
ALEXANDER, W., Stirling.
ALLAN, John, Stirling.
ANDERSON, David S. B., Dunfermline.
ANDERSON, J., M.A., Callander.
ANDERSON, William, New Kilpatrick.
ANDREW, Dr., Doune.
ANGUS, Miss, Helensburgh.
ANGUS, Robert, Old Cumnock, Ayrshire.
ARNOT, James, M.A., Edinburgh.
ASHER & Co., London.

BALD, W., Edinburgh.
BALLINGALL, D., Blair Drummond.
BARCLAY-ALLARDICE, Robert, F.S.A.(Scot.), Cornwall.
BARTY, Dr., Dunblane.
BAIN, James, Toronto.
BAIRD, H., Auchenbowie.
BAXENDINE, A., Edinburgh.
BERRY, J., jun., Buchlyvie.
BERRY, James Garrow, Cambus.
BLACK & JOHNSTON, Brechin.
BLAIR, A. Aikman, Edinburgh.
BLAIR, Robert, Trossachs Hotel.
BOWDITCH, Chas., Massachusetts, U.S.A.
BRIDGES, James, Perth.
BRISBANE, Thos., Stirling.
BROWN, James, Stirling.
BROWN, J. A. Harvie, Dunipace.
BROWN, William, Edinburgh.
BRUCE, James, Edinburgh.

List of Subscribers.

BRYCE, William, Edinburgh.
BRYCE & MURRAY, Glasgow.
BRYDEN, R. A., Glasgow.
BUCHANAN, A., Polmont.
BUCHANAN, J. Hamilton, Edinburgh.
BURDEN, John, New York.

CAMERON, Miss, Stirling.
CAMERON, A. C., LL.D., Paisley.
CAMPBELL, J. W., Stirling.
CAMPBELL, Bailie Finlay, Helensburgh.
CAMPBELL, Jas. Alex., Brechin.
CAMPBELL, Mrs., Alexandria.
CHERRY, Miss, Craigs.
CHRISTIE, Geo., Stirling.
CHRISTIE, James, Glasgow.
CHRISTIE, Robert H., Dunblane.
CHRYSTAL, David, Stirling.
CLARK, James, Doune.
COMBE, Miss Jessie, Glasgow.
COOK, W. B., Stirling.
CORNISH, J. E., Manchester.
COWAN, Donald, Stirling.
CRABBIE, Geo., Port of Menteith.
CURROR, John G., Stirling.

DALRYMPLE-DUNCAN, J., Stirling.
DICKSON, Rev. J. G., Manse, Kippen.
DICKSON, P. T., Aberfoyle.
DOUGHTY, Alex., Aberfoyle.
DOUGLAS, Miss, Callander.
DOUGLAS & FOULIS, Edinburgh.
DOWGRAY, John, Lochgelly, Fifeshire.
DRYSDALE, W., Stirling.
DRYSDALE, Ex-Provost, Bridge of Allan.
DUN, Alexander, Stirling.
DUNCAN, Archibald, Newhouse.

EASTON, Walter, Carronhall.
ELLIOT, Andrew, Edinburgh.
ERSKINE, H. D., of Cardross.

List of Subscribers.

FERGUSON, Daniel, Stirling.
FERGUSON, Councillor Hugh, Stirling.
FERGUSON, Miss, Stirling.
FERGUSON, Rev. John, Aberdalgie.
FERGUSON, John, Glasgow.
FERGUSSON, Rev. R. Menzies, Bridge of Allan.
FERRIES, Rev. George, D.D., Manse of Cluny, Aberdeenshire.
FLEMING, Sir Sandford, K.C.M.G., Ottawa, Canada.
FLEMING, D. Hay, LL.D., St. Andrews.
FOLKARD, H. T., F.S.A., Wigan.
FORRESTER, Robert, Glasgow.
FORSYTH, George, Stirling.
FOWLER, Major, Stirling.
FOX, Chas. Henry, M.D., Edinburgh.

GALBRAITH, T. L., Stirling.
GIBSON, James A., Stirling.
GILLANDERS, John, Denny.
GORDON, Alex., Stirling.
GRAHAM, James L., Stirling.
GRAHAM, John, Inverness.
GRANT, Rev. A. T., Leven.
GRANT, David, M.A., M.D., Melbourne.
GRANT, John, Edinburgh.
GRAY, James, Aberfeldy.
GRAY, William, Doune.
GRAY, Geo., Glasgow.
GRAY-BUCHANAN, A. W., Polmont.

HAMILTON, R., Port of Menteith.
HARVEY, Wm., Stirling.
HENDERSON, George., Stirling.
HENDERSON, Hugh, Stirling.
HENDERSON, Rev. W. T., New Kilpatrick, Glasgow.
HOLMES, W. & R., Glasgow.
HOWART, J. W., Stirling.
HUNTER, James, Kippen.
HUTCHESON, A., F.S.A., Broughty Ferry.

INGE, Rev. John, Alford.

List of Subscribers.

JAMIESON, John, Stirling.
JAMIESON, John, Portobello.
JENKINS, Alexander, Stirling.
JENKINS, John, Stirling.
JOHNSTON, T. W. R., Stirling.
JOHNSTON, Rev. J. J., Port of Menteith.
JOHNSTONE, David, Edinburgh.
JOYNSON, E. Walter, Aberfoyle.

KIDSTON, R., F.G.S., Stirling.
KIDSTON, Adrian M. M. G., Helensburgh.
KING, Councillor, Stirling.

LAING, Alexander, Edinburgh.
LANDER, T. E., Arngomery.
LAWRIE, R. H., Edinburgh.
LAWSON, Wm., Castleview, Stirling.
LEITCH, J. M., London.
LEE, Alex. H., Edinburgh.
LEVY, Andrew, Edinburgh.
LINDSAY, D., Stirling.
LINKLATER, Miss, Callander.
LIPPE, Robert, LL.D., Aberdeen.
LITTLE, Robt, Kirkcaldy.
LOVE, James, Falkirk.
Low, Walter, Ballendrick, Perthshire.
LOWSON, Geo., M.A., B.Sc., Stirling.
LUMSDEN, James, Alexandria.

MACALPINE, John, Ruskie.
MACFARLANE, Charles, East Blackburn.
MACGREGOR, Rev. A. O., Denny.
MACGREGOR, John, Port of Menteith.
MACKEITH, Alex., Glasgow.
MACLAY, James, Glasgow.
MACLEOD, M. C., Dundee.
MACLEOD, N., Edinburgh.
MACADAM, W. N., Edinburgh.
MACADAM, Jas. H., F.S.A. (Scot.), London.
MACDONALD, Dr. Angus, Edinburgh.

List of Subscribers.

MACFARLANE, Bailie, Stirling.
MACKAY, D., Inverness.
MACKAY W., Inverness.
MACKAY, John, Glasgow.
MACKAY, W. H., Port Salisbury, South Africa.
MACKAY, James, North Dakota, U.S.A.
MACKAY, John, Cardross.
MACKEITH, J. Thornton, Ruskie.
MACKENZIE, Mrs., Dunblane.
MACKENZIE, James, Glasgow.
MACKIE, James F., Stirling.
MACKINLAY, R. A., Rothesay.
MACKINTOSH, C. Fraser, LL.D., Inverness.
MACLACHLAN, Archibald, Stirling.
MACLEHOSE, James, & Sons, Glasgow.
MACMILLAN, John, Edinburgh.
MACNAUGHTON, Rev. Geo. D., B.D., Braco.
MACNIVEN & WALLACE, Edinburgh.
MACPHERSON, James, Stirling.
MAILER, James, Stirling.
MAILER, Wm., Stirling.
MAIR, James S., Aberfoyle.
MARTIN, F. J., Edinburgh.
MAXWELL, Mrs., Doune.
MAY, George, Fintry.
MELVEN, William, Glasgow.
MELVILLE, MULLEN, & SLADE, London.
MENZIES, John, & Co., Edinburgh and Glasgow.
MENZIES, Robert, Stirling.
MILLER, John, Stirling.
MILLER, John, Dunedin.
MILLER, Wm., Pollokshields.
MINNOCH, W. H., Stirling.
MITCHELL, Rev. J. Gordon, Norrieston Manse.
MONTEATH, J. Kippen.
MOORE, Mrs. Alex., Port of Menteith.
MOORHOUSE, J. Ernest, M.D., Stirling.
MORRIS, David B., Stirling.
MORRISON, Miss, Stirling.
MORRISON, John, Aberdeen.

List of Subscribers.

MOYES, Alex., Stirling.
MUNRO, John, Stirling.
MURPHY, A. MacLean, Stirling.
MURRAY, J. G., Stirling.
MURRIE, Stewart, Stirling.
M'DONALD, A. B., M. Inst. C.E., Glasgow.
M'GEACHY & Co., Glasgow.
M'LELLAN, Andrew, M.A., Liverpool.

NEWARK LIBRARY, per G. E. Stechert, London.
NIGHTINGALE, Miss, London.

OLIPHANT, T. L. Kington, Auchterarder.
ORMOND, Rev. D. D., F.S.A. (Scot.), Stirling.

PATERSON, Alex., Stirling.
PATERSON, James R., Dalmuir.
PATERSON, Rev. G. W., Aberfoyle.
PATERSON, D., Thornhill, Dumfriesshire.
PLATT, L. J., Stirling.
PULLAR, L., Bridge of Allan.

RAMSEY, Robert, Glasgow.
RETTIE, R. G., Kirkcaldy.
RICHARDSON, J. B., Pitgorno.
RICHARDSON, James, Glasgow.
ROBERTSON, Dr., Stirling.
ROBERTSON, Dr., Bannockburn.
ROBERTSON, W. J., Manchester.
ROBERTSON, R., Glasgow.
ROBERTSON, James, Menstrie.
ROBERTSON, James, Bonnybridge.
RODGERS, W. M., Stirling.
RONALD, Ex-Bailie, Stirling.
RONALD, James E., Stirling.
RONALD, Thos., Bannockburn.
ROSS, David, M.A., B.Sc, LL.D. Glasgow.

SALMOND, Professor S. D. F., Aberdeen.
SAMUEL, John Smith, Glasgow.
SANDEMAN, Ridley, Stirling.

List of Subscribers.

SCHILLING, Julius F., Stirling.
SCONCE, Colonel, Edinburgh.
SCOTT, Rev. W., Stirling.
SCOTT, Robert, Montrose.
SCOTT, Alexander, Stirling.
SEMPILL, Chief-Constable, Newhouse.
SHIRRA, Wm. L., Stirling.
SLEE, Miss, London.
SMALL, J. W., Stirling.
SMITH, James Kemp, Stirling.
SMITH, J. & Sons, Glasgow.
SMITH, Rev. Frederick, Dunblane.
SMITH, Robert, Dundee.
SORLEY, Councillor Robert, Glasgow.
SOTHERAN, Henry, & Co., London.
STARK, Robert, Kirkcaldy.
STEVEN, John, Glasgow.
STEVENS, B. F., Trafalgar Square, London.
STEVENSON, Rev. R., M.A., Gargunnock.
STEVENSON, Robert, Kilwinning.
STEWART, Walter, Edinburgh.
STIRLING PUBLIC LIBRARY, per Robt. Whyte, Secy.
STIRLING, C. C. Graham, Campsie Glen.
STIRLING, J., Port of Menteith.
STIRLING HIGH SCHOOL LIBRARY, per Geo. Young, Secy.
SUMNER, E. R., Aberfoyle.
SWORD, James, Stirling.
SYMON, J. H., Q.C., Adelaide.

TENNENT, Robert, Dunipace.
THE MITCHELL LIBRARY, per F. T. Barrett, Glasgow.
THIN, James, Edinburgh.
THOMSON, Miss E., Denny.
THOMSON, Arthur H., Stenhousemuir.
THOMSON, Alex., Edinburgh.
TODD, Charles H., Aberdeen.
TOWNS, W., East Plean.

WALKER, D. W., S.S.C., Edinburgh.
WATT, John, M.A., Aberdeen.

List of Subscribers.

WEIR, Alexander M., Stirling.
WILLIAMS, Rev. G., Thornhill.
WILSON, Colonel, Bannockburn House.
WILSON, Edward L., Bannockburn.
WILSON, James, Birmingham.
WOOD, Alexander, Saltcoats.
WORDIE, Peter, Lenzie.
WORDIE, John, Glasgow.
WYLIE, Bailie, Stirling.

YELLOWLEES, Rev. John, Larbert.
YOUNG, D., Doune.
YOUNGER, A., Cambus.

PREFACE.

THE beautiful Lake of Menteith, with the picturesque country that surrounds it, and the monastic and baronial ruins on its Islands, are familiar enough to the tourist and the visitor. The interesting histories connected with these places are not, however, so well known, as there is no easily accessible work in which they can be read with anything like fulness and accuracy. The materials lie scattered in Public Records and private charter chests, or are contained in rare or privately-printed books. To bring these materials together in something like a connected narrative, and generally to supply authentic information—so far as it is at present attainable—regarding the Hills and the Lake of Menteith, the Priory of Inchmahome, and the Castle of Inchtalla, is the aim of this volume.

Two investigators of the present century have done much to elucidate the history of the Priory and of the Earldom of Menteith; but it can hardly be said that the work of either is available to the general reader. The Rev. W. M'Gregor Stirling's "Notes on Inchmahome"—published in 1812—has long been out of print, and it is now difficult to procure a copy; while the late Sir William Fraser's elaborate "Red Book of Menteith" was a privately-printed work, and has thus never been readily accessible.

Stirling has the credit of being the first to go beyond the hazy local traditions, and to collect materials for a history of the Priory obtained from the MSS. collections at Gartmore and other places in the neighbourhood. These materials, however, as they appear in his "Notes on Inchmahome," though authentic, are not very abundant.

But he continued his investigations after the publication of his book, and noted the results of these researches in manuscript additions, written on the margins of his own copy of his work. That copy, with the Manuscript Notes, is now in possession of H. D. Erskine, Esq. of Cardross, to whose courtesy the writer has been indebted for an opportunity of examining it. Whatever was new in these Notes will therefore be found embodied in the present narrative. The writer desires also to acknowledge his obligation to Mr. Erskine for giving access to the index and abstracts of the Cardross Charters—of the greatest value for a history of the Priory—as well as for his kind and valued aid in the examination of those ruins in which he takes so deep an interest.

Sir William Fraser's exhaustive examination of the documents in the charter chests of Buchanan, Gartmore, &c., relating to the Earldom of Mentcith, has made his "Red Book," in which the results of that examination are recorded, a storehouse of materials for all future investigators of that subject. Ample use has, in these pages, been made of Fraser's researches, as well as of the Minutes of Evidence in the Airth Peerage Cases, where charters and other documents will be found printed with admirable accuracy. The unsettled question of the Mentcith succession has been purposely avoided.

Sir William also added largely to the previously known history of the Priory. He printed in the "Red Book" a considerable number of charters relating to its affairs. Such of these charters as do not appear elsewhere, and to the originals of which access could not be had, have been accepted as he gives them; but all the other authorities to which he refers have been re-examined, and new ones have been added. In this way, it has been found possible to correct a few inaccuracies, while some additional facts have been brought to light.

A list of works that have been cited as authorities for statements made in this book, and of the various sources, printed and manuscript,

Preface.

from which information has been drawn, is appended. The most fruitful of the sources of new information have been the Chartularies of the Religious Houses of Scotland (the Chartulary of Dryburgh has, as was to be expected, been specially useful), the various Record Publications—Acts of Parliament, Privy Council Records, Treasurers' Accounts, Exchequer Rolls, &c., &c.—and, especially, the local Records of the Burgh of Stirling. Most important of all have been the Protocol Books of that burgh. An Abstract of these Protocols had been made for the use of the burgh, and was recently printed by the late Rev. A. W. Cornelius Hallen, M.A., of Alloa. Neither the print nor the Abstract are always perfectly accurate ; but the writer has fortunately been supplied with trustworthy transcripts of all pertinent Protocols by Mr. W. B. Cook, of Stirling, who has made careful abstracts of all these documents from the original MSS. And that is not the only service for which he has to acknowledge his obligation to that gentleman. In all matters of genealogy and family history he has been specially indebted to Mr. Cook, and in fact, through the whole course of the investigation, he has received from him ungrudging and valuable aid.

Although several Priors have been added to those known to Sir William Fraser, there still remains an unfortunate gap in the list. Perhaps materials for filling that gap may some day come to light, but as yet the author has not been able to find them. He hopes, however, that as few errors as possible have been allowed to enter into what he has written. He has been as careful as he could to distinguish between what is merely probable and what may be regarded as certain, and to set down nothing as fact without some distinct and sufficient authority for it.

The topographical accounts of the district, it may be added, have been written from a somewhat intimate acquaintance with it for many years. And as to the descriptions of the ruined buildings on the Islands—which were also written from personal observation—the author is pleased to find them confirmed, in all essential points, by the high professional authority of Messrs. M'Gibbon & Ross, authors of the *Ecclesiastical and Baronial Architecture of Scotland*, whom he desires to thank for their courtesy in consenting to the reproduction of their plans of Inchmahome and Talla.

A. F. H.

ALPHABETICAL LIST OF WORKS CITED AS AUTHORITIES, OR OTHERWISE REFERRED TO, IN THIS VOLUME.

Anderson's (Robert, M.D.) Works of Smollett, 6th edition. 1820.
Anderson's (James) Diplomata Scotiæ.
Antiquary, The Scottish, vol. xi., 1897; vol. xiii., 1899. Edin.
Arundel MS.: Catalogue of British Museum MSS. Printed London, 1834.
Armstrong's (R. A.) Gaelic Dictionary. London, 1825.
Audsley's Popular Dictionary of Architecture. London, 1882.
Aytoun's (W. E.) Ballads of Scotland. Edin., 1861.

Balfour's (Sir James) Historical Works, edit. 1824. London.
Baring-Gould's (Sabine) Lives of the Saints. 1872-7.
Bell's (H. Glassford) Life of Mary Queen of Scots, 2nd edit. 1831.
Bellenden's Translation of Boece's History and Chronicles of Scotland. Edin., 1821.
Blaikie's (W. B.) Itinerary of Prince Charles Edward Stuart: Scottish History Society. Edin., 1897.
Brown's (Dr. John) Horæ Subsecivæ, 2nd series. Edin., 1861.
Buchan's (Earl of) Anonymous and Fugitive Essays. Edin., 1812.
Buchanan (George), Opera Omnia, ed. Ruddiman. Edin., 1715.
Buchanan's (of Auchmar) History of the Family of Buchanan. 1723.
Burt's (Captain) Letters from a Gentleman in the North of Scotland, edited by R. Jamieson. London, 1822.

Calderwood's History of the Kirk of Scotland: Wodrow Society. Edin., 1842-5.
Calendar of Documents relating to Scotland, ed. by Sir Francis Palgrave. London, 1836.
Chalmers' (George) Caledonia. London, 1807-10.
Chalmers' (George) Life of Mary Queen of Scots. London, 1818.
Chalmers' (George) Life of Thomas Ruddiman. London, 1794.
Chambers' (Robert) Domestic Annals of Scotland. Edin., 1858-61.
Chambers' (Robert) Picture of Scotland. Edin., 1827.
Charters and Other Documents relating to the Royal Burgh of Stirling— A.D. 1124-1705. Glasgow, 1884.

List of Authorities.

Chronica de Mailros: Bannatyne Club. Edin., 1835.
Chronicon de Lanercost, ed. by Stevenson. 1830.
Churchyard's (Thomas) Chips concerning Scotland. London, 1817.
Cuninghame-Graham's (R. B.) Notes on the District of Menteith. Edin., 1895.

Dalrymple's (Father) Version of Leslie's History of Scotland: Scottish Text Society. Edin., 1884-5.
Dargaud's (J. M.) Histoire de Marie Stuart. Paris, 1850.
Dictionarium Scoto-Celticum: the Gaelic Dictionary of the Highland Society. Edin., 1828.
Diurnal of Occurrents: Maitland Club. Edin., 1833.
Dun's (P.) Summer at the Lake of Menteith. Glasgow, 1866.

Erskine of Carnock, Journal of Hon. John, from 1682 to 1687: Scottish History Society. Edin., 1873.

Forbes's (A. P., Bishop of Brechin) Kalendars of Scottish Saints. Edin., 1872.
Fordun and Bower: Historians of Scotland Series. Edin., 1879.
Fordun's Chronicle of the Scottish Nation, ed. by Skene: Historians of Scotland, IV. Edin., 1872.
Fosbrooke's (Thos. Dudley) British Monachism. London, 1817.
Fountainhall's (Lord) Decisions of the Lords of Council and Session, &c. Edin., 1759-61.
Fragmenta Scoto-Monastica. Edin., 1842.
Fraser's (Sir William) The Chiefs of Colquhoun. Edin., 1869.
Fraser's (Sir William) The Red Book of Menteith. Edin., 1880.

Genealogical Magazine, July, 1897.
Gordon's (Sir Robert) Genealogical History of the Earldom of Sutherland. Edin., 1813.
Gordon's (Dr. J. F. S.) Monasticon. Glasgow, 1868.
Graham's (Dr. Patrick) Sketches of Perthshire, 2nd edit. Edin., 1812.
Graham's (of Duchray) Account of the Earl of Glencairn's Expedition. Edin., 1822.
Graham's (Alexander of Duchray) Description of Parish of Port: Macfarlan Papers in Advocates' Library.
Gwynne's Military Memoirs of the Great Civil War. Edin., 1822.

Hay Fleming's (Dr. David) Mary Queen of Scots. London, 1897.
Her Majesty Queen Victoria's More Leaves from the Journal of a Life in the Highlands. London, 1884.

List of Authorities. xix

Henry the Minstrel—Schir William Wallace: Scottish Text Society's edition. Edin., 1884-5.
Hill Burton's (John) History of Scotland, new edit. Edin., 1897.
Holford's (Margaret) Poems. 1811.
Hunter's Woods, Forests, and Estates of Perthshire. 1883.

Innes's (Cosmo) Sketches of Early Scottish History. Edin., 1861.
Innes's (Father Thos.) Essay on the Ancient Inhabitants of Scotland, ed. by Grub. Edin., 1879.
Instrumenta Publica (Ragman Rolls): Bannatyne Club. Edin., 1831.
Irving's (Dr. David) Memoirs of George Buchanan. Edition 1837.

Jebb's (Samuel) De Vita et Rebus Gestis Mariae, &c. London, 1725.
Jervise's (Andrew, F.S.A.) Memorials of Angus and Mearns. Edin., 1861.
Johnston's (Rev. J. B.) Place-Names of Scotland. Edin., 1892.

Keith's (Bishop) Catalogue of the Scottish Bishops. Edin., 1705; and Spottiswoode's edition of same, printed at Edin., 1824.
Keltie's (W. S.) History of the Scottish Highlands. Edin., 1887.
Knox's (John) History of the Reformation. Edition of 1732.

Lanigan's (Dr. John) Ecclesiastical History of Ireland. Dublin, 1829.
Langtoft's (Pierre de) Chronicle, ed. by Wright. London, 1866-8.
Leslie's (Bishop) Historie of Scotland: Bannatyne Club. Edin., 1830.
Liber Cartarum Prioratus S. Andree in Scotia: Bannatyne Club. Edin., 1841.
Liber Ecclesie de Scon: Maitland Club. Edin., 1843.
Liber Insulæ Missarum: Bannatyne Club. Edin., 1847.
Liber Pluscardensis, ed. by Skene. 1877-89.
Liber S. Marie de Dryburgh: Bannatyne Club. Edin., 1847.
Liber S. Thome de Aberbrothoc: Bannatyne Club. Edin., 1848.
Lindsay's (Sir David) Works, ed. by Laing. Edin., 1871.
Lindsay's (Robert of Pitscottie) History of Scotland, ed. by Dalzell. Edin., 1814.

Macbain's (Alex.) Etymological Dictionary of the Gaelic Language. 1896.
M'Gibbon & Ross's Castellated and Domestic Architecture of Scotland. Edin., 1887-92.
M'Gibbon & Ross's Ecclesiastical Architecture of Scotland.
Mackie's (Charles) Castles, Palaces, and Prisons of Mary Queen of Scots. 1853.
M'Nayr's (James) Guide from Glasgow to some of the most remarkable Scenes in the Highlands of Scotland. Glasgow, 1797.

List of Authorities.

Macpherson's (David) Geographical Illustrations of Scottish History. Edin., 1798.
Maitland's (William) History and Antiquities of Scotland. London, 1757.
Major's (John) Historia Majoris Brittaniæ. Edin., 1740.
Malcolm's (David) Memoir of the House of Drummond. 1808.
Manuscript Records of the Burgh, Kirk Session, and Presbytery of Stirling.
Manuscript Protocol Books of the Burgh of Stirling.
Marshall's (Dr. William) Historic Scenes in Perthshire. Edin., 1880.
Maxwell's (Sir Herbert) Robert the Bruce. 1898.
Millar's (A. H.) Castles and Mansions of Scotland. Edin., 1890.
Minutes of Evidence in the Airth Peerage Cases. 1839 and 1841.
Munimenta Alme Universitatis Glasguenis: Maitland Club. Glasgow, 1854.

Napier's (Sheriff Mark) Memorials of Montrose: Maitland Club. Edin., 1848-50.
New Statistical Account of Scotland. Edin., 1845.
Nicolas' (Sir Harris) History of the Earldoms of Strathern, Monteith, and Airth. London, 1842.
Nimmo's (Rev. W.) History of Stirlingshire, 2nd edit., by Rev. W. M. Stirling. Stirling, 1817.

Patten's (W., Londoner) Expedicion into Scotlande. London, 1548.
Pinkerton's (John) Enquiry into the History of Scotland. Edin., 1814.
Pitcairn's (Robert, W.S.) Criminal Trials in Scotland. Edin., 1829.

Ramsay's (John) Scotland and Scotsmen in the Eighteenth Century. Edin., 1888.
Records of the Royal Burgh of Stirling (Extracts from), A.D. 1519-1665. Glasgow, 1887.
Records of the Royal Burgh of Stirling (Extracts from), A.D. 1667-1752. Glasgow, 1889.

Record Office Publications:—
    Accounts of the Lord High Treasurer of Scotland.
    Acts of the Lords Auditors of Causes and Complaints (Acta Auditorum).
    Acts of the Lords of Council in Civil Causes (Acta Dominorum Concilii).
    Acts of the Parliaments of Scotland.
    Calendar of State Papers, James I., 1603-1625, edited by M. A. Everett-Green.
    Calendar of State Papers relating to Scotland, edited by T. Thorpe.
    Documents and Records illustrating the History of Scotland, edited by Sir Francis Palgrave.
    Exchequer Rolls.
    Historical MSS. Commission's Reports.

List of Authorities. xxi

Record Office Publications (continued)—
    Register of the Privy Council of Scotland.
    Register of the Great Seal.

Reeves' (Bishop W.) Ecclesiastical Antiquities of Down, Connor, and Dromore. Dublin, 1847.
Registrum de Dunfermlyn : Bannatyne Club. Edin., 1842.
Registrum Episcopatus Aberdonensis, ed. C. Innes : Spalding Club. Edin., 1845.
Registrum Episcopatus Brechinensis : Bannatyne Club. Edin., 1856.
Registrum Episcopatus Glasguensis : Maitland Club. Edin., 1843.
Registrum Monasterii Sancte Marie de Cambuskenneth, ed. W. Fraser : Grampian Club. Edin., 1872.
Robertson's (Colonel Alex.) Gaelic Topography of Scotland. Edin., 1866.
Robertson's (E. W.) Scotland under her Early Kings. Edin., 1862.
Robertson's (William) Index to Missing Charters. Edin., 1798.
Rymer's (Thomas) Fœdera, &c. London, 1704-35.

Scala Chronica (Sir Thomas Gray of Heton) : Maitland Club. Edin., 1836.
Scotichronicon—Fordun and Bower : ed. Goodall. Edin., 1747-59.
Scott's (Alexander) Poems : Scottish Text Society's edition. Edin., 1896.
Scott's (Rev. Hew) Fasti Ecclesiæ Scoticanæ. Edin., 1868.
Scott's (Sir Walter) Lady of the Lake, Rob Roy, Legend of Montrose, Tales of a Grandfather. Edit. 1892.
Sibbald's (Sir Robert) History of the Sheriffdoms of Fife and Kinross. Cupar-Fife, 1803.
Skene's (Dr. W. F.) Celtic Scotland, 2nd ed. Edin., 1886-90.
Smith's (John Guthrie) Strathendrick and its Inhabitants. Glasgow, 1896.
Spalding's (Commissary John) History of the Troubles in Scotland : Bannatyne Club. Edin., 1828-9.
Spalding Club Miscellany. Aberdeen, 1842.
Spottiswoode's (Archbishop) History of the Church of Scotland, 4th edition. London, 1677.
Statistical Account of Scotland (Sinclair's). Edin., 1791-9.
Stewart's (Duncan, M.A) Short Historical and Genealogical Account of the Royal Family of Scotland and of the Surname of Stewart. Edin., 1739.
Stewart's (J. H. J. and Lieut.-Col. D.) The Stewarts of Appin. Edin., 1880.
Stirling Natural History and Archæological Society's Transactions, vol. xv.
Stirling's (Rev. W. MacGregor) Notes on the Priory of Inchmahome. Edin., 1815.
Strickland's (Miss A.) Lives of the Queens of Scotland. London, 1852.

Theiner's (Augustus) Vetera Monumenta Hibernorum et Scotorum historiam illustrantia, &c. Rome, 1864.

List of Authorities.

Transactions of Highland and Agricultural Society of Scotland, 4th series; vols. xi. and xii. 1879-1880.
Tytler's (P. Fraser) History of Scotland. Edin., 1864.
Walsingham's (Thomas) Chronica, &c. London, 1867.
Wishart's Memoirs of James, Marquis of Montrose. London, 1893.
Wodrow's History of the Sufferings of the Church of Scotland from the Restauration to the Revolution. Edin., 1721.
Wood's edition of Douglas's Peerage. 1813.
Wyntoun's Origynale Cronykil of Scotland, ed. Laing: Historians of Scotland. Edin., 1872.

CONTENTS.

CHAPTER I.

TOPOGRAPHY OF MENTEITH, WITH SPECIAL REFERENCE TO PLACES OF LEGENDARY OR HISTORICAL INTEREST.

PAGE

SECTION I.—Extent of the district—The Earldom—The Stewartry—The name—Various derivations of Teith and Menteith—A new one suggested—Varied spellings of the word—References by early writers—Hector Boece—The Caledonian forest and its white bulls—The huntings in Menteith—Buchanan—Bishop Lesley—The cheese of Menteith—The murder of Duncan II.—Not, as stated by Buchanan and others, in Menteith—Restricted sense of the word, ... 1

SECTION II.—The hill country beside the Lake—Ben-dhu and Ben-dearg masses contrasted—Description of Ben-dearg—View from the summit—Lochan-falloch—Craig o' Port—Auchrig "Stone Avalanche"—Loch and Castle Ruskie—Pass of Glenny and Portend Burn—Crockmelly—Traditional battle in 1653 and its incidents—M'Queen's Pass—The Horseman's Leap—Historical accounts of this skirmish—Duchray's narrative—the *Mercurius Politicus*—Colonel Kid *alias* Colonel Rid—M'Gregor traditions—The Tyeper's Path and Tyeper's Well—Tobanareal—These names explained—Death of William, third Graham Earl there—The Cairn of quartz, ... 13

CHAPTER II.

AROUND THE LAKE.

SECTION I.—The Port and the Northern Shore—The Port—Other ferries—Port made a burgh of barony—The Cross—The Law Tree—St. Michael's Fair—Church of Port—Extracts

Contents.

	PAGE
from the Session records—Ministers of Port from the Reformation—The Church and Church-yard—Lands of Port—Prior's Meadow—Portend and the Earls' pleasaunce—Charles II. at Portend, ...	30

SECTION II.—The Western Shore—Earls' stables—Piper's House—Piper's Strand—Milling—The Fair—The Gallows' Hill—The last execution—The Claggans and the last wolf—Macanrie and Auchveity, with the legend of the King's son and the herd-maiden — Suggested interpretation of the names—Arnchly—Cup and ring marked stone—The legend of Pharic M'Pharic—Battle of Tillymoss or Gartalunane, ... 45

SECTION III.—The Southern Shore—Arnmauch—The legend of its formation—Cnoc-nan-Bocan, or the bogle knowe—Possibly an ancient barrow—Gartur—Cardross—The "Black Colonel" in hiding on Ardmach—Lochend—Tom-a-mhoid—The Loch of Gudy—The Pictish town of Guidi, ... 52

SECTION IV.—The Eastern Shore—Its appearance—Chapel and burying-ground at Inchie—Theft of the roast fowls—Rednock—The old Castle—Menteiths and others of Rednock—Grahams of Rednock—Blairhoyle, sometime Leitchtown—Why so called—Claim of Grahams of Leitchtown to the Earldom of Menteith—Rusky—Clan battle (Menteiths and Drummonds) at Tar of Ruskie, ... 58

CHAPTER III.
THE LAKE AND ITS ISLANDS.

The only *lake* in Scotland—*Lake* a recent innovation—Earlier names—Description—Dr. John Brown on the Lake—Different points of view — Extent and depth — Feeders and outlet : Inchmahome—Island of St. Colmoc—Various forms of the name—"Isle of my Rest" a misinterpretation—Account of the island—The Monastery gardens—Nuns' Walk and Nuns' Hill—Legend of the nun—No nunnery—Suggestion to account for the name—Queen Mary's Tree, Garden, and Bower—Large old trees—Their description and measurement: Inchtalla—Why so called—Older forms of the word—General description of the island—Inch-cuan—the Earls' kennels—James the Sixth (First of England) and the Earl of Menteith's "earth dogges,"... 67

Contents.

CHAPTER IV.
THE RUINS OF THE PRIORY ON INCHMAHOME.

Ground plan—Position of the Church—The nave—The entrances—The bell-tower—The north aisle—The sacristy and vestry—The east choir window—Choir interior—Entrance from the south—South side of Church—Windows—The Chapter House—Used as burial-place of later Earls of Menteith—The Prior's Chamber or Queen Mary's bedroom—The avenue to the vault—Statues of the eighth Earl and his Countess, not erected—The cloister—The cells of the Canons—The dormitory—Refectory—Garden—Monuments in the choir—That of Earl Walter Stewart and his Countess described—Also monument of Sir John Drummond, erected by his widow—St. Michael and St. Colmoc on the monument—Other tombstones, ...   101

CHAPTER V.
THE PRIORY OF INCHMAHOME UNDER ITS EARLY PRIORS— 1238 TO 1528.

Early religious settlements on Inchmahome—Who was Colman?—Coming of the Augustinians—Possibly brought by the first Earl Murdach—Founding of the Priory by Walter Comyn, Earl of Menteith, in 1238—Writ of Pope Gregory IX.—Abstract of its provisions—The Canons-Regular of the Order of St. Augustine—Their dress—The divisions and employments of the conventual day—Chapels and Churches belonging to the Priory of Inchmahome—Early revenue according to Bagimont's Roll—Prior Adam swears fealty to Edward I.—Prior Maurice in 1305—Three visits of King Robert Bruce to Inchmahome in the time of Maurice—Perhaps this Maurice, then Abbott of Inchaffray, who performed mass at Bannockburn—Gift of Cardross by Sir Malcolm Drummond—Prior Christinus—Deforcement of the representative of the Sheriff of Perth—Visit of Robert the High Steward—Marriage of David II.—His gift to the Priory—Blank in the annals of the Priory—Prior John—Prior Thomas—His difficulties and his supporters—Deposed—Prior Alexander and his leases—Prior in Parliament—Prior David—His numerous litigations and their results—Prior Andrew—His leases—Names of the Canons in his time—Last of the ecclesiastical Priors, ...   130

CHAPTER VI.

THE PRIORY UNDER COMMENDATORS—1529 TO 1628.

Commendator Robert Erskine—His induction in 1529—Assumed identity with the Master of Erskine—Previously rector of Glenbervy—Afterwards Dean of Aberdeen—Probably one of the Erskines of Dun—Canons of Inchmahome in Commendator Robert's time—George Buchanan's early connection with the Priory lands—The leases of 1513 and 1531—John Erskine, Commendator of Inchmahome, Dryburgh, and Cambuskenneth—Marriage of the Earl of Argyle at Inchmahome—Visit to the Priory of Mary Queen of Scots—Imaginative writing regarding it—Stories about her stay and education here examined—Dargaud, Miss Strickland, Dr. John Brown, Glassford Bell, Mackie, Conaeus, &c.—The facts as ascertained—Dr. Hay Fleming's investigations and authorities — Result of the discussion — Two leases granted by John and the Chapter — Commendator becomes Lord Erskine, afterwards Earl of Mar and Regent of Scotland — Resigns Commendatorship — David Erskine becomes Commendator—His parentage—Bull of appointment—Commendator of Dryburgh—Joins the reformers—Dilapidation of Monastery revenues begins—Tacks by the Prior and Chapter—The "Prior's Manse" in Stirling—David Erskine receives sasine of it from the Magistrates—Its situation identified—Occupied by George Buchanan—The surviving Canons—Chapter probably extinct before 1600—Some properties and leases—The Commendator and his "Thirds"—His confiscation and exile—Henry Stewart appointed Commendator—Pension to Patrick Bathok—Commendator David reponed—Resides at and enlarges Cardross—His interest in education—Last lease in which names of Canons appear—Demits his office—Death—Henry Erskine made Commendator—His parentage—Reason that has been assigned for his appointment to the office—Portrait by Jameson—Fiar of Cardross—Death in 1628, ... 159

APPENDIX TO CHAPTER VI.—ON THE SUBSEQUENT HISTORY OF THE PRIORY LANDS.

Transference of the lands to the family of Lord Erskine begins—Various complicated transactions—Royal charter of the lord-

Contents. xxvii

PAGE

ship and barony of Cardross granted to the Earl of Mar—Ratified by Act of Parliament—Names of the lands constituting the property of the Priory at this time—Purpose of the grant—Traditional stories regarding the marriage of the Earl of Mar and Lady Margaret Stewart—The Italian conjurer and the lady's portrait—Additional charters, with right of assignation—Fee of the lordship assigned to Henry Erskine—Visit of King James the First to Cardross—David, son of Henry, becomes second Lord Cardross—His house garrisoned by General Monck—New charters—Henry, third Lord Cardross—His fines, imprisonment, and other persecutions—House occupied by royal troops—Unsuccessful attempt to found a colony in America—Insolvency—Cardross disponed to the Earl of Mar—Dryburgh sold—Joins the Prince of Orange in Holland—Returns home with him in 1688—Death in 1693—David, fourth Lord Cardross—Becomes Earl of Buchan—Dispones Cardross to his uncle, Colonel the Hon. John Erskine—The Colonel tries to clear off the burdens on the property—It falls, by judicial sale, to his son, John Erskine of Carnock—His second son James was the first Mr. Erskine of Cardross and direct ancestor of the present proprietor, ... 193

CHAPTER VII.

The Ruins on Inchtalla: the Old House and its Furnishings.

Inchtalla, residence of Malise, first Graham Earl of Menteith—Probable period of erection of present buildings—Moulded and carved stones from the Priory built into the walls—Building on the court-yard plan—The High House—Its former heraldic devices—The vaulted under rooms—The upper storey—Stair of access—Indications of a defensive wooden hoarding on the south front—The Kitchen—The arched fire-place—The oven—The Tower, with its stair—The buildings on the west side of the court-yard—Their possible uses and arrangement—The Hall House on the north—Probably the most recent erection—The Hall and its furniture in the time of the last Earl—Inventory of chairs, candlesticks, &c.—The rooms on the upper floor—The East Chamber, hung with blue, and its furnishings—The West

xxviii   *Contents.*

                                                                    PAGE

or Green Chamber and its furnishings—The Tower—The
Laigh Back Room—Contents of the great chest—My Lord's
Chamber and its furnishings—The Wardrobe—The Brew-house
on the east side of the court—Its utensils—The sleeping
apartments over the Brew-house and in the "to-falls," with
their furniture—Indications of the manner of living in the
Earl's house at the end of the seventeenth century—Liquors—
Bread and baking—Supplies of salt herrings—Cooking
utensils—Dishes mostly of pewter—Paucity of silver vessels
accounted for—Domestic crafts—My Lord's wardrobe—
Female properties absent—The last Countess and the frogs—
The dispersal of the property, and the neglect of the house
since the death of the last Earl in 1694, ...   203

CHAPTER VIII.

THE EARLIER EARLS OF MENTEITH.

The ancient Earldom—Gilchrist—Muretach—Maurice senior and
Maurice junior—Their agreement—Maurice at the corona-
tion of Alexander II.—His daughters—Walter Comyn—
His connection with the national affairs—Founds the Priory—
At the coronation of Alexander III.—Seizes the young King
and Queen at Kinross—Rumours regarding the cause of his
death—Marriage of his widow—Her attempts to secure the
Earldom unsuccessful—Walter Stewart obtains the Earldom—
Efforts of the Comyns to retain it—The estates parted in
two—Sir Edmund Hastings receives the Comyn portion from
Edward I. and assumes the style of Lord of Enchimchel-
mock—His brother, Sir John Hastings, receives the other
portion—Life and achievements of Walter Stewart—As a
crusader—At the battle of Largs—Voyage with the Princess
Margaret to Norway—One of Bruce's Commissioners, but
swears fealty to Edward in 1292—Death, and burial at
Inchmahome—Earl Alexander—Taken prisoner at Dunbar—
Released and takes the oath to Edward—His sons hostages
for him—Remains faithful to the English King—Earl Alan—
Fights in Flanders—Taken prisoner at Methven—Stripped
of his estates—Dies in captivity—Earl Murdach—A favourite
of King Robert Bruce—Killed in the battle of Dupplin—
Countess Mary—Brought up at Rusky by her uncle, Sir
John Menteith—Marries Sir John Graham, who becomes

Contents.

PAGE

Earl of Menteith—Gallantry of this Earl at Neville's Cross—His capture, trial, and execution—Their daughter, Lady Margaret—Her four husbands—Her last husband, Robert Stewart—Robert becomes Earl of Menteith, Earl of Fife, and afterwards Duke of Albany, and Governor of Scotland—His life and achievements—The death of the Duke of Rothesay, and Albany's connection therewith—Ancient and modern estimates of Albany's character—Murdach, second Duke of Albany—Appointed Governor—Narrative of events in his life—His arrest and execution by James I.—Traditional statements regarding the place of his arrest—Motives of the King in the extermination of the Albanies—Forfeiture of the Earldom, ... 216

CHAPTER IX.

Sir John Menteith of Rusky and the Capture of Wallace.

Sir John Menteith's birth and parentage—An early supporter of Bruce—Takes the side of Baliol, and is made prisoner at Dunbar—Serves Edward in his French wars—An "Adversary of the King" in 1301—Submits to Edward in 1304—In favour with Edward—Keeper of Dumbarton Castle—The Capture of Wallace—The circumstances of the betrayal and Menteith's connection therewith discussed—His rewards from the English King—Goes over to Bruce—Story of his attempted treachery to Bruce in Dumbarton Castle not proved—His embassies and other employments thereafter—Estimate of his character—The hatred of his memory cherished in Scotland—"Turning the bannock" as an insult to Menteiths, ... 253

CHAPTER X.

The First Six Graham Earls of Menteith—1427 to 1598.

Erection of the new Earldom and Stewartry—Malise, first Earl—His descent—A hostage in England—His son Alexander takes his place—In favour with James III.—At the battle of Sauchie—His wives—Gifts to Lady Jonet and his son, John—Countess Mariota—His family—Alexander, second Earl—Infeftment—

xxx   *Contents.*

PAGE

Suppression of crimes—" Band " with the Earl of Arran and others—Redemption of lands—Family—William, third Earl—Marriage and family—The fight with the Appin Stewarts in which he lost his life—Various accounts of it—The traditional stories—Sir Walter Scott's account—The Appin version—Date of the incident—John, fourth Earl—Active in State affairs—Queen Mary's visit in his time—Alleged journey to France—Joins the Lords of the Congregation—Fights with them at Leith—Subscribes the Book of Discipline—His widow and family—William, fifth Earl—Earldom during his minority—At the Coronation of James VI.—At the battle of Langside—Marriage—Political activities—Feud between the Grahams and the Leckies—John, sixth Earl—Ward of the Crown—His marriage—Description for the Government in 1592—Quarrels and lawsuits—Death, and family, ...   268

CHAPTER XI.

THE LAST TWO GRAHAM EARLS, 1598 TO 1694.

William, seventh Earl—Vicissitudes of his life—Minority, infeftment, marriage—Arrangement of his charters, redemption of lands, and other business of the Earldom—Patronage of the Church of Aberfoyle—His rise to political distinction and honours—Royal pensions—The King's promises and how they were kept—His enemies among the Scottish nobles—Claims the Earldom of Strathern—Claim admitted and letters patent issued—Scot of Scotstarvet's accusations—Title of Strathern recalled—That of Airth granted—Accused of treason—Found guilty—His submission—Stripped of his offices and pensions, banished from the Court, and confined to his own house—Pecuniary ruin—To some extent regains the Royal favour—Refuses to sign the National Covenant—Exerts himself in the cause of Charles I.—Dispersal of his estates—Lives at Inchtalla—Disagreements with his Countess—His curious accounts of her delinquencies—His son, Lord Kilpont, murdered at Collace—His family—William, eighth and last Earl—His poverty and eccentricities—Petitions for payment of pensions—His professed delight in Covenanter-hunting—Curiosities of his correspondence—Complaints of impecuniosity—Correspondence with Graham of Claverhouse regarding the adoption of the latter, and with the Marquis of Montrose and Sir James Graham about the marriage of his niece and the succession

Contents. xxxi

PAGE

to the Earldom—Divorces his first wife and marries again—How he practised economy—Regulations for the management of and expenditure on his household—Countess gets tired of his fussiness and leaves him—A marriage contract drawn up—Traditionary story of the "Roeskin Purse"—Death and testament—Disposition of his estates and personal property, ... 290

APPENDIX TO CHAPTER XI.—THE MURDER OF LORD KILPONT AT COLLACE.

Lord Kilpont, son of the seventh and father of the eighth Earl of Menteith—His birth and marriage—Acts as assistant justiciar of Menteith—Captures a notorious robber—Receives the King's thanks for his services in this matter and against the Covenanters—Assembles the men of Menteith and the Lennox to watch the Irish levies of Montrose—Goes over with this force to Montrose—Murdered by Stewart of Ardvoirlich at Collace—Buried in the Chapter House at Inchmahome—Varying accounts of the murder—The story as told by Wishart, the Chaplain of Montrose—Montrose's tribute to Kilpont—The communication to Sir Walter Scott from a member of the Ardvoirlich family—The story as told in the Acts of Parliament in a statement approved by Ardvoirlich himself, ... 317

CHAPTER XII.

SOME MISCELLANEOUS MATTERS OF GREATER OR LESS INTEREST.

Feud between the Menteiths and Drummonds in the fourteenth century—Alleged and probable causes—The battle of the clans at the Tar of Rusky—Slaughter of the Menteith chiefs—Interference of the King—Terms of the arrangement of pacification—The Beggar Earl of Menteith—Relationship to the last Earl—Appears at Holyrood and claims the title—Claim disallowed by the House of Lords until further proof—Never again attends the election of Scottish representative peers—Sinks into poverty—Becomes a "gangrel"—Found dead in a field near Bonhill—Account for his funeral—Subsequent

claimants of the Earldom—Titles of Menteith and Airth still dormant—The last Earl and the Grahams of Duchray—Fracas at the Bridge of Aberfoyle—Two local Legends: (I.) The Butler and the Witches—(II.) Rival Long-bows—Quaint mode of fishing for pike—Royal visitors to the Lake and neighbourhood—Summary of royal visits previously referred to—Bruce's sword at Cardross—The Jameses in Menteith—James V. and the King of Kippen—Prince Charles Edward in Menteith—His alleged visit to Cardross—Queen Victoria and Princess Beatrice in Menteith—Their two visits to the Lake—Her Majesty's opinions of the scenery and the people, ...	323
NOTES AND CORRECTIONS, ...	355
INDEX, ...	359

LIST OF ILLUSTRATIONS.

		PAGE
1.	Inchmahome from North Shore of Lake,	41
2.	Cup-marked Stone near Milling (from photograph by R. Kidston, F.G.S., &c.),	49
3.	View of the Lake from the South East,	56
4.	The Lake and Inchmahome from Portend,	63
5.	The Admiral's Point,	71
6.	The Nuns' Hill,	79
7.	Queen Mary's Tree,	83
8.	Queen Mary's Bower,	87
9.	Inchtalla,	94
10.	Inchcuan,	97
11.	Plan of the Priory Buildings (from M'Gibbon & Ross's Ecclesiastical Architecture),	102
12.	West Doorway of the Priory,	105
13.	The Aisle Arches,...	109
14.	The Chapter House—Interior,	112
15.	The Chapter House from the East,	114
16.	The Vaulted Kitchen, Inchmahome,	119
17.	Ground Plan of Priory (from M'Gregor Stirling's Notes on Inchmahome),	122
18.	Recumbent Monument of Walter Stewart, Earl of Menteith, and his Countess,	125
19.	The Priors' Manse, otherwise called George Buchanan's House, in Stirling (from drawing by T. Allom),	184
20.	Plan of Buildings on Inchtalla (from M'Gibbon & Ross's Domestic, &c., Architecture),	204

SEALS.

21.	Priory of Inchmahome,	131
22.	Sir Edmund Hastings,	226
23.	Walter Stewart, Earl of Menteith,	231
24.	Robert, Duke of Albany,	245

List of Illustrations.

SEALS *(Continued.)*

25. Malise, First Graham Earl of Menteith, 269
26. Alexander, Second Graham Earl, ... 275
27. William, Third Graham Earl, ... 278
28. William, Seventh Earl, ... 291

SIGNATURES.

29. Commendator John Erskine, ... 170
30. Commendator David Erskine, ... 179
31. Commendator Henry Erskine, ... 192

The Lake of Menteith.

CHAPTER I.

Topography of Menteith : with Special References to Places of Historical and Legendary Interest.

"The varied realms of fair Menteith."

SECTION I.—EXTENT, NAME, AND EARLY ACCOUNTS OF THE DISTRICT.

ENTEITH—in the most comprehensive sense in which the name was and is still employed—may be defined approximately as the country drained by the river Teith and its tributaries, together with the western and northern portions of the watershed of the Forth as far down as its junction with the Teith.[1]

This extensive district, which measures about twenty-eight miles in length from west to east, with a maximum breadth of about fifteen miles, has for backbone the ridge—mountainous in the west and decreasing in height towards the east—which lies between the basins of Loch Katrine, Loch Achray and Loch Vennachar and the course of the

---

[1] Balquhidder, however, although in the drainage area of the Teith, was reckoned a portion of the district of Stratherne.

Teith on the north, and Loch Ard and the river Forth on the south. From this central ridge Menteith extends northwards over the valley of the Teith, and on the south takes in a considerable portion of the vale of Forth. It comprises the modern parishes of Callander, Kilmadock, and Lecropt, with portions of Logie and Dunblane, all lying north of the central ridge; and Aberfoyle, Port of Menteith, Kincardine, and part of Kippen, on its southern slopes.[1]

The territories over which the ancient Earls of Menteith had jurisdiction were, however, of still wider extent than even this ample region, including, as they did at various times, large tracts of country in Argyllshire and the island of Arran.

The Stewartry of Menteith, on the other hand, was of smaller extent. It included that portion of the territories of the old earldom which, on the execution and confiscation of the Albanies, was seized by King James the First and formed into a royal lordship under this designation. It comprised the more easterly portions of the old territory and the valley of the Teith, with the Castle of Doune as the chief messuage; while only the western region, for the most part lying on the south side of the central ridge, was assigned to the new earldom.

The name of the district evidently connects itself with that of the river which is one of its principal natural features. As a rule in local nomenclature, it is the rivers and watercourses which give their names to the surrounding countrysides, not the region-name which originates that of

---

[1] This district of Menteith, along with that of Stratherne, formed the old Celtic province of Fortrenn. The four provinces of ancient Alban were: (1) Stratherne and Menteith; (2) Athole; (3) Angus and Mearns; (4) Fife and Fothreve. — Skene's Celtic Scotland, vol. i. p. 290; vol. iii. p. 133.

the river. As to the significance of the river-name Teith, however, etymologists have not yet reached agreement.

The derivation of the word most generally given—although not always absolutely accepted—is that suggested originally by the Rev. Dr. Robertson, the writer of the Old Statistical Account of the Parish of Callander (who, by the way, spells the name *Teath*—an orthography probably more correct than the now invariable *Teith*). He says the Avon Teath is "the warm river"[1]—deriving the word from the Gaelic *te* or *teth*, which means "hot." Of this appellative two explanations have been given. One applies the quality of warmth rather to the river-valley than to the waters of the stream. Fringed with woods and shut in, on north and south alike, by continuous hill-ranges, it is sheltered from the cold blasts which sweep the mountains, and thus affords a contrast to the cold uplands on either side so marked as to deserve the epithet of "warm." This explanation, besides being rather far-fetched, is contrary to the usual rule of deriving the name of the country from that of the river. The other explanation is that given by the Rev. Dr. Graham of Killearn in his "Perthshire Sketches." He writes the Gaelic name as *Avon-Thaich*, and while distinctly stating that "the etymology is uncertain," he explains the derivation from *Te* or *Teth* by "the *boiling* appearance which it (the river) presents, on account of the rapidity of its current from Callander to Ochtertyre."[2] Within these limits the Teith is certainly a clear and rather rapid stream—"swift"

[1] Old Statistical Account of Scotland, vol. xi., p. 574.
[2] Sketches of Perthshire, by the Rev. P. Graham, D.D., 1812; p. 64.

is Sir Walter Scott's poetical epithet[1]—but a "boiling appearance" is not its characteristic. In respect of the smoothness of its flow, its freedom from rushes and cataracts, it is distinctly in contrast with its own two head streams, and notably with the tumultuous water which rushes down the Pass of Leny from Loch Lubnaig.

Other derivations are not wanting. One authority[2] says the name is probably from the Gaelic *taic*, which means "strength or vigour." But *strength* is a quality predicable of all large rivers, and is not peculiar to the Teith. Colonel Robertson[3] finds in the word a reference to an old Celtic river-god, "whose name means *water*." Leaving the river-god—whose existence does not admit of proof—out of the question, it may be said that a root-word with an apparent resemblance to that of Teith is to be found in other river-names in Scotland, Wales, and Cornwall. But all this is extremely vague, and indicates no particular feature of this stream from which it might be supposed to derive a characteristic name.

Such a characteristic quality, however, is pointed at in a derivation submitted—it is believed for the first time[4] —by Dr. A. C. Cameron, a very competent Gaelic scholar. He says:—"The Teith in Gaelic is *Uisge-Theavich*, that is, 'the quiet and pleasant water'; the root being *teamh*

---

[1] "Along thy banks, swift Teith! they ride."—Lady of the Lake, canto v. st. xviii.
[2] Johnston's Place Names of Scotland, 1892, p. 232.
[3] Robertson's Gaelic Topography of Scotland, p. 144.
[4] In a letter to the present writer. It may be said that when Dr. Cameron sent his explanation of *Uisge-Theavich*, he was not acquainted with the locality, and unaware of the character of the stream and its feeders. He merely interpreted the Gaelic name by which the river had been known to him from boyhood.

('quiet,' 'pleasant,' as opposed to 'rough,' 'wild') + *ich* (=English termination—*ous*)." Now, the character of the two streams which unite to form the Teith is sufficiently indicated by their names. That which comes from Loch Vennachar has the Gaelic name of *Eas-gobhain* —"the smith's cascade"; while the Loch Lubnaig branch is known as the *Garbh-uisge*, or "rough water." They are both—the latter especially—rude and brawling torrents. But the river formed by their union is of a totally different character. From the junction, where it assumes the name of Teith, it becomes still and placid; it flows, or scarcely flows, in quiet deep pools, through the meadows of Callander. Dr. John Brown's characterisation of it—as seen from Callander Bridge—is as true as it is poetical, "lying *diffuse and asleep*, as if its heart were in the Highlands and it were loath to go."[1] To this smooth stream, the name of *quiet and pleasant* might well be given in contrast to the *wild and rough* waters which unite to form it. The name thus given has adhered to the river throughout its course, and although below Callander its stream becomes more rapid, it nowhere merits the epithet of "boiling." There is not a cataract in its whole course.

Thaich, or Taich, according to Dr. Graham, was a name applicable not only to the river, but to the whole of the district which is known to us as Menteith. He says:— "It may be proper to remark that the name Menteith, by which the whole territory included between the Forth and the Teith, from their junction, a little above Stirling, to the western extremity of Loch Con, upon the confines of

[1] Horæ Subsecivæ, by John Brown, M.D., second series, 1861, p. 170.

Buchanan, is denominated, is entirely unknown in the Gaelic; the district is uniformly called *Taich*."¹ The Rev. W. M'Gregor Stirling makes the same affirmation —evidently on Dr. Graham's authority:—" The name of Monteath "—so he spells it—" even in the present day is not known to the Gael, who call it Taich."² Others have repeated the statement. It is, however, too absolute. Gaelic-speaking people know and have long known the district by the name of Menteith, as well as by that of Taich or Taicht.³ *Taichia* is the usual Latin form of the name. It occurs in a Patent under the Great Seal, dated 31st July, 1631, whereby King Charles the First created William, seventh Earl of Menteith, Earl of Stratherne and Menteith. Throughout this document, the Earl is styled *Comes Taichie* lie *Menteth*.⁴ But in all the earlier official documents it is Menteith—in varied forms of spelling.

The very earliest form in which the word occurs is *Meneted*, in which shape it appears, according to Innes, in a manuscript that dates in the latter part of the twelfth century.⁵ In a charter, dated 1234, it appears as Mynteth and also Mynynteth, and as Meneteth in 1240. From the

¹ Graham's Sketches of Perthshire, p. 64.
² Notes on the Priory of Inchmahome, by the Rev. W. M'Gregor Stirling, p. 88, *note*.
³ If Taich is not to be taken simply as the river name applied to the surrounding country, it may be, as suggested by Dr. Cameron, a compound of *Teamh* and *faiche*, meaning the "pleasant country." Pleasant enough it is as compared with the wild region beyond, and attractive for the foray-loving Highlanders, who were wont to descend from their fastnesses to spoil its more fertile fields—" the varied realms of fair Menteith." But it seems better to connect the name of the country with that of the river.
⁴ Patent printed in the Red Book of Menteith, vol. i. p. 323.
⁵ The passage referred to occurs in a manuscript which Innes attributes to Giraldus Cambrensis. This manuscript contains a description of Alban, said to

The Lake of Menteith. 7

twelfth to the end of the seventeenth century, the word occurs in written documents in over thirty different forms of spelling.

A list of these will show the variety in which the old scribes indulged. The date of the first occurrence of each form is given. Many of them, of course, are repeated with greater or less frequency.

Meneted (12th century), Manenthe and Manethe (1213), Mynynteth and Mynteth (1234), Meneteth (1240), Menteth (1250), Meneth (1253), Menetyef (1255), Menthet (1262), Menethe and Menetheht (1286), Mentheht (1290), Menethet, Menetheth, and Menetht (1329), Menetethe (1342), Menetoth (1354), Menetetht (1390), Montatht (1392), Mentethe (1403), Mentetht (1410), Menteith (1421), Monteth (1450), Menteithe (1473), Menteitht (1501), Mentheth (1503), Mentehet (1508), Mentech (1512), Monteith (1513), Mentethyt (1597), Munteth (1597), Monteathe (1622), Montide (in a letter from Louis XIII. of France to the Earl of Menteith, 1634), Montieth and Monteeth (English—letters from the army of the Parliament—1653).[1] The spelling Monteath does not appear before 1724, when it was employed by Alexander Graham of Duchray in his description of the Parish of Port.

Disregarding the early substitution of *y*, and the later and rare substitution of *u* and *o* for the *e* of the first syllable, and

---

have been supplied by Andrew, Bishop of Caithness, whose death date was A.D. 1185. The phrase employed by the Bishop, speaking of the divisions of the country, is "pars etiam tertia est Stradearn cum *Meneted.*" Innes's Essay on the Ancient Inhabitants of Scotland (Edin. 1879). Appendix No. 1, p. 412.

[1] Others could be added, but the list is long enough for its purpose. All the names in it are taken from early charters, Acts of Parliament, Exchequer and other official documents.

excluding the anomalous *Manethe* and *Manenthe*—which appear in documents of Henry III. of England, and may therefore be set down as errors of ignorance on the part of the English scribe—an analysis of these forms, taking account both of the spelling and the frequency of recurrence, seems to yield two, of which the others are but varieties of spelling. These are *Meneteth* and *Menteth*. The former is more frequent in the earlier writings, and therefore may perhaps be nearer the original word.

Assuming that the last portion of the word represents Theavich or Teith—whether the district or the river—the origin of the first part may be found in one or other of the Gaelic words *monadh* (hill), *mòine* (moor or moss), or *muin* (back). The *hill-land, moorland, back-land* of Taich would fitly enough designate the region. The indefinite sound of the vowel in the first syllable, indicated by the occasional change in spelling from *e* to *y, u, o,* and even *a,* and still surviving in the popular pronunciation, would also give countenance to any of the derivations suggested. Perhaps, however, we shall not be far wrong if we accept Monadh-Theavich as the most likely original of the word Menteith.[1]

The references to the district of Menteith by early Scottish writers are extremely scanty, and afford but little information regarding the appearance or character of the country. Hector Boece merely mentions it as lying to the

---

[1] This derivation receives support from the statement, on the authority of Macbain's Gaelic Dictionary, that the Cornish forms of *monadh* were *menit* and *meneth*, and the Welsh form was *mynydat*. The forms of the old Pictish Goidelic in use among the people by whom these early place-names were given may have been similar.

west of Stirling, and as having been partly covered in more ancient times by that old Caledonian forest which gave so much trouble to the Roman soldiers, and which sheltered the famous white bulls. Both bulls and forest had in his time all but disappeared. His description of those fierce inhabitants of the wood may be suspected of being mythical, but it is exceedingly graphic, and—in the quaint Scots in which Bellenden's translation dresses it—deserves quotation. After stating that "the wod of Calidon ran fra Striveling throw Menteith and Stratherne to Atholl and Lochquhabir," he proceeds:—

"In this wod wes sum time quhit bullis, with crisp and ourland mane, like feirs lionis; and, thoucht thay semit meik and tame in the remanent figure of thair bodyis, thay were mair wild than ony uther beistis, and had sic hatrent agains the societe and company of men, that thay come nevir in the woddis nor lesuris quhair thay fand ony feit or haind thairof; and, mony dais eftir, thay eit nocht of the herbis that wer twichit or handillit be men. Thir bullis wer sa wild, that thay wer nevir tane but slicht and crafty laubour; and sae impacient, that, eftir thair taking, thay deit for importable dolour. Als sone as ony man invadit thir bullis, thay ruschit with so terrible preis on him, that thay dang him to the eird; takand na feir of houndis, scharp lancis, nor uthir maist penitrive wappinis."[1]

Menteith appears always to have been a hunting district. It continued to be so in the times of the Stuart kings, who had a royal forest and hunting-hall in Glenfin-

[1] Bellenden's Translation of Boece's History and Chronicles of Scotland, edit. 1821: The Cosmographic, chap. x.

lass, as well as huntings in the forest of Aberfoyle. The Chamberlain's Accounts contain numerous entries of expenses for building and repairing the hunting seats and maintaining the forests with their rangers and keepers. But there were no white bulls then to hunt. The staple game were deer and foxes, though Lesley makes mention of wolves as still existing in his time.

Buchanan's account of the district is equally meagre with that of Boece, or rather more so. It amounts only to the statement that Menteith lies between the mountains of Strathearn and the Forth, and that it receives its name from the Teith, which runs through the midst of it.[1]

Bishop Lesley adopts Boece's description of the Caledonian forest and its wild bulls, and adds that more ancient writers had affirmed the existence of bears and wolves in this great forest, stating that the bears were long before his time utterly extinct, although wolves were still to be found. Other points of interest he mentions:—"Neist this (*i.e.* Stirling) westwarde lyes Monteith, nobilitat and mekle commendat throuch the name of sik cheise as nane fyner, quhairin, by uthir singular thingis that it hes, ane famous suerlie and kinglie castell, lykewyse ane certane monaster of midway rentis" (the original Latin is *mediocrium reddituum*, "of moderate revenues") "it conteines."[2]

The famous and kingly castle of course refers to Doune, and the monastery of moderate revenues is obviously Inchmahome. These are now in ruins, but not more so than

[1] Buchanan's Opera Omnia a Ruddiman, 1715; vol. i. p. 10.
[2] Lesley's Historie of Scotland, translated by Father Dalrymple, Scottish Text Society's edition, 1885; vol. i. p. 28.

the reputation of Menteith for its cheese. That appears to have utterly departed. Nevertheless the note is of interest, as confirming what we know from other sources that Menteith was a comparatively wealthy district, whose herds of grazing cattle were a temptation too strong to be resisted by the hungry Highland clans that inhabited the mountains to the north and west. In the earlier times the Earls of Menteith would be responsible for guarding this valuable property; and after a portion of their domain became the property of the Crown, the officers of the Stewartry had a kind of militia appointed to watch the Highland marauders.[1]

This may be a suitable place to notice an error that has found its way into all the local histories and into many of the general histories of Scotland, and for which Buchanan appears to be, in the first place, responsible. He makes Menteith the scene of the murder of Duncan II. in 1094.[2] This prince, who dethroned the usurper Donald Bane, was treacherously slain by Maolpeder, Earl of Mearns, at the instigation, it is said, of Donald. Hector Boece does not venture to indicate the locality of the tragedy. He merely says that Duncan was killed "slepand in his bed, eftir he had roung ane yeir and ane half";[3] but Buchanan—who, like Boece, calls the murderer Macpender—distinctly puts the scene of the occurrence in Menteith (*Taichia*). One is inclined to wonder what the thane of the Mearns was doing

---

[1] Exchequer Rolls, vol. ii. p. 487 : payment of £4 3s for watchmen " to watch thieves coming from Lorne to Menteith." Other entries to the same effect.

[2] Buchanan's Opera, vol. i. book vii. p. 118.

[3] Bellenden's Boece, book xiii. chap. 16.

in the region of Menteith. It seems not unlikely that Buchanan was led to his statement by a misapprehension of his authority. That authority appears to have been the *Scotichronicon*, which affirms that Duncan perished by the treachery of his uncle Donald and by the instrumentality of one Malpedir, Earl of Mearns, at *Monathethyn*.[1] Now, Monathethyn, and still more its MS. variants *Monthechyn* and *Monathechin*, are so very like Monadhthaich, that there need be little wonder that a writer who was acquainted with Gaelic—as Buchanan was—should, without stopping to investigate, transcribe the word in Latin as Taichia.

Maitland repeats the tale, and gives additional definiteness to the scene by placing it "in the Castle of Menteith"[2] —wherever that may have been. Chalmers pointed out the proper locality of this murder as *Monachedin*, now called *Mondynes*—a place on the banks of the Bervie in Kincardineshire or Mearns; the exact spot being marked by a monolith of over 6 ft. in height above ground, which is said to have been set up to commemorate the event.[3] Not-

---

[1] Scotichronicon a Goodall, lib. v. cap. xxviii. : *Qui cum per unum annum et sex menses regnasset, avunculi sui Dovenaldi dolo quem saepius bello viceras, per adminiculum cujusdam comitis de Mernis, nomine Malpetri, Scottice Malpeder, apud Monathethyn caesus interiit.*

[2] Maitland's History and Antiquities of Scotland, 1757, vol. i. p. 345.

[3] Chalmers' Caledonia, 1807, vol. i. p. 423. See also Robertson's Scotland under her Early Kings, vol. i. p. 158 ; and Skene's Celtic Scotland, vol. i, p. 438. Wyntoun (Origynale Cronykil of Scotland, edited by Laing, 1872, book vii. chap. iii. line 387) mentions the fact of the murder, but gives neither the name of the place nor of the murderer. *Monachedin*, however, appears as the name of the place in what is perhaps the earliest authority of all—a list of the Kings of Scots and Picts in the Register of the Priory of St. Andrews, written A.D. 1251 :— "*Donekan Mac-Malcolm regnavit 6 mens. hoc interfecto a Malpeder Macloen comite de Mearns in Monachedin.*" See Innes' Essay on the Ancient Inhabitants of Scotland : Historians of Scotland, 1879, vol. viii. app. 5, p. 424.

withstanding this correction, the error still persists and is found in some quite recent works.[1]

The name Menteith is still in use as a convenient geographical term, although the district has no longer a judicial or civil existence. When it had, the name was applicable to the whole of the country already described. While it is still employed in that wide sense, the local significance of the term is now frequently confined to the country lying more immediately around the Lake of Menteith. As it is with this narrower region that the subject of this book is specially connected, it will be proper to give some account of it—its topography, history and traditions—before dealing in detail with the Lake and the Islands.

SECTION II.—THE HILLS OF MENTEITH, AND SOME OF THEIR TRADITIONS.

> "Many a tale,
> Traditionary, round the mountains hung,
> And many a legend peopling the dark woods."

WHAT we have called the hilly backbone of the province of Menteith, after leaving the gap which makes a sort of break in its continuity at Aberfoyle, runs, at considerable

---

[1] Dun's Summer at the Lake of Menteith, 1866, p. 15; Keltie's History of the Scottish Highlands, 1887, vol. i. p. 36.

elevation, between Loch Vennachar and the Lake of Menteith. It is divided into two distinct masses by the ravine of Glenny and the depression at the summit, over which passes the rough track between the lakes. These may be distinguished by the names of their principal summits, as the Ben-dhu *(black mountain)* and the Ben-dearg *(red mountain)* masses. The names indicate a natural and striking contrast in colour—Ben Dhu bearing on its southern front a ridge of bare and dark-coloured rock, while Ben Dearg to the east shows ruddy-tinted rock and soil, and brown heath to its top. The dark front of Ben Dhu, cut into five or six portions by sharp notches on the top, retires at its eastern extremity towards the north, leaving room for the heathy slopes and moors of Mondhui. Back in hollows of this mountain mass towards the north and west, lie the fine Loch Drunkie—of old times held by wild Macfarlanes and Macphersons—and the solitary mountain tarn known as Loch Rheoidte ("the frozen lake").

The eastern or Ben-dearg section of the hills is what is usually designated specifically the Hills of Menteith. Though not entitled, from their height alone, to rank among first-class Scottish mountains, yet their appearance is in no small degree impressive. Seen from the south, they appear to rise with almost startling suddenness and steepness from the level of the lake. As the lake itself is but little above sea-level, and as there are no gradually rising foot-hills to diminish the apparent height, they have the full scenic advantage of their measured elevation. A dense wood of firs, which runs up a great portion of this steep southern face, but allows the bare, brown summits to show above, adds to the effect of the view of the hill from this side. When this outer wall has been scaled and the interior region is explored, the true mountainous characteristics are revealed. Boggy hollows, steep grassy or heath-clad slopes, stony or rocky crests, make up its general character. Although it affords grazing for sheep and cattle, cultivation has never existed, except around the skirts of the mass and up a few short and narrow openings. From of old it has been the haunt of wild beast and wild fowl, and if the wolves and boars, which legend affirms to have frequented its recesses, are now extinct, it is still tenanted by some of our wilder animals. The usual winged and four-footed game preserved for sport is, of course, abundant. The eagle is probably extinct, but falcons are said yet to breed in the cliffs of Auchyle. Foxes are numerous, and badgers, and possibly wild-cats, are still to be found.

The heights of this region—which comprises an area of several square miles—arrange themselves in a rough way in three main portions. The most northerly, which rises from the shores of Loch Vennachar and the banks of Eas Gobhain, rises to its greatest elevation in Ben Gullipen (*gailebhein*—great rough hill?), 1344 feet in height. The central ridge, rising by a long ascent from the Pass of Glenny to the east till it attains its greatest height of 1401 feet, is Ben Dearg, sometimes written Ben-dearig, and pronounced generally by natives of the district as "Ben-dhirack." The prospect from this summit is magnificent. Northwards rise the numberless peaks of the Grampians in confused array. Ben Ledi is close at hand, across Loch

Vennachar, with Loch Lubnaig coiling round its eastern foot. Behind are Ben More and Stobinean, with the "Braes of Balquhidder." More to the right, Stuc-a-chroin, Ben Voirlich, and Uamvar, backed by Ben Chonzie, and the Comrie hills, are seen, with the peaks of the Atholl hills in the distance. Towards the left, the mountains on the borders of Perth and Argyll shires may be descried. Westwards, the eye takes in Ben Venue and Ben Lomond, through the opening notes Ben Arthur and the mountains at the head of Loch Long, and lingers on the waters of Loch Katrine and Loch Achray, and other lakes on which the shadows of these mountains lie. Looking southwards, the prospect is of a totally different and beautifully contrasting kind. Instead of the billowy sea of mountain peaks which fills the view to the north, there is the fair Vale of Menteith, fertile and finely cultivated, adorned with woods and pleasure grounds, shut in on the south by the green hills of Fintry and the Lennox range, but open in all its length from the sources of the Forth to Stirling Castle. Still further to the east, the eye may travel along the slopes of the Ochils, and follow the carse of Stirling till it rests on the broad waters of the Firth, and, if the atmosphere be sufficiently clear, may mark the towers and hills of Edinburgh rising in the distance. And—not the least charming feature in the scene—close at hand, almost under foot, as it were, lies the Lake of Menteith, mirroring on its placid surface its wooded and ruin-covered islands. The view everywhere from Ben Dearg is brightened and beautified by the numerous lakes that fill the hollows of the mountains. More than a dozen of these are visible from the summit.[1] A very small one lies close at hand. This—which is about half-a-mile in circumference—is called by the very appropriate name of Lochan-falloch, or, the *hidden little lake*. It lies in a deep cleft on the north edge, about 300 feet beneath the summit, so concealed from outside view that not even the position in which it lies can be observed from anywhere below.

The southern portion of the mountain mass—about 1200 feet in greatest height—falls in a steep and straight, almost wall-like face to the shores of the lake. The transition from mountain to lowland is as sudden as the contrast is complete. This southern front is known by the names of Glenny and Auchyle Hills. In the New Statistical Account of the parish[2] it is called the Craig of Port. At Auchrig, on the east side of the hill, there is what the writer describes as a *stone-avalanche*. "The front of the mountain has more or less slid away from the main body, and in one place violently burst. Here conglomerated sandstones (vulgarly called plum-pudding) of large dimensions and irregular shapes lie piled above each other in dizzy poise. The spectator from above can see glimpses of the wide extended vale beneath, through the apertures. Some of the rocks are richly festooned with ancient ivy. They are the favourite haunt of foxes, and often re-echo the mellow note of the fox-hound. A very large spring of water issues from their base, even in the driest season.

---

[1] Among them are Vennachar, Lubnaig, Drunkie, Achray, Katrine, Con, Ard, Menteith, with the smaller lochans, Falloch, Letter, Ruskie, Watston, Macanree, &c.

[2] Published in 1845. Account drawn up from notes supplied by Rev. W. M'Gregor Stirling.

B

From this station, in a clear day, Arthur's Seat may be descried, having its base sunk behind a flat country, which, melted down by distance, somewhat resembles the ocean, and gives to that rock the appearance of the Bass or Ailsa."[1]

A locality of much historic interest lies also at the eastern termination of the hill. About 300 feet lower than the summit of Ben Dearg, and at almost the height of the moorland over which the road from Port of Menteith to Callander passes, lies the lonely little loch of Ruskie, with its island castle, now almost entirely gone, one of the seats of that Sir John Menteith whose connection with the betrayal of Wallace has caused his name and memory to be held in execration by his countrymen. This little lake, about a mile in circumference, occupies a secluded and, in ancient times, not easily accessible position. Tradition therefore avers that here Sir John, who had another residence called the Castle of Menteith somewhere in the vale below,[2] built himself a stronghold for the greater security which the troubled times and his own share in their events seemed to require. It may be presumed, however, that the old Earls of Menteith had some sort of tower on the island before it came into the possession of Sir John. But, by whomsoever or for what purpose it

---

[1] Notes on Inchmahome, p. 70, New Statistical Account of Scotland, vol. x., Parish of Port.

[2] This Castle of Menteith is reputed to have been the ancient stronghold of Rednock. It must be remembered that these statements regarding Sir John's castles rest on the authority of tradition alone. In no extant document is any mention made of his residence or residences. Both Rusky and Rednock belonged to the more ancient Earls of Menteith, and Sir John was a younger son of Earl Walter Stewart.

was built, Rusky Castle can never have been anything but a small peel-tower. The

> "escutcheoned walls
> Of frowning Rusky's ancient halls"[1]

had their existence only in the imagination of the poetess. There is no room on the island for any such spacious buildings as the lines seem to imply. A portion of the residential buildings, as well as the offices, may, however, have been on the shore, while the stronghold occupied the island. If that were so, all traces of them must have long ago disappeared; although the eye of the local antiquarian can still discern on the shore the course on which the ancient chiefs were wont to train their horses.[2]

The centre of interest of the Menteith hills—as it is their geographical centre—is the deep and thickly-wooded defile which separates the Craig-dhu hills on the west from those of Craig-dearg on the east. This opening into the hills is cut by a rushing mountain stream, which rises about the summit of the *col* that connects the two mountain masses. The stream, known as the Burn of Glenny, and in its lower part as Portend Burn, is the principal feeder of the Lake of Menteith. It tumbles down the steep hillsides over a succession of cataracts, and then pierces its way, in many places entirely concealed from sight, through clefts and chasms in the rock, which make passage

---

[1] Wallace, or the Field of Falkirk, by Miss Holford, canto v. st. 15.
[2] Dun's Summer at the Lake of Menteith, 1866, p. 24. For Sir John Menteith, see *infra*. Part of the stone-work of the old Castle is said to have been removed, about the beginning of the present century, for the purpose of building some houses at Blairhoyle.

from one side to the other impossible. These dark and romantic chasms can best be seen by forcing a way up the rugged channel of the burn—not an easy matter at any time, and possible only when the water is not in flood—and are perhaps most striking in their appearance just before the stream has succeeded in escaping from its rocky entanglements to the alluvial flat, across which it quietly meanders to the lake.

Towards the foot of the glen, and on the eastern side of it, a bold outpost of the hills detaches itself from the principal mass. This fine rounded knoll, clothed with bracken and grass to near the summit, which shows bare in contrast, and big enough to be reckoned a hill were it not for the greater elevation behind it, is named Crockmelly—a name apparently made up of *Cnoc* (sometimes written *Croch*) and *maol*, and therefore meaning "the bald or bare hill." Between Crockmelly and the stream are two places whose names are referred by local tradition to incidents in an affray which happened here in connection with the rising of the Earl of Glencairn in 1653. At that time Scotland was under the rule of the Commonwealth. But General Monk, who had over-run the country and held it with a firm hand, was called away to take command of the English fleet in the war that broke out with the Dutch. Taking advantage of his absence, the Earls of Glencairn and Balcarres endeavoured to raise the Highlands in the royal cause. Glencairn made his appearance in Menteith, where he was joined by Graham of Duchray with his men and some of the neighbouring clans. While these were encamped about Duchray and Lochard, the Governor of

Stirling Castle marched to meet them, with a squadron of horse and about a regiment of foot—a force apparently quite sufficient to deal with the rising, as the Grahams and their friends did not number quite three hundred men, all told. The English troops, however, were hemmed in at the pass of Aberfoyle, and driven back with considerable loss.

It is with this historical affair that tradition connects the incidents at Glenny. While on the march to Aberfoyle, along the northern shore of the Lake of Menteith, and in the narrow passage between Crockmelly and the lake, the English force was suddenly attacked by a small party of the Grahams of Glenny, whom their laird had ambushed in the pass on the front of the hill and among the rocks and trees of the glen. The Grahams were too few in number to be able to stop the march of the enemy, but the fire from their ambush was so annoying that the English commander ordered his horse to charge up the hill, and clear the pass. It is said that one of the Graham party, called M'Queen, had signalized himself by the accuracy of his aim and the deadly effect of his fire. He was therefore made the object of special pursuit by the horsemen. He did not escape. He was overtaken, and cut down at a spot which thenceforth has borne the name of "M'Queen's Pass."

Another native was more fortunate. Chased by a horseman right over the shoulder of the hill, he fled down the other side towards the glen of Portend, making for a place where, as described by the author of "Inchmahome," the rivulet has cut a deep and narrow chasm in the rock, the strata of which have a dip a little removed from the perpendicular, with the consequence that one of the sides projects in proportion as the other leans backwards.[1] To this deep fissure the wily Graham led the pursuing trooper. And just in time he reached the rock overhanging the hidden chasm. The soldier was at his heels, and his arm already raised to cut him down, when Graham swerved to the side, and horse and rider, unable to check their impulse, went headlong over the precipice. Thus local tradition accounts for the name of the " Horseman's Rock," by which the place is still known.

The laird of Glenny, though unable to arrest the advance of the English, had yet time to warn Duchray of his approach, so that the latter was enabled to take up an advantageous position at the foot of Lochard.

Such is the traditional account of the engagement at Glenny. Whether the details of the affair are accurately preserved or not, circumstances—to be by and bye referred to—seem to favour the belief that some such skirmish may have actually taken place here, although no mention is made of it in the detailed narrative of the events at Aberfoyle that has come down to us. This narrative, it may be stated, is attributed to John Graham of Duchray, himself the leader of the local clansmen, and may therefore be taken as authoritative in regard to the incidents of

---

[1] Notes on Inchmahome, p. 69. The following sentences complete the author's description of Portend Glen :—" They (*i.e.*, the sides of the glen) are both richly adorned with varied coppice, through which, from the noon-day twilight beneath, the sky is seen in glimpses. Huge moss-grown stones are scattered in wild and picturesque confusion ; and the din of the several rapids they form, by interrupting the course of the water, contributes to the romantic effect of this sequestered scene."

the fight. It is titled " Account of the Earl of Glencairn's Expedition as Governor of His Majesty's Forces in the Highlands of Scotland in the years 1653 and 1654, by a Person who was an Eye and Ear Witness to Every Transaction."[1]

As Duchray and Aberfoyle are so nearly connected with Menteith, it may not be out of place here to give a brief abstract of the substance of this narrative. It states that the first to join Glencairn in his rising was the laird of Duchrie with forty footmen, followed immediately by the tutor of M'Gregor with eighty men. These assembled at Duchray, where they were joined by Lord Kenmure with forty horsemen from the west, Colonel Blackadder with thirty horse from Fife, and the laird of M'Naughton with twelve horsemen. In addition there were between sixty and eighty Lowland men, without horses, but well provided with arms, under Captain Hamilton, brother to the laird of Milnburn. The total force thus amounted to less than 200 foot and 42 mounted men. The narrative then proceeds:—" Colonel Kidd, governor of Stirling, being informed that the king's forces were come so near him, marched with the greatest part of his regiment of foot and a troop of horse, to a place called Aberfoile, within three miles of Lord Glencairn. His lordship having intelligence, did march with the small force he had to the pass of Aberfoile, and drew up his foot on both sides very advantageously: and the horse, which were commanded by Lord

---

[1] The "Account" is adjoined as an Appendix to the Military Memoirs of the Great Civil War, by John Gwynne. These two curious works were printed from the MSS., and published at Edinburgh in 1822.

Kenmure, formed the wings. He gave orders for Captain Hamilton's cravats[1] and Deuchrie's men to receive the first charge, which they did very gallantly: and at the very first made the enemy retire. The general, perceiving this, commanded the Highland forces to pursue as also Lord Kenmure's horse: on this the enemy began to run in earnest:—they lost about sixty men on the spot, and it was said about eighty in the pursuit: no prisoners were taken on either side."[2]

This account of Duchray's, it will be observed, makes no allusion to the affair of Glenny, but in a letter to the *Mercurius Politicus* from the military correspondent in Scotland (dated at Dalkeith 3rd Sept., 1653) there is reference to another slight skirmish, which seems to have occurred at some place in Menteith nearer to Stirling than Lochard is. " The Lords Lorne and Kenmore are busy about the west of Stirlingshire; and were, with about 260 horse and foot, *within seven miles of the garrison, fired at some of ours, and killed a horse out of the ambuscade.* Colonel Read is marched out against them, with three companies of his own regiment and three troops of horse." This may well enough refer to the ambuscade at Glenny. We may make some allowance for the geographical knowledge of the English correspondent, as well as for the course of local tradition which represents as a private affair of the Laird of Glenny what was really a reconnaissance of the Highland force. The Colonel commanding the English troops was apparently not with his men on the occasion. It was to punish the insult that he marched immediately after-

[1] Croats. [2] Military Memoirs of the Great Civil War, &c., p. 160.

wards to Aberfoyle. Three days later the same correspondent writes as follows :—" In my last I acquainted you with the Lord Lorne and Kenmore's coming near to Stirling and Colonel Read marching towards them : since which there hath been a little skirmish, wherein they killed us two horse, and wounded us about twenty men and some horses : but they were well requited. When the craggs could shelter them no longer, they left our men upon the plain ground. There appeared fifty of their foot and some horse : divers of their foot run along the hills, from hill to hill, flanking of our men, and gauling us upon our retreat, which occasioned our loss. Colonel Read yet lies in the field near Port, by the isle of Menteith, near which the engagement was." This is no doubt the English version of the engagement at Aberfoyle. The circumstance of the Highlanders running along the hillsides and harassing the retreat of the enemy is characteristic. The statement of the Parliamentary loss in killed and wounded, as might be expected, differs greatly from the estimate of Duchray. It is to be observed also that the Commander, whom Duchray calls Colonel Kidd, is here named Colonel Read. The English writer must be credited with knowing the name of the Parliamentary officer. Duchray probably made the not unnatural error of taking *Rid*, which used to be the Scottish pronunciation of Read, for *Kidd*, or it may be that the transcriber or printer of his manuscript mistook the letter R for K. It is certain that Read—*Scotticè* Rid—was the governor of Stirling at that time. In a minute of Town Council, of 18th July, 1653, he is styled, "Colonell *Rid*, governour of this burgh."[1]

[1] Extracts from the Records of the Royal Burgh of Stirling, A.D. 1529-1666, p. 209.

For some time longer the Highland troops remained in the district. The *Mercurius Politicus* notes, under date 6th Nov., 1653, that the leaders still " lie about the island of Monteath with about 1000 foot and horse: about a third part of them want arms, instead whereof they have clubs " —surely a sorry rabble wherewith to overturn the government of the Lord High Protector. On the 26th of November occurs this final note—" To give you some account of our present posture, Kenmore is going northward: *but has left his beagles under one John Graham of Docra, to steal horses and plunder the country.*" Thus contemptuously is the Laird of Duchray dismissed from the pages of the *Mercurius Politicus*.[1] As the letter is written from Stirling, it was probably penned while the writer was still suffering from the soreness of Read's defeat by Duchray at Aberfoyle.

Down the pass of Glenny has swept many a Highland foray. By this track the predatory tribes of the wild mountain region beyond Loch Vennachar came down to harry the fertile region of Menteith and the Vale of Forth. The immediate neighbourhood especially, the domain of the Duke of Montrose, was the favourite scene of operations of those expert blackmailers and cattle-lifters, Rob Roy and his kin. It is to be expected, therefore, that memories of M'Gregors, and MacFarlans, and other marauders, should linger in the glen. And so they did till recently; but the inhabitants have now become very few, and the population of the vale below has greatly changed, so that orally preserved tradition has now become scanty. The harvest of such tradition, however,

[1] Military Memoirs, &c., Appendix pp. 199 to 214, *passim*.

has been already pretty well gathered, and the result has found a place in national as well as local literature. It is not intended to repeat any of these tales here: but whoever desires to read the story of the "bold outlaw," and the not less curious histories of his sons, will find an authentic account, together with a history of the clan in general, in Sir Walter Scott's Introduction to "Rob Roy": while the local legends of their exploits in Menteith have been told, with imaginative embellishments, in Mr. P. Dun's "Summer at the Lake of Menteith."

The old path leading up from the glen and over the ridge is still to be traced in the heath. It is known as the *Cheepers* or *Tyepers* path. At the top of the ridge it splits—one track taking down the hill in a north-easterly direction to the east end of Loch Vennachar, while the other curves round towards the north and west, and leads between Lochs Drunkie and Vennachar to Loch Achray and the Trossachs. On the height of the pass is a spring known as the Tyepers Well. This name seems to be merely a bad corruption of the old Gaelic word *tiobar* (pronounced *tibbar* or *tipper*), meaning "a well," or more specifically, "a well on a height." The word therefore exactly describes this spring and its situation, and furnishes also the explanation of the Tyepers Path—"the well road." This *tiobar* was most probably the spot where William, the third Earl of Menteith of the Graham line, was slain by Donald the Hammerer and his followers in or about the year 1544.[1] Writers who have mentioned this event have not been very definite in their localisation. Sir Walter

[1] The story is told in detail in the Life of that Earl, *infra*.

Scott says that the Earl and his men went in pursuit of the Stewarts by the difficult and dangerous path which leads from the banks of the Loch of Monteith through the mountains to the side of Loch Katrine. "They came up with Donald's party in the gorge of the pass, near a rock called Craig-vad or the Wolf's Cliff."[1] Others name the place Tobanareal, which is said to be "a spring on the summit of the ridge which separates Menteith from Strathgartney, between Loch Katrine and the Lake of Menteith."[2] The ridge, up which the Stewarts were making their way towards their native Appin, when overtaken by the Grahams, is that which lies between the Lake of Menteith and Loch Vennachar—although there is a track, as has been already noted, leading round the north side of the hill to Loch Katrine. *Tobanareal* is evidently a corruption of the original name. The first part no doubt is meant for *Tobar*. In the earliest mention both of the story and the place, the name is written *Tipard'nerheil*.[3] And this leads us to the etymology of the name, which seems to be a slightly corrupted form of *Tiobair-na-iorghuill*, meaning "the fountain of the fray."[4] If this is correct, the name must have been given to commemorate the incident, and was perhaps that by which it was afterwards known to the Stewarts. If it

---

[1] Tales of a Grandfather, 1892, vol. i. p. 424.

[2] Fraser's Red Book of Menteith, vol. i. p. 311.

[3] History of the House of Stewart, by Duncan Stewart, M.A. This book was published in 1739, but must have been written previously to 1730, which was the date of the author's death.

[4] In *iorghuill* the *gh* is silent, so that the word sounds as if written *irrail*. (Communication from Dr. A. C. Cameron.)

The Lake of Menteith. 29

ever prevailed in the neighbourhood, it has long been
lost, and the name has reverted to the more ancient and
simple *tobair*, now degenerated into *tyeper*.

In a hollow below this spring there is a cairn of white
quartz stone, gathered evidently with some care and trouble,
which one would like to be able to identify as the burial
place of some of those who fell in the fray at Tipardnerheil:
but the shepherds of Glenny say that it marks the spot
where a man was robbed and murdered when returning
by the hill-track to Loch Vennachar-side from a fair at
Aberfoyle.

CHAPTER II.

Around the Lake: Civil and Ecclesiastical Notices of Port: Traditions of the Shores.

"Green meadows and lake with green islands."
"Not a feature of these hills
 Is in the mirror slighted."
  "Tradition's dubious light
That hovers 'twixt the day and night."

SECTION I.—THE PORT; AND THE NORTHERN SHORE.

AT the north-west corner of the lake, and under the shadow of the hills, lies the village, or rather hamlet, of Port—so called, no doubt (Gaelic *poirt*, "a ferry," also "a landing-place"), because it was the landing-place for the monks of Inchmahome in their communication with the church which they possessed there, or when visiting the lands of their domain. There were two other landing-places on the north side of the lake. One was on the lands of Portend, where the pleasure-grounds of the Earls of Menteith were situated. This afforded the shortest passage from the shore to the islands, and may have been the private ferry of the Earls of Inchtalla. A third, and perhaps more public port, was at the extreme north-west corner of the lake. At Gateside, as the place is called, there was long a ferry to the islands: there was the house of the boatman, who used also, down to recent times, to be the lessee of the fruit gardens on Inchmahome.

The Port, although it gives name to the parish, was never anything but a very small village, and is now even smaller than it once was. The church, the manse, the inn, the schoolhouse, and a few cottages, make up the whole. Nevertheless, this small and secluded hamlet was erected into a burgh of barony by James the Third more than four hundred years ago. In a charter under the Great Seal,[1] dated at Edinburgh on the 8th of February, 1466, that monarch, for the singular favour he bore to his beloved kinsman, Malise, Earl of Menteith, and for provision to be made for himself and his lieges in the high land of Menteith,[2] during the season of the huntings and at other times, made the town of Porte, in Menteith and in the sheriffdom of Perth, a free burgh, to be had and held by the foresaid Malise, his successors, and the inhabitants thereof, in all time coming, as a pure and free burgh in barony, with all the usual liberties, privileges, and just pertinents. There was a well-known royal forest in Glenfinglas in the Stewartry of Menteith, the keepership of which was usually held by the captain of the castle of Doune; but the royal huntsmen can scarcely be supposed

[1] This charter has been printed in full in the Red Book of Menteith, vol. ii. p. 297.
[2] Or, "at the head of Menteith": the Latin words are, *in summitate de Menteith*. In the charter of James I., 1427, erecting certain lands into the earldom of Menteith, mention is made of the "foreste de baith le sidis de Lochcon." The situation of this forest might be very aptly described as "*in summitate de Menteith*"—at the head of Menteith.

The Lake of Menteith.

to have gone by way of the Port for the chase in Glenfinglas. There was, however, another forest for red deer, known as the forest of Menteith, which lay in the district of Aberfoyle. Whether this also was a royal forest is not quite clear;[1] but at any rate it lay within the bounds of the Earls of Menteith, and would be approached from Stirling by way of the lake. It is therefore most likely that it was to make provision for the royal comfort when hunting there that the King gave his beloved kinsman his free, if small, burgh in barony.

The cross of the burgh is said to have been the trunk of an old hawthorn tree, which stood by the lake side, opposite the manse of Port, and was known as "the law tree." Around this tree an annual fair was held in the month of September, and called after St. Michael. A writer, however,[2] who rests on the authority of oral tradition, asserts that up to the time of the last Earl of Menteith, in the end of the seventeenth century, St. Michael's fair was held on the farm of Milling, on the western shore of the lake. The fair is now discontinued.

There was a church at Port long prior to the Reformation.[3] It was one of four dependent on the Priory. The

---

[1] In the Exchequer Rolls (vol. vii. p. 614) there is noted a sum of £4 expended on repairs for the *Hunting-lodge at Duchray* in 1469—which seems to show that this also was a royal forest in the time of James III. From the same authority we learn that the keeper of the forest of Menteith in 1467 was one Donald Neyssoune (vol. vii. p. 485). The fermes of the lands of Duchray were in the hands of the king in 1461 (vol. vii. p. 69).

[2] Dun's Summer at the Lake of Menteith, p. 29.

[3] In the Protocol Book (John Graham's) of Stirling, there is registered the solemnization of the marriage, on the 21st April, 1541, of Archibald, Earl of Argyle, and Margaret Graham, daughter of William, Earl of Menteith, at the church of Inchmahome, after parties had been proclaimed three times "*apud ecclesiam de Port et Dolarie.*"

earlier records of the Kirk-Session, after the Reformation, have unfortunately been greatly mutilated, but of what remains, Mr. M'Gregor Stirling has printed several interesting extracts,[1] which throw some curious light on the manners and habits of the parishioners.

In the Episcopalian period, one of the ministers was Mr. James Donaldson, who had been presented to the charge by Bishop Leighton of Dunblane. As was to be expected from a friend of Leighton, he set himself to improve the morals of the people, which appeared to stand greatly in need of reformation. The prevailing sin was drunkenness, aggravated by its commission on the Sabbath day. The people assembled at the Port, and betook themselves to the ale-houses instead of to the church. Some, after their visit to the ale-house, came in late to worship, and had to sit bareheaded before the minister. Others did not attend the afternoon service. Elders were appointed to search the ale-houses, and also to keep watch on the roads leading from the village so as to prevent people going away without attending afternoon service. When they did remain, however, it was found that they were too apt to proceed, after the service was over, to wash down their diet of divinity in the public-house. So that the Session (23rd Feb., 1668) "acted and ordained that no bear nor ell seller within the paroch, shall sell ell after sermon, except in case of necessitie, folk be thirstie ore fant, they drink a chapon of ell, or those that are sick, or those that are strangers." It may be suspected that some members of the Session were not themselves without sin in this

[1] Appendix viii. to Notes on Inchmahome.

matter. At any rate, on 12th April, 1668, they thought proper to pass the following self-denying ordinance:— " The Session also considering the necessitie of reforming their own lives and manners befor they endeavore any such thing amongst others, have ordained that none of their number shall, after both sermons endit, goe into any ell house except in case of real necessitie, or for searching, under the pain of twentie shilling Scots for the first tym, and thereafter for everie tym this is to be doubled *toties quoties*." But even this self-denial on the part of the elders, added to the discipline of the church, was found insufficient to repress " that old sin and scandall of this paroch of drinking the wholl Lord's day." So recourse was had to fining the ale-sellers if they sold to any but sick persons and strangers, and to these only as much as would quench their thirst—a quantity which seems to have been limited to the regulation "chapon." Possibly, after that, "sickness" increased on Sundays at the Port. Unfortunately, we do not know to what extent Mr. Donaldson and his Session succeeded at length in repressing "the old sin" of the parish, because the records were carried off by Mr. Patrick Bell, his successor, and only partially recovered.

For some time after the Reformation the church of Port was served by readers. The name of William Streuling appears as reader in 1567, and Andrew Dougall was filling the office in 1574. Dougall was succeeded by William Stirling—whether the same as the first-mentioned is not known. This Stirling was somewhat of a pluralist. He had been presented to the parsonage of Aberfoyle in 1571, and held at the same time the vicarage of Kilmadock, with a manse in Dunblane; and to these offices was added the charge of Port in 1574. He was one of three nominated by the Privy Council in 1589 "for the maintenance of true religion in the Stewartries of Stratherne and Menteith": and shortly afterwards he was removed to Strageyth.

The first regular minister of the parish bore also the name of William Stirling. He was a graduate of Glasgow, where he was laureated in 1585. His first charge was Kincardine, whence he was translated to Port in 1597. He held the cure till 1616. His successor was James Seytoun, A.M.—laureated at Edinburgh, 29th July, 1603; became tutor in the family of Livingston of Dunipace, by whose influence he was admitted minister of Denny in November, 1607; translated to Logie in January, 1610, and finally to Port of Menteith in December, 1616. He died in 1638, when about fifty-five years of age. On the 2nd of July, 1638, King Charles I. presented to the charge Thomas Henderson, A.M., who had been a student of Glasgow University, where he was laureated in 1626. Henderson died in April, 1664, at the age of fifty-eight, survived by his wife, Jean Setoun of Wester Spittaltoun, a son and three daughters. "The utencils of his house were estimat at x lib.: frie geir j^c lib." He appears to have been, for the times, fairly well blessed with this world's goods.

The next minister was James Donaldsone, A.M., already referred to. He had graduated at St. Andrews in 1660, was licensed by George, Bishop of Edinburgh, in 1666, and was presented by Robert Leighton, Bishop of Dunblane, to the parish of Port, where he was inducted on the 15th of November, 1667. Donaldson was evidently an earnest and painstaking clergyman, and the parish enjoyed the benefit of his ministrations for fourteen years. In 1681 he was translated to Dumbarton, where it is to be feared he did not enjoy the comfort and peace that had been his lot in the quiet vale of Menteith. The tide of popular fury was rising against the Episcopalian clergymen—the "curates," as the populace called them—and the revolution of 1688 allowed the Presbyterians the freedom they had formerly been denied. In the "rabbling of the curates," no doubt some good men had to submit to ill-treatment along with the worthless creatures that had been in many cases intruded into the pulpits. Donaldson suffered with the rest. He was rabbled and deposed in 1690.

On Donaldson's departure from Port, James Ramsay, who had succeeded Leighton in the Bishopric of Dunblane, presented his own son, Robert Ramsay, A.M. The latter had graduated at Edinburgh in 1668, and had been licensed by Alexander, Bishop of Edinburgh, on 21st May, 1673. He was admitted to the parish of Port on the 25th of January, 1682, but remained only a few months in the parish, as he was translated to Prestonpans in September of the same year. He continued to exercise the office of the ministry in Prestonpans till the 10th of May, 1689, on which date he was deprived by the Committee of Estates for not reading and obeying their proclamation of the 11th of April. He betook himself to the Canongate of Edinburgh, where he died in 1699, about fifty-one years of age.

Next came Patrick Bell, who had studied at Glasgow, 1678-1683. He was presented to the parish by Alexander Higgins of Craigforth, and admitted to the charge on the

15th of May, 1683. He was the last of the Episcopalian clergymen. It was he who carried away, when he left the parish, the Session Records—which were only recovered after many tedious delays and complicated legal proceedings, and in a very imperfect and fragmentary condition, by the Kirk-Session in 1706. Mr. Bell was deprived by the Privy Council, 3rd October, 1689, for not reading the Proclamation of the Estates, for refusing to pray for their Majesties King William and Queen Mary, and not observing the Thanksgiving. Shortly after, he was served heir, in succession to his elder brother, of the estate of Antermony, of which his father, Alexander Bell, had been proprietor. He married Annabelle, daughter of Stirling of Craigbarnet, and was the father of John Bell of Antermony, the author of a one-time famous book of Travels in Asia.[1] Arthur Forbes, who had studied at Glasgow, and was licensed by the United Presbytery of Stirling and Dunblane in 1696, was ordained minister of the parish, 10th February, 1697. It was by him and his Kirk-Session that the existing fragments of the earlier Records were recovered from Mr. Patrick Bell. He died in the summer of 1724. After an interval of two years, Forbes was succeeded by John Fergusson, a native of Cowal, and a student of Glasgow. He was called in August, 1725, but was not ordained till July of the following year. Mr. Fergusson was proprietor of the estate of Craigholl. He died 2nd October, 1768. The next minister of the parish was Robert Stirling, who seems to have been a native of the district. He was licensed by the Presbytery of Dunblane on the 27th of

[1] Travels from St. Petersburgh to Various Parts in Asia.

July, 1762, and his first appointment was that of assistant to Mr James Oswald, minister of Methven. He was presented to the parish of Port by the patron, David Erskine, W.S., and ordained 13th July, 1769. He completed thirty-two years of service in the parish, and died on the 23rd of July, 1801. Before his death, however, he had the assistance of his son, William M'Gregor Stirling, who was presented by James Erskine of Cardross, and ordained assistant and successor to his father on the 15th of August, 1799. Mr. M'Gregor Stirling was a man of genial and kindly disposition, and of literary and artistic tastes. He was a zealous antiquarian, and set the first example of the careful and systematic study of the local records. All subsequent writers on the Priory and the Castle have been greatly indebted to his researches. His first important publication was entitled "Notes, Historical and Descriptive, on the Priory of Inchmahome; with Introductory Verses, and an Appendix of Original Papers."[1] It is frequently referred to in this volume. In 1816 appeared his "Chart of British History, with a Memoir," and in 1817 he edited a revised edition of "Nimmo's History of Stirlingshire" (first published in 1777), so enriched with additional matter as to make it practically a new and much more valuable work. "Papers illustrative of the Political Condition of the Highlands from 1689 to 1696" was printed by the Maitland Club in 1845. Mr. Stirling married—a second time—in 1823, and the circumstances of his marriage unfortunately led to a Presbyterial enquiry which resulted in a sentence of deposition. The sentence, how-

[1] Edinburgh, 1815: William Blackwood.

ever, was reversed by the Assembly of 1824, and arrangement was made for his retirement and the appointment of an assistant and successor. He withdrew to Edinburgh, where he busied himself in his favourite antiquarian and literary pursuits. He died of fever at Stockbridge on the 23rd of January, 1833, in the sixty-second year of his age. The assistant and successor appointed was William Wyllie, a licentiate of the Presbytery of Ayr. He was presented by David Erskine of Cardross, ordained 22nd September, 1825, and held the cure till his death on the 5th of March, 1843. Mr. Wyllie was succeeded by the Rev. Allan Turner, D.D., who died in 1867. The successor of Dr. Turner, and present incumbent of the parish, is the Rev. James Johnston, M.A.[1]

The present Church of Port was erected on the site of its predecessor in 1878. It is in thirteenth century Gothic, simple in treatment, and with an elegant spire, which comes well into the landscape as seen from the lake or the islands. It succeeded a building erected in 1771, near the beginning of the ministry of Mr. Robert Stirling. This, plain as it was, seems to have been considered a very good specimen of church building at the time, as it was taken as the model of a new church at Drymen built in the following year.[2] The site is probably that of the earliest Church of Port. In the churchyard are several old and interesting tombstones, the old church bell suspended from a tree—the new building has a chime of

---

[1] The authority for these facts regarding the ministers of the parish is, mainly, Scott's Fasti Ecclesiæ Scoticanæ, vol. ii. pt. ii.

[2] Guthrie Smith's History of Strathendrick, p. 92.

musical bells—and the mausoleum of the Grahams of Gartmore, built on the west border of the enclosure, hard by the lake.

The northern shore of the lake, westward from the Port, consists of a narrow strip of comparatively level land lying close under the steeply-rising hills. The lands of Port, as this was formerly called, are interesting, for several reasons. Here, about the middle, was the Prior's Meadow, which was no doubt a valuable possession of the monastery in olden times. In 1646, it was held in feu from the Priory by the Earl of Menteith.[1] On the Prior's Meadow is a small mound, which is supposed to be artificial, but the purpose of its construction is unknown. Tradition avers that it was formed with consecrated earth brought over from Ireland. In this tradition we may at least find, if nothing else, a recognition of the fact that Colman, who gave name to the island of Inchmahome, was an old Irish saint and bishop.[2]

Here, too, around Portend, was the pleasaunce of the Earls of Menteith. The surface of Inchtalla was barely large enough to carry the buildings which lodged the family; and, while they had the western portion of Inchmahome as garden ground, their more spacious pleasure grounds were on the northern shore of the lake. Relics of this ancient use are to be seen about Portend in the great old trees—oak, chestnut, walnut, sycamore, and others—which

---

[1] The monasterie and precincte with the yairdis and the Priouris medowe fewit to the Erll of Monteythe—xx s. (Rental of the Feu-duties of Inchmahome—October, 1646.)

[2] See *infra*, chap. v.

Inchmahome from North Shore of the Lake.

still remain dotted over the fields and bordering the old avenue which led to Coldon and the landing-place from Inchtalla. Coldon—or Cowdon—is a small conical hill, set close to the margin of the lake, and covered with wood. From this circumstance the name is said to have been been derived—Gaelic *coille*, "wood," and *dun*, "a hill-fort." There are vestiges of early fortification on its top and sides.

On the 1st of May, 1493, Michael Dun, mair of the sheriffdom of Perth, gave sasine to Alexander, as heir of his grandfather Malise, the first Earl of Menteith, of the earldom and its pertinents, "ad ripam lacus de Inchmahomok prope *le Coldone* supra solum terrarum de Porth," by the delivery of earth and stone in the usual manner, "apud litus lacus de Inchmahomok, inter prescriptum lacum et le Coldone."[1]

At this shore of Coldon, it may be noted in passing, there is a fine echo—the walls of the Priory of Inchmahome sending back the sound of words loudly spoken at the water's edge.

Portend appears to have been the home farm as well as the pleasure ground of the ancient earls. Here the cows for the domestic supply of milk to the Castle were kept, as we learn from the instructions of the last earl to his wife—"fyve kyne for the use of the house to be keiped in Portend." There was probably also a small mansion house, or superior farm-house, which received a royal visitor, in the person of Charles II., in the month of February, 1651. That sovereign, on the 10th of February,

[1] Instrument of Sasine printed in Red Book, vol. ii. p. 301.

1651, ratified at Portend a warrant to William, Earl of Airth, for payment of a debt due to him by his Majesty's father of saintly memory, who had deprived the earl of his dignities of Stratherne and Menteith, and assigned him the new and obscure title of Airth. Charles was at that time engaged in the, as yet vain, attempt to recover the kingdom from the Commonwealth, and was anxious to keep his own and his father's friends attached to his cause. So he gave to the earl, who had suffered much for and at the hands of Charles I., this warrant for the payment of a sum of £7000 assigned to him by "our umquill father of ever blessed memorie," and for an annual pension of £700 till the principal sum was paid in full and at one payment, adding, "we doe hereby promise on the word of ane prince to sie it faithfullie payed when ever we fynd occasione."[1] It is scarcely necessary to say that he never found occasion. Afterwards, when he had come to the throne, two warrants were issued for the payment of £500 sterling to the earl's grandson, William, second Earl of Airth—which also were never more than waste paper.[2]

Past Portend flows the burn which is the principal feeder of the lake; and, on the other side of that stream, at the head of the fine north-western bay, is Gateside, where was the cottage of the boatman, and what used to be the common or public ferry to the islands.

---

[1] Warrant printed in the Red Book of Menteith, vol. ii. p. 68.

[2] Warrants dated, 14th July, 1662, at Hampton Court; and 2nd June, 1665, at Whitehall. For further information about the royal debts to the earl, see *infra*, chap. xi.

The Lake of Menteith. 45

SECTION II.—THE WESTERN SHORE.

THE country on this side of the lake is bare of trees, and not inviting in prospect, as it stretches away to the westward in moorish humps, diversified with bogs. But it has much to interest the historian and antiquarian. Close by the shore were the Earls' stables, occupying the south side of a promontory projecting into the lake, south from the farm house of Milling, and at the nearest point of land to the kennels of Inchcuan. Further round the shore was the place where dwelt another important feudal official —the Earls' piper. Vestiges of the Piper's House still remain. And here is the curving gravel strand, more than half-a-mile in length, along which he used to strut in the early mornings, with his pipes in full blast, to waken the sleepers on Inchtalla with his stirring strains. Mellowed by their passage across half-a-mile of water, we can suppose that these strains fell upon the ears of the listeners not ungratefully.

The farm of Milling has other interesting localities. As has been said, the Fair of St. Michael was formerly held here on the shore of the lake; and a little to the west is the bold knoll of the "Gallows Hill," full in view of Inchtalla, so that the earls could see the execution of the criminals whom their justice or injustice had condemned. Tradition assigns the last execution on the Gallows Hill to the time of the last Earl of Menteith, who is said to have unjustly caused an innocent youth to be hanged on a charge of horse-stealing. That tradition, however, is unsupported by any tittle of ascertained fact, and the story, as told by the legend, represents that eccentric and hypochondriac nobleman in a character quite inconsistent with anything that is known of his real nature. A still more legendary interest attaches to the Claggans, where, it is affirmed in the locality, the last wolf in Scotland was killed. But that same statement is made of other places, so we must take it with the usual grain of salt. And so also must we take the interesting legend of Loch Macanree and Auchveity.

This story bears all the marks of having been invented by the rustic imagination to account for the apparent meanings of the names. Macanree appears to be good enough Gaelic *(Mac-an-righ)* for "King's Son," and Auchveity seemed to be by interpretation "The field of Betty." The problem, therefore, was to bring these two persons together. And this is how it was solved.

Once upon a time this country to the west of the lake was royal forest, wherein the King and his court used to enjoy the delights of the chase. One one occasion the King's son had gone out to the hunt and raised a fleet stag, which, instead of keeping to the hillside, rushed off to the low and boggy ground in the neighbourhood of the lake. The royal prince followed on, reckless of possible danger in the ardour of his chase, and rapidly outstripping his attendants, till his horse sunk deep in the bog beside the little lochan. The prince was in the utmost danger of being engulfed, horse and all, when a strapping herdmaiden, who was tending her cattle at the Shiels of Gartrenich, not far off, hastened to the rescue. She grasped the prince with her strong hands, plucked him from the tenacious mud, and set him on firm ground. In reward for this gallant deed, she received from the King the piece of land near which the feat was done, and which thenceforth was called from her own name, Auchveity, or Betty's field. The lochan also, to commemorate the circumstance, received its name of Loch Macanree—the lake of the King's son. The legend is delightfully indefinite as to the time when this interesting incident occurred, and as to the particular prince who was the hero of it.

As it has its origin, no doubt, in the attempt to account for a popular etymology, a little more philology may be pardoned. Auchveity may quite well be interpreted *the field of the marsh*—a name quite characteristic of the place. As to Macanree—the fact that in pronunciation the accent is invariably placed on the *second* syllable, with a suspicion of an indefinite vowel sound between the *n* and *r*, would lead us to look somewhere else than to *Mac-an-righ* for the origin of the word. It may possibly be found to be *Magh-an-oraidh, i.e.,* "the field or plain of worship." This explanation may be supposed to receive confirmation from the fact that the site of the ancient Chapel of Arnchlay—one of the chapels dependent on the Priory of Inchmahome—is hard by. The *larach* or foundation-site of this old chapel is still to be seen.

Near this is the curious and interesting stone called the Peace Stone—for what reason so called is unknown. The stone was buried in a trench about the beginning of the present century, by the farmer on whose fields it lay, but is again exposed to the light of day. The local legend is that long ago a Gaelic seer—whose name, Pharic M'Pharic, at any rate looks Celtic enough—prophesied the burial of this stone by two brothers, who, for their impiety, would die childless, that the stone would by and bye rise to the surface, and then would be fought a great battle on Auchveity. The first part of the prophecy has been fulfilled—the farmer brothers who buried the stone both died without issue, and the stone is again above the surface; but the great battle has not yet come off. Apart from the legend, however, the stone is of great interest to archæologists. It lies about half-a-mile south from the farm-house of Milling, at the boundary of the arable land. It is roughly circular on the surface, measuring about four feet in diameter. The surface is entirely covered with cup and ring marks—twenty-two cups in all—varying in size from an inch to two inches in diameter. The cups and rings are very symmetrically formed. Nearly in the centre is a fine one surrounded by four circular grooves. Others have incomplete triple and quadruple circles, with radial duct dividing them. There are other curious curves that sometimes interlace, and near the lower side of the stone are five or six cups with straight channels running out from them over the edge. The markings are much weather-worn, and the stone, of course, points to the work of a period long anterior to any of the ecclesiastical buildings in the neighbourhood.[1]

An historical battle site is the Moss of Talla or Tilly-

---

[1] Standing Stones, &c., by A. F. Hutchison, in Transactions of Stirling Natural History and Archæological Society, vol. xv.

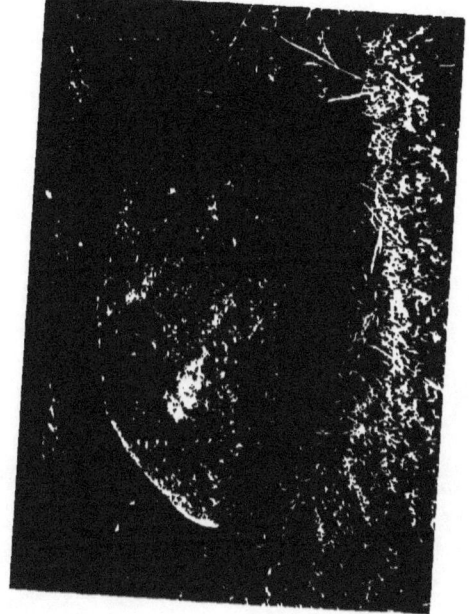

The Milling Cup-marked Stone.

The Lake of Menteith.

moss, lying further to the west and not far from the river Forth. At this place, on the 11th of October, 1489, the Earl of Lennox, with the force he had collected to avenge the death of James III., pitched his camp. He was on the way to Dumbarton Castle, which was being held for him by his son, Matthew Stewart, and Lord Lyle. On his approach to Stirling from the north, he found the passage of the Forth impossible, as the town was held in strong force by the friends of the young King, James IV. He therefore marched to the west on the north side of the river, intending to cross it near its source, and encamped at the Moss of Talla. The King and Lord Drummond were at Dunblane when word was brought them that Lennox was lying at Talla. The King immediately sent to Stirling for "culverins," hastily collected a small force, and with Lord Drummond rode out from Dunblane to attack the insurgents. They fell upon them in the darkness of the night and utterly routed them, driving them across the Forth to Gartalunane.[1] Lennox himself and the other principal conspirators were pardoned and taken into favour by the King. Only Thomas Galbraith, laird of Culcreuch, was executed as a traitor, and his lands bestowed on Adam Hepburn, brother of the Earl of Bothwell. Next day, the King rode back to Stirling, going by way of Kippen, at the church of which place he gave thanks for his success, and bestowed an angel (= 24 shillings) on the church as a thank-offering.[2]

[1] Buchanan's History of Scotland, book xiii. chap. 5; Tytler's History, 1864, vol. ii. chap. v. p. 250.
[2] Accounts of the Lord High Treasurer of Scotland, p. 122.

SECTION III.—THE SOUTHERN SHORE.

THE ground to the south of the lake rises gradually from the shore to the height of land between the Lake and the Vale of Forth, and is, for the most part, heavily wooded. The long, curving, sandy bay on the south-west terminates about the middle of the lake in the promontory of Arnmaack, which runs out from the shore to within a short distance of Inchmahome, and divides the lake almost into two portions. This long peninsula is said by local tradition to have been the work of fairies. This is how the story is told by Mr. M'Gregor Stirling. "The Earls of Menteith," he says, "were possessed of what was called the '*red-book*,' to open which was to be followed by something preternatural. One of them (whether from accident or design is a matter of doubt) unclasped the fatal volume, when lo! the fairies appeared before him, demanding work. His lordship set them to make a road from the mainland to the islands. They began on the southern shore, and had made what is now called Arnmaack, a pleasing peninsula, tufted with a grove of Scotch firs of considerable height; when the Earl, fearing either that they would become mutinous should they run out of work, or that they might, by completing their task, spoil the insular situation of his fastness, or both, bade them twist a rope of sand. They began the latter task without finishing the former, which still remains half done; but finding their new employment too much for them, and covered with shame, they resolved to depart."[1]

[1] Notes on Inchmahome, p. 81.

The Lake of Menteith. 53

It is added that the Earl, in commiseration of their shame arising from the impossible task he had set them, granted them a new dwelling-place on the north side of Ben Venue, and there they have dwelt since, in the well-known Coir-nan-Uriskin.

As this veracious story refers the construction of Arnmack to one of the Earls of Menteith, it must have taken place well within the historical period. But history—sooth to say—makes no mention of the circumstance. In one respect the fairies showed good sense, that is, in constructing their passage-way to the islands from the south rather than from the north shore. The Coldon shore is the nearest point of the mainland to the islands; but there the water is extremely deep, whereas on the south side it is comparatively shallow.

Arnmack seems to signify "the portion or field of the swine"; and, if this be its correct etymology, it may have been used as a preserve, in the woods of which were fed the herds of that useful domestic animal; or, the name may contain a reference to the story of some ancient boar-hunt, now forgotten.

The fancied abode of the supernaturals—if, again, we are to give credence to etymology—was further east on the same side of the lake. More than half-way from Arnmack to the south-east angle of the lake is another and smaller, though very conspicuous promontory, clothed with ancient trees, and known by the name of *Cnoc-nan-bocan*, which, being interpreted, means "the knowe of the bogles." This knoll has all the appearance of an ancient "barrow." It has never been examined. Should it turn out, on exploration, to be a sepulchral mound, the name which has so long clung to it would receive a sufficient explanation.[1]

Southwards from Arnmack lies Gartur, originally the property of the monastery of Inchmahome, and now again belonging to the estate of Cardross, but for some time occupied by a branch of the Graham family, in whom was said to be the succession by heirs-male to the earldom of Menteith. The last male representative of this line died in 1818. All the south side of the lake is occupied by the lands and woods of Cardross, once the dominical lands of the Priory of Inchmahome, and ever since the time of the Commendators held by members of the family of Erskine. Cardross itself is a stately old mansion, containing many interesting relics, and the estate and its owners have been closely associated with many important events in the history of the country. But it would be going too far afield to refer to these here, although something may be said regarding them in a later portion of this book. It is enough to point out one or two interesting localities in the more immediate neighbourhood of the lake.

To return for a little to Arnmack, it may be pointed out that in the "Journal of the Hon. John Erskine of Carnock, from 1683 to 1687,"[2] it is called Ardmach, which seems to mean "the high field"—a designation of which it is difficult to see the propriety. This Mr. Erskine—

[1] A mound on the estate of Craigengelt, in the parish of St. Ninians, which was popularly known as "The Ghaist Knowe," was dug into in 1838, and discovered to be a barrow, with sepultures of the bronze age.

[2] The Journal of the Black Colonel was printed by the Scottish History Society in 1893, from the original MSS. in the possession of H. D. Erskine, Esquire of Cardross. It is of great interest, and valuable as a contribution to the history of the times of persecution.

View of the Lake from the South-East.

The Lake of Menteith.   57

the "Black Colonel," as he was called—was zealous in
the cause of civil and religious liberty at that time, and
suffered persecution in consequence. In the summer of
1684, he was in hiding in the neighbourhood of Cardross,
and found shelter in the woods of Ardmach, where he slept
o' nights "among the fairn." While here he seems to
have been in friendly communication with the last Earl
of Menteith; so that that nobleman can scarcely have been
the ferocious persecutor of the Covenanters that, in his
letters to Graham of Claverhouse, he makes himself out to
be. Perhaps he made an exception in the case of a friend, or
it may have been that he merely put on his airs of severity
to recommend himself to the powers that then were.[1]

At the south-eastern extremity of the lake lies the
pleasant mansion-house of Lochend—a place frequently
mentioned in the early writs of the Priory. Here the late
genial and gallant Admiral Erskine, so long the Member
of Parliament for the County of Stirling, used to dwell.
The house and grounds afford most charming views of the
lake. The wide expanse of water is backed by the bold
hills of Glenny on the north; while to the westward the
middle distance is broken by the peninsula of Arnmack,
running out as if to meet the graceful wood and ruin-
covered islands; and Ben Lomond rears his lofty cone in
the background of the view.

Southwards from Lochend, half-way up the rising ground
behind, is a locality whose name carries us back to very
early times. This is the *Tom-a-mhoid*, or "moot-hill"—
the place where the open-air courts and other meetings

[1] See *infra*, chap. xi.

were held, and local justice administered. As an occasionally necessary adjunct to this administration of justice, there is—or was—an aged ash-tree, which tradition pointed out as that on whose boughs malefactors, in the olden times, were "justified."

At Lochend the lake is drained by the water of Goodie, which a little below its efflux from the lake, used to spread out into a shallow lake called the Loch of Goodie (Gude, Gudy, Gwdy, Gwidi).[1] An attempt has been made to claim for some position on this stream or lake the site of the ancient Pictish town of Guidi, referred to by the venerable Bede.[2] Wherever that much-disputed site may have been —Inchkeith, Inchcolm, Inchgarvy, Edinburgh, Queensferry, Camelon, or elsewhere—the vale of Goodie has nothing to answer to the circumstances of Bede's description, except the—possibly accidental—resemblance in the name.[3]

IV.—THE EASTERN SHORE.

THE whole of this side is beautifully wooded, and diversified with green and bosky knolls. The waters of the lake curve

[1] In grants by the Dowager Queen Margaret to her brother-in-law, James Stewart, of the captaincy of Doune Castle, &c., dated at Stirling 1st and 8th September, 1528, mention is made of the "fischeing of the lowis (lochs) and stankis of Lugnock (Lubnaig), Loch Banacher (Vennachar), and Gude." (Red Book of Menteith, ii. 385, 387.)

[2] New Statistical Account of Scotland, vol. x. p. 1100. This account of the Parish of Port of Menteith is said to have been "principally drawn up from an account written by a late incumbent, the Rev. W. M'Gregor Stirling."

[3] Bede's words (Lib. i. cap. 12) are:—"Orientalis (sinus) habet *in medio sui* urbem Guidi; occidentalis *supra se*, hoc est ad dexteram sui, habet urbem

in and out, forming pretty little bays whose gravelly shores are overhung with trees. The road to the Port winds along the margin, and affords most pleasing glimpses of the lake and its wooded islands. Not far from the exit of the Goodie is a fine tree-clad promontory jutting out boldly into the deep waters, near which is said to have stood the old Chapel of Inchy, another of the dependent chapels of Inchmahome. No fragment of this ancient chapel is now left, but it is traditionally said to have its site at or near the place which is now the garden of the farm-house of Inchie. A Chapel-well to the east of this attested its existence. The promontory is reputed to have been the burying-ground connected with the chapel.

The most general local tradition affirms that it was in a house at Inchie where that wedding feast was laid out which was devoured by the hungry followers of Donald the Hammerer—the cause of the engagement on the hills of Menteith, in which William, the third Graham earl, lost his life. But another tradition, perhaps equally entitled to credit, says that the depredation was committed at the office houses of the Earl's stables, on the opposite side of the lake: while a third, but less likely, traditional statement has it that the roasted fowls were carried off from the house of Talla itself.[1]

On the eastern shore of the lake is the fine estate of Rednock, with what has been a strong old castle now in ruins.[2]

Alcluith." Alcluith is easily identified with Dumbarton, but the site of Guidi has not yet been finally determined.

[1] See chap. x.

[2] This castle is said to have been built by George Graham, the first Graham of Rednock.

Rednock was long in the possession of the early earls of Menteith or cadets of their family. In 1213, on the death of Murdach, the second known earl, the succession was disputed by his two sons, both named Maurice—a quarrel which was settled by the intervention of King William (the Lion). The arrangement agreed to provided the earldom to the younger brother, while the elder Maurice was to hold of the King, for life, certain lands, among which is mentioned the town of Radenoche.[1] After the death of this Maurice, Rednock reverted to the earldom. The lands and Castle of Rednock are said traditionally to have been the property of Sir John Menteith of Ruskie. Although this does not admit of documentary proof, it is not unlikely, for Sir John, as a younger son of Walter Stewart, the fifth Earl of Menteith, may have been in possession of this property, which at that time formed part of the earldom.

When the new earldom was formed in 1427, Rednock was not included in it. It was part of the lands annexed to the Crown as the Stewartry of Menteith. It was still held, however, under the Crown, by families of the name of Menteith, who regularly paid their feu-firms to the royal Chamberlains of the Stewartry, as we learn from regular entries in the Exchequer Rolls. It appears from these records to have been divided into two portions. One of these was held by a John of Menteith in 1456.[2] It is difficult to make out the identity of this John. He can-

---

[1] *Inspeximus* of this agreement by Henry the Third, dated 20th September, 1261, in the Record Office—printed in the Red Book, ii. 214.
[2] Exchequer Rolls, vol. vi. p. 278.

not have been in the direct line of the Ruskie descent, as that terminated in two female heirs much about this time. Walter, one of the Ruskie Menteiths slain by the Drummonds in the clan-battle at Tar of Ruskie previous to 1360, left a son at that time under age. This may have been the Walter of Menteith who, in 1403, witnessed a charter of Robert of Rusky:[1] and John may have been a son or grandson of this Walter. John of Menteith was condemned to death and escheated in 1457.[2]

In 1473, King James the Third granted to James of Menteith for the service he had done in killing the King's rebel, Patrick Stewart, the ten pound lands of Rednok, to "bruke and joiss the saide landis heretablye in feuferme."[3] The Exchequer Rolls show that the ferms for these lands continued to be paid by successors of this family of Menteith, down to some time in the sixteenth century.

Another portion of the lands of Rednock were set in assedation in 1480 to John Menteith and Jonet Drummond his spouse, and a third and smaller portion to one Gilchrist M'Kessone. These Menteiths and M'Kessons continued to hold of the Crown till 1499. In that year James the Fourth made a grant to Sir Patrick Hume of Polwarth of the lands of Argaty and Lundy, and also of the £3 6s. 8d. lands of Rednock, otherwise called Inchanach, set to Patrick Menteth (son of John), and the 33s. 4d. lands of Rednock, set to Gilchrist Mackesson in reward for the services he had rendered the King in his wars.[4] In 1582, these

[1] Charter in Red Book, vol. ii. p. 272.   [2] Exchequer Rolls, vol. vi. p. 356.
[3] Printed in the Red Book, vol. ii. p. 300, from original at Rednock.
[4] Exchequer Rolls, vol. xi. p. 161.

lands are mentioned as still pertaining to Patrick Hume of Argaty and Rednock; but in 1584, David Hume of Argaty was executed and his lands confiscated, for communicating with the banished Commendator, David Erskine, and his friends.[1]

In 1515, William Edmonston, the keeper of Doune Castle, received sasine of the lands of Rednock.[2] Archibald Edmonston of Rednock appears in the Rolls in 1566.[3] He was one of the tenants of the Stewartry who complained, on the 17th of January, 1566, of the conduct of the steward in insisting on lifting the rents of their lands, which had been spoiled and utterly wasted by the Clangregor and other lawless persons.[4]

Rednock is found, in 1584, in the possession of George Graham, second son of John, fourth Earl of Menteith, who was known as the "tutor of Menteith" from the circumstance that he was legal guardian to his nephew the sixth earl during his minority. This George is said by Sir William Fraser to have been the ancestor of the Grahams of Rednock. Mr. Graham Easton, however, affirms that George was not of Rednock, but of Easter Rednock only—the real Rednock being one Gilbert, who was the ancestor of the Grahams of Leitchtown.[5] He is

---

[1] Register of the Privy Council of Scotland, vol. iii. p. 672 : Pitcairns' Criminal Trials, vol. i. pt. iii. p. 136. In the latter work, the "dome" is given as follows :— "the said David suld be tane to ane gippet, at the croce of Edinburghe, and thair hangit, quarterit and drawin ; and all his landis, takis, stedingis, rowmis, possessionis and guidis, to be eschete to the Kingis use."

[2] Libri Responsionum for 1515 ; Exchequer Rolls, vol. xiii. p. 579.

[3] *Ibid*, vol. xiv. p. 334.

[4] Register of the Privy Council of Scotland, vol. i. p. 418.

[5] Genealogical Magazine for June, 1897, pp. 73 and 79.

The Lake and Inchmahome from Portend.

designed or designs himself " George Graham of Rednock, tutor of Menteith," in a document of date 1584.[1] His elder son James had charters of confirmation from the King (James VI.) of Easter Rednock in 1584 and 1598. James was succeeded by his brother John, whose daughter Marion married John Graham of Duchray, and thus Rednock came into the possession of that family, whose descendants have possessed it since.

Contiguous to Rednock, on the east, is Blairhoyle. This name is a reversion to the most ancient designation of the lands—Blairquhoille. Judging from the name, it must have been covered with woods in the early times. It was in possession of the Crown as part of the Stewartry till 1517, when James the Fifth granted it to John Leech, a member of an old Perthshire family. John's father, Finlay Leitch, had fallen at Flodden, and it was probably to mark his appreciation of the loyalty of the father that the King gave the property to his son. John Leitch was succeeded by a son of the same name, whose only daughter carried the estate to her husband, Robert M'Gibbon. Baron M'Gibbon, as he was called, again had an only daughter. She married one Patrick Graham, and their descendants, in regular succession, held the estate till about twenty years ago, when the then James Graham of Leitchtown sold it to A. H. Lee, Esquire. Mr. Lee changed the name of Leitchtown to the older and more euphonious style of Blairhoyle.

For this branch of the family of Graham a claim has been maintained to the dormant earldom of Menteith.

[1] Red Book of Menteith, vol. i. p. 321.

Mr. Walter Malise Graham Easton—who traces his own descent from the Leitchtown Grahams—has published elaborate pedigrees to prove his contention that George Marshall Graham, of Toronto, Canada, eldest son of James of Leitchtown, is now "*de jure* fifteenth Earl of Menteith and ninth Earl of Airth."[1] This thorny question is not for the pages of a book like this. It must be left to the experts in genealogy.

North from Rednock and Blairhoyle is Ruskie. To the lake and island Castle of Ruskie reference has already been made. But there is another spot of some historic interest yet to be referred to. This is the Tar (Gaelic *tor*—a small hill) of Ruskie, where the famous clan battle between Drummonds and Menteiths—in which three brothers of Sir Alexander Menteith of Ruskie were slain—was fought, about the middle of the fourteenth century. Some account of this fight and its consequences will be found in a subsequent chapter.[2]

[1] Genealogical Magazine, June 1897, pp. 74, et *seqq.*   [2] Chap. xii., *infrd.*

CHAPTER III.

The Lake and the Islands : A Chapter of Description.

"Meek loveliness is round thee spread,
A softness still and holy."

"Islands that together lie
As quietly as spots of sky
Among the evening clouds."

"My dear Lord, Labe has made me in love with the Yles of Menteith. He says the greatest things in the world of it."—*Graham of Claverhouse.*

IT has often been said that the Lake of Menteith is the only *lake* in Scotland. The substitution of the English word *lake* for the more Scottish *loch* is, however, of quite recent origin, and is due not to local but to literary influences. This change was the more easily effected, because even Loch of Menteith—used by Sir Walter Scott and others—was so comparatively recent that it had not had time to take firm hold before it was displaced by the more Anglified form, Lake of Menteith.

The oldest documents in which the name of the lake occurs are in Latin, and in these it is called *Lacus de*

Inchmahomok (1485[1] and 1493[2]). The first occurrence of the name in the vernacular is in the rental of the feu-duties of Inchmahome, in 1646, in which are included the "*loche of Inchemahummoe* and fischeing thairoff."[3] In Timothy Pont's Map of the Province of Lennox—printed at Amsterdam 1654—it appears as *Loch Inche mahumo*; and so, also, it is written in several other seventeenth century maps.

Graham of Duchray (1724[4]) is the first writer to call it Loch of *Monteath*. As *Loch* it appears in the old Historical Account of the Parish (1799). Dr. Graham uses both Loch and Lake in his Sketches of Perthshire (1812), and varies these with Lake of Inschemachame and Inchmahave in his Account of the Natural History of the district;[5] while the New Statistical Account (1845) reverts to Lake of Inchmahome. During this century the country people of the surrounding district were in the habit of speaking of it as the *Loch o' Port*, and by that name it is still known to the older among them.

The transference of the name of Menteith to the Loch of Inchmahome has no doubt been the chief reason for the limitation that has grown up in the territorial significance of the former word, by which it has been diminished of its

---

[1] Grant by Earl Malise, 8th December, 1485, to his son John of the lake of Inchmahomok.—Red Book, i. 297.
[2] Sasine of Earl Alexander, 6th May, 1493.—Red Book, ii. 302 and 303.
[3] Printed in Red Book, ii. 368.
[4] Description of Parish of Port, by Alexander Graham, Esq. of Duchray (Macfarlarlan Papers in the Advocates' Library) quoted in Notes on Inchmahome, Appendix ix.
[5] Appendix x. to Notes on Inchmahome.

ancient amplitude, and is now generally restricted to the vicinity of the lake.

The lake lies beneath the Ben-dearg portion of the Hills of Menteith, and so close to them that only a narrow strip of meadow land intervenes between the northern margin and the foot of the steeply rising hill. Although the surface of its waters is only some 55 feet above the sea level, and not more than five or six feet above the level of the Carse of Forth, yet the ground all around rises more or less gradually on all sides from the shore, so that the lake occupies a cup-like depression of considerable depth. These rising banks, clothed on the east and south with luxuriant woods, which shelter it from storms and screen it from the view in those directions, give it that air of retirement and seclusion which is its chief and most charming characteristic. The idea of peacefulness thus suggested is intensified by the strength of the mountain mass that shuts it in on the north. But though generally calm and at rest, it can put on a scowl occasionally. When stormy blasts from the west blow across the bleak moorlands and strike its waters into foam, the lake looks angry enough. The prevailing sentiment of the scene, however, is that which has been so finely interpreted by the late Dr. John Brown: "Set in its woods, with its magical shadows[1] and soft gleams, there is a loveliness, a gentleness and peace about it more like ' lone St. Mary's Lake,' or Derwent Water, than of any

---

[1] This fine phrase has much to answer for. "The magical shadows" have been written to death by all the writers of "gush" who have since essayed to describe the scene.

of its sister lochs. It is lovely rather than beautiful, and is a sort of gentle prelude, in the *minor* key, to the coming glories and intenser charms of Loch Ard and the true Highlands beyond. . . . . On the unruffled water lie several islets, plump with rich foliage, brooding like great birds of calm. You somehow think of them as on, not in the lake, or like clouds lying in a nether sky —'like ships waiting for the wind.'"[1]

This tender little sketch of the scene has been taken from the Port. That is the usual point of view; and, indeed, the prospect, either from this, or from any point on the eastern shore, is charming. But it may be doubted if it presents the lake to the best advantage. The entire western portion, with its shapely bays, is cut off from sight. To see the whole expanse of water at one view, let the spectator look at it from the top of Coldon Hill, on the north shore opposite Inchmahome, or climb to the summit of the knoll on the hill of Glenny, just above the farm-house at Portend. These positions both afford very complete and delightful views of the lake. But a still finer, perhaps—with more of the picturesque, if less of the bird's-eye—is to be had from the Aberfoyle road, where it reaches the height above the farm-house of Milling, about a mile to the west of the lake. This is probably the best point from which to look at the lake. The prospect is wider and opener than from the Port; it has less of that feeling of formality which is inseparable from a bird's-eye view; at the same time, it partially

[1] Horæ Subsecivæ, by John Brown, M.D., second series, p. 170. (Edin., 1861.)

The Admiral's Point, Lake of Menteith.

conceals the rather bare and weak portions of the western shore, and places the finely wood-fringed southern and eastern sides full in sight, while the islands seem to group themselves in the most effective way.

The lake is approximately circular in outline, with the long promontory of Arnmawk breaking the line of continuity of the southern shore. It is between five and six miles in circumference, with a maximum length of about a mile and a half from east to west, and a mile from north to south. Generally shallow, in some places it is abruptly deep. Towards the eastern side, after a few yards of shallow water at the shore, it sinks at once to a depth of 46 feet. In the south-western bay, between Inchtalla and the southern shore, it is about the same depth. But greater depths are reached in the northern parts of the lake. Soundings opposite Gateside, in the north-west bay, give 63 feet of water, and between Inchmahome and the landing-place at Coldon the maximum depth of 88 feet is attained.[1]

The principal feeder of the lake is the Portend Burn, which enters at the north-west corner. Some smaller rills also add their little tributes to its waters. At a gap in the encircling rim of rising ground, at the south-western extremity, the superfluous waters are carried off by the Goodie, which winds its slow way through the fields and mosses of the Carse for nearly nine miles, till it joins the Forth in the neighbourhood of Gargunnock.

Some description of the appearance and natural features

[1] These depths are taken from soundings made for the Rev. W. M'Gregor Stirling in 1815.

of the islands in the lake will be necessary, before dealing in detail with their ruined buildings, and the history of those who reared and inhabited them.

Inchmahome, the largest of them, lies nearly in the middle of the lake. It takes its name from St. Colman or Colmoc, to whom its earliest Church would therefore appear to have been dedicated.[1] Colmoc is a diminutive form of Colman. The kindly Celts had a habit of adding this affectionate diminutive—*oc*, and also prefixing the endearing *ma* or *mo* ("my") to the names of their well-beloved saints. So *Innis Macolmoc*, the original of the island name, means *the island of my dear* (little) *Colman*.[2] It is very nearly in this form in which it is written in what is perhaps[3] the earliest extant document wherein it is mentioned, the Papal Instrument of 1238, which authorised the foundation of the monastery. There it is called Inchmaquhomok. For a century after that the name appears only in the Gallicised or Latinized forms of Isle de St. Colmock, Insula Sancti Colmoci, and Insula Beati Colmoci—all attesting the understood meaning of the word. The Gaelic word reappears in documents first as Inchemecolmoc and Inchemacholmock, and then, by a gradual process of softening, through Inchmaquhomok, Inchmahomock, Inchmaquholmo, Inchmaquhomo, Inch-

---

[1] See *infra*, chap. v.

[2] Compare the name of a parish not far off—*Kilmaronock*, the cell or church of my dear little Ronan.

[3] This qualification is necessary, because there is a reference in the Chartulary of Cambuskenneth (pp. 160, 161), assignable to the year 1210, to a *persona Macholem*, whom Sir William Fraser and others agree to accept as parson of Inchmahome. But may the reference in this case not be to St. Colme's Inch in the Firth of Forth rather than to St. Colman's Isle in Menteith?

mahomo, and Inchmahummo, reaches its present form of Inchmahome.

It is noticeable that the form Inchmachame, which Mr. M'Gregor Stirling adopts, and to which he gives the poetical meaning of "Isle of my Rest," does not occur till 1610.[1] There need be little doubt that it is a mere corruption, *more Scotico*, of the ancient pronunciation. The attenuation of the broad *o* into the indefinite Scottish sound of *a* is too common to stand in need of illustration. In this connection, moreover, the intermediate form, Inchmahummo, is instructive. It is almost a pity to disturb an interpretation which has given occasion to so many pretty and poetical imaginations. But M'Gregor Stirling is entirely responsible for this version of the name, and on no more definite ground than the circumstance that he found the spelling *Inchmachame* in the Charter of James VI., and probably that Inchmahame was the local pronunciation in his day. From this he jumps to the conclusion that "Insche-ma-chame, or Innis-mo-thamb, 'Isle of my Rest,' was probably the name in pagan times," and accounts "for the subsequent change to Inchmahome, or Inchmahomo, by supposing it a Latinized and monkish corruption of the original Gaelic."[2] The Gaelic Inschemachamhe, however, would be pronounced as if written Inchmachave, and so we find Dr. Graham, who was a good Gaelic scholar, and who seemed to adopt M'Gregor Stirling's version of the name, actually writing it.[3]

The following are the various forms in which the name

[1] In a Charter of James VI.
[2] Notes on Inchmahome, p. 119. [3] *Ibid*—Appendix x. p. 189.

The Lake of Menteith.

appears in charters and other documents, with the dates of the earliest occurrence of each :—

Insula de Inchmaquhomok (Deed of Foundation), 1238; Isle de St. Colmock (Prynne's Collections III., 653—referred to by Spottiswoode), 1296; Isle de Saint Colmoth (Ragman Roll, p. 117), 1296; Insula Sancti Colmoci (Charter of Earl Alan), 1305; Inchemecolmoc (Letter of Malise of Stratherne), 1306; Insula Beati Colmoci (Charter of David II.), c. 1340; Insula Sancti Colmaci (Writ of Robert the High Steward), 1358; Inchemacholmock (Exchequer Rolls), 1358; Inchmaquholmok (Acta Concilii), 1478; Inchmaquholmo (Acts of Parliament), 1481; Inchmahomok (Register of the Great Seal), 1489; Inchmaholmo (Acta Concilii), 1490; Inchemahomo (Lease by Prior Andrew), 1526; Inchmoquhomok (Writ of Earl Alexander), 1534; Inchemaquhomo (Discharge by Queen Mary), 1548; Inchmahomo (Lease by Commendator John), 1548; Inchemahomok (Charter of Commendator David), 1562; Inschemachame (Charter of James VI.), 1610; Inchemahummoe (Rental of the Feuduties), 1646; Inchmahumo (Pont's Map), 1654. Of these, Inchmahomok and Inchmahomo are far the most common from the sixteenth century onwards. The final syllable seems to have been retained in the pronunciation till last century. Graham of Duchray, in 1724, still uses Inchmahomo.

There can be no doubt whatever that *insula sancti Colmoci* was the interpretation of the name in the earliest times to which written evidence extends.

Mr. M'Gregor Stirling himself eventually gave up his cherished derivation from Innis-mo-thamb, and with it, of course, the poetical interpretation "Isle of my Rest." In a manuscript addition to his "Notes on Inchmahome" (p. 32) he says, "This etymology (Innis-mo-thamb) must give way to Isle of St. Columba, or St. Cholmoc. A saint of the name of Columba, and whose birth was English and noble, is mentioned by Fordun as having been buried at Dunblane about the year 1000 A.D. *(Scotichronicon, sub anno* 1295)." He is probably wrong about the particular saint who gave name to the isle; but at any rate he admits that his former derivation and interpretation of the island name cannot be maintained.

The island is about five acres in extent; generally level in the eastern portion, but rising into pleasant knolls towards the south and west. With its fine old trees, through which the ruins of the priory buildings are partially seen, it makes a very attractive picture as seen from the shore of the lake. It is divided into two nearly equal portions by a road or avenue, running north and south, fenced on either side by a stone wall, and showing beside the western wall some remnants of a row of ancient trees by which it seems to have been bordered. This appears to have been a common road or piece of neutral ground, separating the gardens and other grounds of the monastery on the east from those of the Earls of Menteith, which lay on the west side—that nearest to their castle on Inchtalla.

The gardens of the monastery and of the island generally continued to be cultivated for profit till well on to the middle of the present century. In Mr. M'Gregor Stirling's time, they were held in lease, he tells us, by one Alexander M'Curtain, who is said to have been "a lineal descendant of the hereditary gardeners of the Earls of Menteith."[1] The fruits grown were gooseberries, cherries, plums, pears, apples, Spanish filberts, &c.; the filbert being "the long, red, thin-shelled variety, of which the kernel is much admired." These gardens, however, were afterwards allowed to go to utter ruin, and became a mere tangled wilderness. Although, about twenty years ago, the grounds were cleared and fenced, and the wilderness brought into better order, it is to be feared that most of the old fruit trees are now dead or non-productive. But should the visitor chance to be on the island in the springtime, his eye will be delighted by the luxuriant growth of fine daffodils, which literally cover the meadows as if with a carpet of gold.

The mutual road already referred to has traditionally acquired the name of "The Nuns' Walk"; and at the southern extremity of it is a sunny eminence called "The Nuns' Hill." These names may be of comparatively recent origin. Neither of them, at any rate, has any warrant in historical fact, for there were no nuns on Inchmahome. However, a local legend is not wanting to account for the name at least of the Nuns' Hill. This, in brief, is how the story is told. A nun of Cambuskenneth —unfortunately for this detail in the story, there was no nunnery at Cambuskenneth either—had fallen in love with a son of one of the earls of Menteith, and he with her;

---

[1] John M'Keurtane seems to have been a sort of Chamberlain to the earl at the end of the 17th century, for it was to him that "The just accompt of my Lord's Close and Stockings, taken at the Isle on the 20th of December, 1692," was delivered. Appendix vi. to Notes on Inchmahome.

The Nuns' Hill, Inchmahome.

and the two had set a tryst to meet on a certain evening at this particular spot on the island shore. Before the day of tryst, however, the young lord was fatally wounded in a clan fight on the hill of Glenny. In his dying moments he confided to his confessor the story of his love for the nun, and the time and place of the proposed meeting. When the hour of tryst arrived, the holy father arrayed himself in such habiliments as might give him a general resemblance to the appearance of the dead youth, and hied him to the shore. Then as the maiden stepped from the boat, which had borne her across the lake, to receive, as she imagined, the warm embrace of her expectant lover, she was seized by the monk and hurled back into the water. The other members of the holy fraternity must have known of the plot of their zealous brother, or have been informed of the deed when it was done; for the story goes on to tell that next day they recovered the body of the hapless nun from the waters of the lake, and buried it in an upright posture on the hill. Why they should have thought it necessary to do so is not quite clear. Anyhow, a large stone near the top of the hill used to be pointed to as marking the place of this interment. The stone is not now to be seen.

If the names Nuns' Walk and Nuns' Hill are, however, of ancient date, a suggestion may be here offered to account for them. In the usual conventual arrangements, the hour of dinner was twelve o'clock. After that, the monks were set free for recreation until the bell rang for Nones—about two o'clock or later. This recreation usually took the form of walking about the gardens and precincts of the monastery when the weather was fine, and, in winter or bad weather, sitting round the Refectory fire, talking, disputing, or telling stories. May we not suppose then that, at this time of the day, the monks were in the habit of taking their recreative stroll under the shadow of the great trees which bordered this pleasant path, or of sunning themselves on the green knoll which terminated it on the south? This might give origin to the names of *Nones* (now corrupted into *Nuns*) *Walk* and *Nones Hill*.

There are in the grounds of the Priory and in the Earls' Gardens several memorials of the brief visit of the young Queen Mary to the island after the Battle of Pinkie. A fine old sycamore, standing near the west doorway of the Priory ruins, is known as "Queen Mary's Plane." The reason why it has been so called is not known. Tradition does not venture to say that it was planted by the Queen —as is alleged regarding other Queen Mary trees in various parts of the country—but it may have been planted, or perhaps merely named, in commemoration of her visit. This tree is easily distinguishable by its bright red and scaly bark. It measures about 80 feet in height, and girths 14 feet at one foot from the ground, and 11 feet 9 inches at the height of five feet; and it is still in vigorous health.[1]

[1] The number of sycamores to which Queen Mary's name is attached is remarkable. There are, for example, a Queen Mary's Plane at Scone Palace, another near Craigmillar Castle, and one on the island of Loch Leven, all of which she is said to have planted. Whether she really did so or not, it seems to be certain that the fashion of planting sycamores in gardens and pleasure grounds was introduced into Scotland from France by the Queen and her entourage. Previously, the tree—if it existed at all in Scotland—was extremely rare there.

Queen Mary's Tree.

The Lake of Menteith.

The other memorials are Queen Mary's Garden and Tree, and Queen Mary's Bower. The garden is a square enclosure, measuring about 30 yards on each side, and surrounded with a stone wall. There are also the ruins of a small building at the north-west corner. In the centre of this enclosed space is an old box-wood tree, planted—tradition affirms—by the hands of the young Queen herself. The tree, which is yet flourishing, is about 20 feet in height, and the trunk measures 3 feet 2 inches in circumference. Some filberts and other old fruit trees still survive within the garden walls.

Outside, and to the west of the wall, on an eminence which slopes to the lake shore, is situated the Bower. This is a small oval plot, some 18 feet by 12, and about 33 yards in circumference, now enclosed with a paling. In the centre is a thorn-tree, and round about the narrow walk runs a double row of box-wood, now grown to a considerable height. This box-wood, it must be said, is not that which originally—or, at any rate, formerly—adorned the Bower. The plundering propensities of visitors, or (shall we rather say?) their affectionate desire to carry away with them a relic of the childhood of the unhappy Queen, had caused it almost to disappear, when, between thirty and forty years ago, the Bower was replanted from the gardens of Cardross. The plants, however, with which this was done, had been reared from cuttings taken from the original box-wood of the Bower.

There has been a good deal of imaginative writing on the connection of the child-Queen with this quaint survival from the ancient gardens of the Earls of Menteith.

Some will have it that the Bower was designed by the youthful Queen herself, and planted by her own little hands. Others, less daring, have restricted their fancy to the belief that it was here that she and her Maries were wont to disport and amuse themselves with their child-gardening. "What is this?" asks Dr. John Brown. "It is plainly *the child-Queen's Garden*, with her little walk, and its rows of box-wood, left to themselves for three hundred years. Yes, without doubt, 'here is that first garden of her simpleness.' Fancy the little, lovely, royal child, with her four Maries, her playfellows, her child maids of honour, with their little hands and feet, and their innocent and happy eyes, pattering about that garden all that time ago, laughing, and running, and gardening as only children do and can. As is well known, Mary was placed by her mother in this Isle of Rest before sailing from the Clyde for France. There is something 'that tirls the heartstrings a' to the life' in standing and looking on this unmistakable living relic of that strange and pathetic old time. Were we Mr. Tennyson, we would write an Idyll of that child-Queen, in that garden of hers, eating her bread and honey—getting her teaching from the holy men, the monks of old, and running off in wild mirth to her garden and her flowers, all unconscious of the black, lowering thunder-cloud on Ben Lomond's shoulder."[1]

This is very beautiful, and imagination delights to follow the writer in his fancies of those happy days of childhood. One would not willingly spoil the charming picture. We may safely enough believe that the infant

[1] Horæ Subsecivæ, by John Brown, M.D., second series, p. 172.

Queen Mary's Bower.

Queen did once on a time toddle about these old-world gardens, and as we look at the Bower, imagination is justified in conjuring up her figure on the quaint little pathway. But the place can neither have been made by her nor for her. She was brought too hurriedly to the island to permit the construction of a little garden expressly for her use; and as she was but a baby, four years and nine months old, her own little hands were not yet fit for making bowers or even for much playing at gardening. Neither, it is to be hoped, were "the holy men" so cruel as to set her to lessons at that tender age. And, it must be added further, that she was not more than three weeks altogether on the island, and that at a season of the year not generally the most propitious for flower-gardening in this climate.[1]

The chief natural glory of Inchmahome is in its fine old trees—chestnuts, walnuts, and sycamores, of great size and age, besides oak, ash, hazel, thorn, and other trees. That some, at any rate, of the largest of these ancient trees were planted by the monks may be surmised from two circumstances. In the first place they are of those kinds—not indigenous to the country—which were most favoured by the monkish arboriculturists; and, in the second place, they have evidently been arranged in lines to suit the walls and gateways of the building. As the visitor steps ashore at the little landing-place, he will observe a number of "felled specimens of chestnuts of immense size, whose bark-stripped trunks and hollow butts serve as fire-

[1] For Mary's stay at Inchmahome, see *infra*, chap. vi. On the shore, below "the Bower," there is an excellent echo—given back by the ruins on Inchtalla.

places for the pic-nics of tourists." These were felled nearly half-a-century ago. But there are others still standing in more or less healthy condition. These were carefully examined some years ago for the Highland and Agricultural Society of Scotland, by an expert in forestry, from whose reports the following particulars are taken.[2]

There has evidently, says this authority, been a line of large walnut trees and Spanish chestnuts extending across the garden ground at the western gate of the Priory. Immediately outside of this gateway stood two "sentinel" trees —a fine old walnut to the right, and a chestnut as its companion to the left. The measurements of the walnut are given as 80 feet in height, 10 feet in girth at one foot from the ground, 8 feet 1 inch at three feet, and 8 feet at six feet high. The chestnut is described as having a good bole, but decaying; and its dimensions are given as 85 feet in height, 19 feet 10 inches at one foot, 16 feet 10 inches at three feet, and 16 feet 6 inches at six feet from the ground. Of the two trees thus reported on in 1879, the walnut, which in the report was said to be decaying and oozing a good deal near the root, has entirely disappeared—cut down and removed some years ago—and the chestnut is now a mere fragmentary ruin. Opposite these sentinels stands the sycamore already mentioned as Queen Mary's Tree.

Running south, along the west side of the Nuns' Walk, is a line of three great chestnuts. The first was reported

---

[2] Reports on Old and Remarkable Trees of Scotland, by Robert Hutchison of Carlowrie: Transactions of Highland and Agricultural Society of Scotland fourth series, vols. xi. and xii. These trees were carefully re-measured for the purposes of this work in October, 1898, and it is these revised measurements that are given in the text.

by Mr. Hutchison to be "decaying" when he examined it. It still stands, but the measurements are not so great as those he gives. It rises to a height of about 70 feet, with a stem which measures nearly 14 feet at one foot, 13 feet at three feet, and 12 feet 4 inches at six feet from the ground. The next is the picturesque tree known as the "antlered chestnut." The top has suffered injury, and the bare branches projecting above the foliage, and resembling the horns of deer, give it the appearance that is known as "stag-headed." Though stated in the report to be "much decayed," it still retains its vigour, and, in fact, appears to be in very good health. It has slightly increased in size since 1879. Its dimensions now are—height, about 80 feet; bole, 25 feet; girth—at one foot from the ground, 20 feet 6 inches; at three feet, 20 feet; and at six feet, 17 feet. The third tree—not mentioned in the report—has a bole of 20 feet, a circumference of 16 feet 7 inches at one foot from the ground, and of 14 feet 6 inches at the height of five feet. It is in vigorous health. The largest oak tree on the island is on the Nuns' Hill. Its dimensions are not remarkable. At one foot from the ground it girths 13 feet, and at five feet 11 feet 8 inches. Other varieties of wood there are in abundance, hazels, ashes, larches, elder trees, some pines, and two Wellingtonias recently planted. The last named somehow strike one as not being quite in keeping with the feeling of the place.

The whole island now belongs to the Duke of Montrose, to whose ancestor it passed by the will of William, the eighth and last Earl of Menteith. Of old only the western half belonged to the earls—the eastern part being the property of the Priory, and, therefore, subsequently of the lairds of Cardross, to whom the Priory, with its possessions, passed after the extinction of the monasteries. In 1646[1] the "monasterie and precincte with the yairdis" were held in feu from David, second Lord of Cardross, by William, seventh Earl of Menteith and first of Airth, and they must have passed, at a later date, into his possession in some way that has not been certainly ascertained.

Immediately to the west of Inchmahome, separated from it by a narrow channel, lies the island now called Inchtalla, although throughout the seventeenth century, when it was the residence of the later Graham Earls of Menteith, it was designated by its proprietors always simply " The Isle " (Ysle, 1642 ; Yle, 1646 ; Isle, 1679 ; The Isle, 1692 ; The Isle of Menteith, 1694 ; Isle of Monteath, 1724.) *Talla*, or Tulla, as it is printed in Stobie's Map of Perthshire, is a recurrence to an older name, which therefore appears never to have been lost. It is first met with in writing in the Stirling Protocol Books, under date 23rd October, 1476, in the shape of *Inchtolloch*.[1] In the *Registrum Magni Sigilli*, in 1485, the form is practically the same—*Inchtulloche*. In 1494 it appears with *Eilan* substituted for Inch and the termination softened, Ellantallo. Throughout the fifteenth and sixteenth centuries this name is retained, with, of course, the usual licenses in spelling.[2]

[1] Rental of the Feuduties of Inchmahome.
[1] This interesting document is quoted *infra*, chap. x.
[2] The varied forms—in the order of date—are, Inchtolloche, Inchtulloche, Illintulaich, Ellantallo, Ylyntullo, Ilyntullocht, Ilantullo, Yll Intulla, Tulla, Talla ; then come Isle, Earl's Isle, and Isle of Menteith.

"The Isle"—Inchtalla.

As to the interpretation of the name, *Inch* and *Eilan* are, of course, the same in meaning, both signifying "island." *Tulloch* is the usual form in which the Gaelic *tulach*, a "mound" or "knoll," is represented in place-names. But that derivation is inapplicable here. *Tallach*, however, is the adjective form from *talla*, a "hall" or "great house." In the Highland Society's Gaelic Dictionary, *tallach* is translated "*aulis instructus ; ad aulam pertinens.*" It is, therefore, a very appropriate epithet for this island, which was literally covered with the "halls" of the earls. This derivation, besides giving a satisfactory explanation of the name, accounts for the *ch* in the older forms of the word. We may conclude then that *Inchtalla* means " the island of the halls," or more simply "the castle-island."

Inchtalla is of an oval or rather egg shape, broadest in the north, and tapering to a point at the southern end. It must have afforded a fairly secure, if rather confined, retreat for its turbulent lords in the olden times. It was crowded with buildings—a small central court being the only uncovered bit of ground on the island. In consequence the earls' gardens, for use as well as for pleasure, had to find room on the neighbouring island of Inchmahome, while the park and pleasaunce was on the north shore of the lake, where was the shortest passage from the mainland to Inchtalla. But though the buildings were thus crowded there could have been no want of air with the open lake all round. So close were they to the water that the strong winds, which occasionally blow from the west, must have dashed the spray against the walls. This is perhaps the explanation of the curious fact that the windows on the ground floor of the buildings looking to the west are so small and so few.

The island had become a dense jungle of natural wood, which not only covered the margins and filled up the central court, but invaded the interior of the ruined buildings. Seedling trees had grown up everywhere on the walls and in the areas of the old castle. These not only impeded entrance and rendered it difficult to get any view of the interiors, but by their continued growth were gradually loosening the stones and mortar, and accelerating the period of complete overthrow. Last autumn (1898) Mr. Erskine of Cardross caused this mischievous growth to be cleared away. It is now, therefore, again possible to obtain some idea of what these ancient buildings may have appeared, and it is to be hoped that the process of rapid decay may be for some time longer arrested. In a subsequent chapter an attempt will be made to describe them in detail and—so far as materials for the purpose are available—to identify the various chambers and their uses.

Not far from the western shore of the lake lies the third and smallest of the islands. It is called *Inchcuan*, or "Dog Island," because it is supposed to have been used for the kennels of the earls' hunting dogs. If that were so, the kennels could not have been on a very extensive scale, as the islet is a tiny one, only a few yards in circumference. There seems, however, to be some ground for believing that at the time when Talla was an inhabited house—or, at any rate, when it was built—the surface of the lake was at a somewhat lower level than now, for a corner of the south-

Inchcuan or Dog Island.

west building on that island now overhangs the water, so that the area of Inchcuan may have been rather larger then than it now is. But at the most it can never have been anything but a very small patch of ground—quite insufficient, one would think, for the kennels of a lordly establishment. And there is reason to believe that fox-hunting on the hills of Menteith was a favourite sport with the earls. William, the seventh earl, had a special breed of terriers, whose reputation had reached the ears of King James the Sixth long before their master had become a famous politician, or was anything but a Scottish nobleman, employing a good deal of his time, as is likely, in the field sports of the country. On the 17th of August, 1617, the King wrote from Houghton Tower to the Earl of Mar, then Lord High Treasurer of Scotland, in the following terms:— "These are moste earnestlie to require you, as yee will do us moste acceptable service and procure our exceeding greate contentment to searche oute and sende unto us two couple of excellent terrieres or earth dogges, which are both stoute and good fox killers, and will stay long in the grounde. Wee are crediblie enformed that the Earle of Monteth hath good of that kinde, who wee are sure wilbe glade to gratifie us with them."[1] His Majesty, we doubt

[1] Letter printed in Red Book, vol. i. p. 335. Original in charter chest of the Earl of Mar and Kellie. King James perhaps got his information about the Earl of Menteith's terriers when he was staying with his friend, the Earl of Mar, at Cardross. Mar himself, at a later date, had to go further afield for "earth-doggs." On the 5th of November, 1631, he wrote to the Laird of Glenorchy, from Stirling, saying that he was to be resident in that town a good part of the winter, and that his greatest sport was likely to be fox-hunting. "Thairfor," he says, "I will ernestly intrett you to send me with this berar a couppill of good earth doggs." And he adds in a postscript—"Quhat ye send me latt itt be good altho itt should be bott on."—Innes's Sketches of Early Scottish History, 1861: Appendix, p. 514.

G

not, got his two couple of Menteith earth-dogs, and we trust had exceeding great contentment therewith. The Earl's pack, however, could not well have been all accommodated on Inchcuan. It may be that the island was only occasionally used—perhaps as an infirmary for sick dogs or a place of detention for obstreperous animals—while the usual kennels were at the stables on the western shore of the lake, just opposite Inchcuan. No vestige of these stables now remains, but the little promontory, on and beside which they were clustered, still bears the name of "the stable ground."

CHAPTER IV.

The Ruins of the Priory on Inchmahome.

"Rising from those lofty groves
Behold a ruin hoary."

"Buried midst the wreck of things which were—
There lie interred the more illustrious dead."

"All is silent now : silent the bell,
That, heard from yonder ivied turret high,
Warned the cowled brother from his midnight cell ;
Silent the vesper chant—the litany,
Responsive to the organ ;—scattered lie
The wrecks of the proud pile, mid arches grey."

N the north side of the Island of Inchmahome, a few yards from the little landing-place, and standing on ground rising slightly from the level of the lake shore, are the ruins of the Priory. It was not one of the great ecclesiastical foundations of the country, but merely—so to speak—a family priory, and does not exhibit any imposing building or ornamentation. Still, with all its simplicity of style, the Church has been a not inelegant specimen of Gothic architecture, and standing on its island site, with its lofty tower, it must have showed to great effect across the surrounding waters.

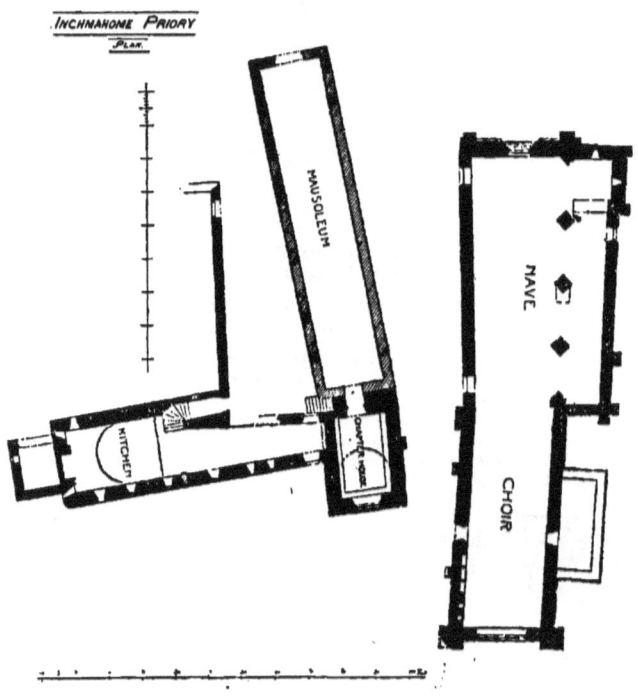

Plan of the Priory Church and Buildings.
(By permission, from M'Gibbon & Ross's Ecclesiastical Architecture of Scotland.)

The Church stands, as is usual, due east and west. It measures in all about a hundred and fifty feet in length by thirty-five feet in breadth, and consists of a nave with aisle on the north, and a choir. The nave is seventy-five feet in length, and of unequal width—contracting from over twenty-seven feet at the west end to less than twenty-four feet at the east. It is entered by two doors. One of these is at the south-west angle of the Church, and over this there has evidently, from the marks on the wall above and at the sides, been a stone-built porch or, as Mr. M'Gregor Stirling calls it, a quadrangle. The main door is in the western wall. This great doorway has been a really fine example of early English Gothic. Although wasted by the unavoidable decay of centuries, it is still sufficiently entire to afford an idea of its original elegance. The width of the arched entrance is just half the height, six feet in the one case and twelve in the other. The breadth of the carved and clustered pillar work which surrounds the opening is six feet. The shafts, with their moulded caps and bases, have been wrought with great care, and notwithstanding the centuries that have passed since they were cut, are still wonderfully entire. On either side of this doorway are two shallow recesses, with double Gothic archings supported on pillars of very graceful construction. The spandrils between the upper arches are ornamented with recessed quatrefoil and trefoil decorations. A former writer on the Priory[1] says that there used to be "five images" on the wall above the doorway. Nothing of the kind is now to be seen. It must be added that it is hard

[1] Dun's Summer at the Lake of Menteith, p. 8.

to believe that there ever was any such sculptured work in this position. The bottom of the great west window appears to have come down so near to the top of the arching of the gateway as to leave no room for it. That window itself has now fallen down, with the whole upper part of the gable in which it was placed. Traces of it, however, may still be observed from the interior of the Church, and these show that it had a breadth of about fifteen feet.

At the north-west corner of the Church is a square tower rising to the height of four storeys. This is known as the Bell Tower. It is twelve feet square, inside measurement, and has walls of nearly three feet in thickness. Not a vestige of the stair by which the upper storeys must have been reached is now in existence; so that the fine view which some former writers have spoken of as obtainable from the Bellman's window[1] must be taken on their credit. There are now no means of reaching this window high up in the west side of the tower. The ground portion of the Bell Tower is said to have been used for the incarceration of evil-doers by the last Earls of Menteith. The tower does not seem to have been part of the Church as originally designed and built, but an addition made at some later —perhaps not much later—period. This is inferred from the circumstances that it is built outside of and has covered up one of the four fine arches that separated the nave from the aisle on the north.[2] To the shelter thus

---

[1] Among others, Sir W. Fraser (Red Book i. 509), long before whose time access to this window was quite impossible.

[2] Perhaps it may be more correct to say that the Church buildings from the first included a tower at this corner, which at a later period was rebuilt and

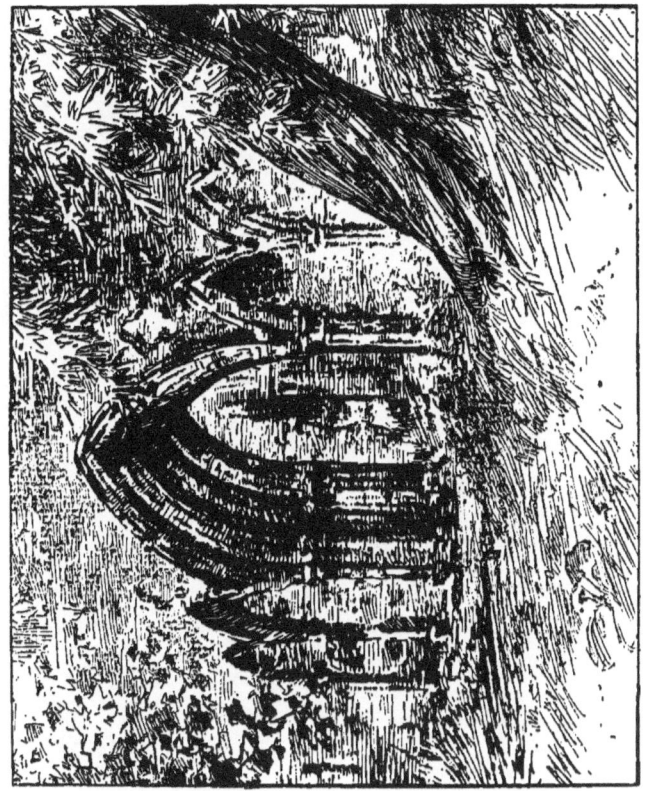

West Doorway of the Priory, Inchmahome.

afforded we may trace the preservation of the two westmost of these arches till the present time. The other two fell rather more than a century ago.[1] Judging from the fragmentary remains of the arches, they must have been in excellent taste and of cunning workmanship, and a great adornment of the Church.

Marks of ragling on the east side of the Bell Tower still show where the roof of the aisle terminated on the west, and the foundations of the outer wall and buttresses were disclosed by the excavations of Admiral Erskine. A considerable part of the north wall—to the east of the arches—is still pretty well preserved. It shows three clerestory windows, one single and two with double lights, of plain design. Outside of this wall has been another building, apparently divided into two chambers. The corbels on the wall show where the roof of this building had joined the Church; and the base mouldings, which the excavations showed were carried round it, indicate that it was a portion of the original design, and not a mere lean-to addition afterwards made. This Mr. M'Gregor Stirling has called the Chapter House, but this identification cannot be regarded as correct. The Chapter House was more likely, according to the usual arrangements of monasteries, to have been adjacent to the cloisters, and near the residence of the prior and canons. If that were the case here, we shall have to look for it on the south

---

divided into storeys. This is the opinion of Messrs. M'Gibbon & Ross, founded on the appearance of the base course of the tower. (Ecclesiastical Architecture of Scotland, vol. ii. p. 177.)

[1] The New Statistical Account, published in 1845, says that these arches fell about fifty years previous to that time.

side of the Church. The building now in question was most probably the sacristy and vestiarium or vestry, from which the officiating priests entered the choir. The door of entrance still remains, nearly opposite where the High Altar must have stood. This sacristy building or aisle did not extend to the extreme east end of the wall. It left space for a long two-light window coming down into the lower storey and helping to light the choir. Neither this window nor the other three in this portion show any ornamentation. Though well-proportioned, they are all severely plain.

The great choir-window is in the east gable of the Church. This gable—with the exception of its flanking buttresses, which are much decayed—is still comparatively entire. The window has been a very fine one, with beautiful pointed arches. It is in five divisions, of which the central one is eighteen inches, and the others each twelve inches in width. The tracery, if there had been any, is gone; and the whole has been built up with rubble work—at what time is not now known, but certainly previous to the present century.

The interior of the choir—which measures sixty-six feet in length by twenty-three feet eight inches in breadth—like that of the nave, has been stripped of almost all its original adornments. There still remain, on the south side, a sedile or stall and two ambries, which are now used to preserve some fragments of carved stones that have been found in the ruins. Here, also, is the Piscina or sink into which the celebrating priests emptied the water in which they had washed their hands, and by which all consecrated waste stuff was carried away. The choir is now pretty well filled with graves

Arches of the Aisle.

and tombstones of deceased Grahams, Drummonds, and others. Some of these are noteworthy, and deserve a more detailed description. This is reserved till the rest of the buildings have been described.

The south side of the Church is in a very dilapidated condition. It looks as if it had suffered from violence as well as from natural decay. The choir portion of it has been best preserved. In the centre of this is an arched doorway, by which the monks entered from the Chapter House and their dwellings on the south. Between this door and the east corner are two windows which have been separated by a buttress. They both reach from the top of the wall to the level of the doorway arch. The first has two lights and the other one only. Both are well designed, and bear evidences of fine workmanship. On the other side of the door are also two windows, but smaller, and now much injured. A moulded projection or string runs along the face of the wall at the base of these windows. All the nave portion of the south wall is very much ruined. It appears, however, to have been blank—with the exception, perhaps, of the higher part, in which there were no doubt windows for the admission of light into the nave. Along this were the cloisters of the original building. They have long ago disappeared, but the corbels for the roof are still visible.

A building to the south of the Church, towards the eastern end, usually known as the Vault, deserves some attention. The common statement regarding it is that it was run up hurriedly in 1644, to receive the remains of Lord Kilpont, who was murdered by Stewart of Ardvoirlich in Montrose's camp at Collace.[1] But this seems very unlikely, for several reasons. The house bears no trace of having been "run up hurriedly." It is as good a bit

of building as any of the rest, and appears to be equally old. If it is in better preservation, that appears to be

[1] New Statistical Account.

The Chapter House, Inchmahome.

due to the fact that it has been built on and over a very strong semi-circular vaulting which has kept the structure together. It is of two storeys, and burial vaults are not generally so constructed—especially when built *extempore*, as this one is said to have been. The under storey is lighted by a very good three-arched window—giving an amount of light that could hardly be considered necessary for a mere tomb. The vaulting of the interior has been very carefully constructed; and round the wall runs a bench of stone. These indications seem to mark it out as the ancient *Chapter House* of the Priory. It measures twenty-four by fifteen feet—not a very large chamber, but quite sufficient to accommodate the Chapter of Inchmahome. The stone floor and central bench would of course be removed when, at some period subsequent to the Reformation, this Chapter House began to be used as a burying-place for the Earls of Menteith. That it was so used scarcely admits of doubt. Sir William Fraser—who does not, however, give his authority for the statement—says that the body of Lord Kilpont was interred in the Chapter House of the Priory, "the burying-place of the family."[1] Here, perhaps, also Lord Kilpont's father, the seventh earl, was buried: and the inference from the will of the last earl makes it almost certain that his remains were here interred.

The room over the Chapter House is lighted by a window of two arches in the east. It had a door in the west end, which appears to have been reached by a stair, which can yet be traced, coming up from the Frateries on the ground floor to the south. This pleasant apart-

[1] Red Book of Menteith, vol. i. p. 398.

ment was probably the Prior's Chamber. It was close to and most likely in connection with the apartments of the canons, which seem to have occupied the second storey of the long building running to the south, over the vaulted kitchens yet to be seen. This chamber goes by the name of "Queen Mary's Bedroom," because it is alleged that the little Queen slept there during her stay on the island. The tradition is not unlikely to be well founded. There was no resident prior at the time. The Prior's Chamber, however, was no doubt the pleasantest and best room in the monastery, and as such, would be given up to the use of the young Queen; while her personal attendants and retinue could be lodged close beside her in the apartments of the canons.

Running out from the door of the Chapter House are two parallel stone walls, enclosing an approach, and terminating on the west in a stone-built gateway. The time of the building of these long walls and gateway is not in doubt. The last Earl of Menteith died, without issue, in 1694, and left his personal estate to his nephew, Sir John Graham of Gartmore, with the following instructions:—

"As also that Sir John shall be obliged to cause an exquisite and cunning mason to erect two statues of fine hewn stone, at length from head to foot, whereof one for ourself, and the other for our dearest spouse, Dame Catherine Bruce, now deceased, upon the west gable of our burying-place, in the easter isle,[1] and make an entry from the said burial-place near to the east end of the

[1] Inchmahome is generally about this time designated "the *easter* isle," in contradistinction to Inchtalla, "the wester isle."

gravel walk, with a stone dyke on each side, and a fine entry of hewn work upon the west end thereof, bearing our name and arms, and our said spouse's."[1]

The gravel walk referred to is that which leads from the landing-place on Inchmahome from the wester isle across the Menteith portion of the grounds to the Nuns' Walk. This walk is still distinctly traceable beneath the turf with which it is now covered.[2] As it came out on the dividing road somewhat to the south of the straight line from the Chapter House door, that accounts for the awkward angle the approach thus constructed makes with the line of the Priory buildings. It has cut obliquely through portions of the cloister, and of what M'Gregor Stirling supposes to have been the dormitory of the monastery. The parallel walls and the gateway have been built, and the niched stones on the "entry," designed for bearing the names and arms of the deceased Earl and his wife, are in their places; but the stones are blank—they bear neither names nor arms, and apparently have never done so. Whether the "exquisite and cunning mason" was ever commissioned to execute the two statues, there is no evidence to show, beyond a statement of Mr. M'Gregor Stirling's[3] to the effect that he had been told

---

[1] The testament was dated 20th October, 1693, and recorded 11th December, 1694. It is quoted by M'Gregor Stirling (Notes on Inchmahome, p. 94), from Wood's Edition of Douglas's Peerage.

[2] In Wood's Douglas's Peerage the words are "gravel walk," but in the Disposition as printed in the Airth Peerage Minutes of Evidence (1839) they appear as "gavel wall." The latter is probably the correct reading, as "gravel" is not a Scotch word. It is difficult, however, to understand what is meant by the *east* end of the gable wall, unless it be intended merely to indicate that the "burial-place" was near the east end of the Church.

[3] Notes on Inchmahome, p. 94.

by the proprietor of Gartmore in his time that among the Menteith papers preserved at Gartmore was a receipt for the price of cutting two figures in stone to be placed in Inchmahome. There are certainly no statues now at the west gable of the Chapter House, or "burial-place," as it then was, and we have not heard of any fragments of what might once have been statues having ever been found there.

The remaining monastic buildings on the south side of the Church are in a state of great dilapidation, and any attempt at identifying their uses must be to a large extent conjectural. They seem to have been arranged in the shape of the letter L. The long narrow limb—about a hundred feet in length—running due south from the Chapter House, has lost its upper storey. But the ground floor—at least, the southmost part—easily identifies itself. It was the great kitchen of the monastery. Portions of the vaulting of this kitchen yet remain, and the great fire-place and chimney are entire. The upper storey we have supposed to have been occupied by the canons as their private rooms. It was to these chambers or cells that they were in the habit of retiring between the hours of nones and vespers, to read or write, or otherwise employ themselves. This is the building which goes by the traditional name of the Nunnery. That is an obvious misnomer. Graham of Duchray was, no doubt, right when he called it "the dwellings of the Churchmen."

Of the wing running westwards from the northern portion of this long building, only some fragments of wall remain. In this Mr. M'Gregor Stirling has placed

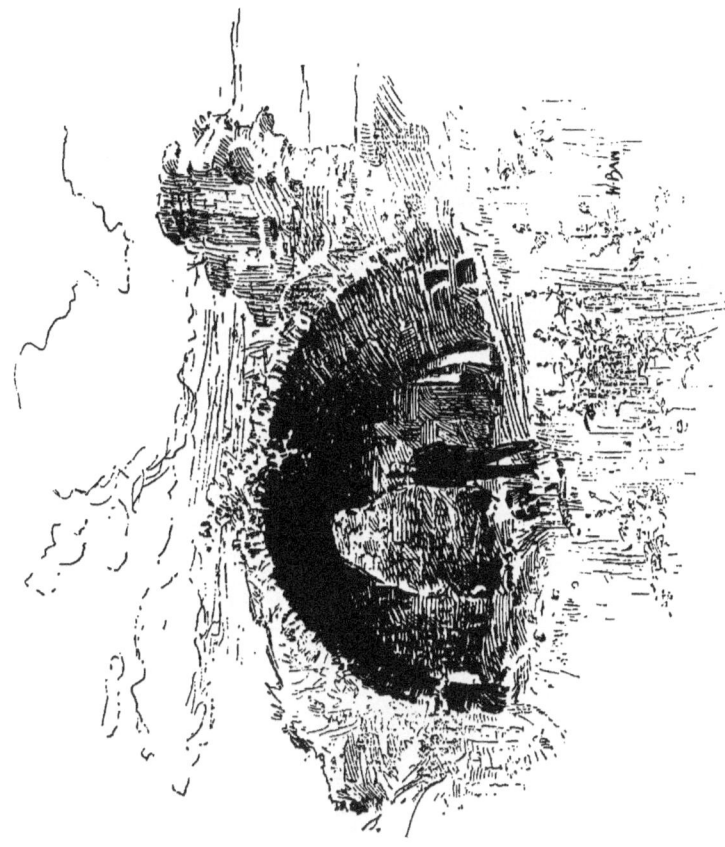

The Vaulted Kitchen, Priory Buildings.

the Dormitory and the Refectory. Perhaps in his time there were indications, not now to be seen, which led him to this identification. We can advance nothing either to support or contradict it beyond this, that there has evidently been an entrance—or perhaps two—from the kitchen into what he supposes to have been the Refectory. The Dormitory he places on the north side. The upper (northern) wall of it has been entirely removed to make way for the last earl's "approach" to the family burial-place. The west wall also has disappeared.[1] In the south wall is an entrance into the Refectory, and in the south-east corner another, which may have led either to the kitchen or to the apartments above. The Refectory has lost entirely its west and south walls. Of the two doors in the eastern wall, one seems to have led directly to the kitchen, and the other opens on the foot of the stairs which led up to the Prior's Chamber and the apartments on the second storey. The vegetable garden is placed to the south of the Refectory, but there were most probably extensive gardens on the east side of the buildings as well.

The choir of the Church—including a space of nearly seventy feet in length by over twenty-three feet in breadth—is the last resting-place of Stewarts and Grahams of the family of the Earls of Menteith and its branches, and of Drummonds, a family related to the earlier earls, and closely connected with the district and the Priory.

[1] It may be doubted whether there ever was a dormitory building on the north side of the refectory. More likely the whole space between the north wall of the refectory and the south wall of the Church was taken up by the cloisters and the cloister-garth; while the dormitory was in the upper storey of the building, approached by the staircase, a portion of which is still to be seen near the entrance to the kitchen.

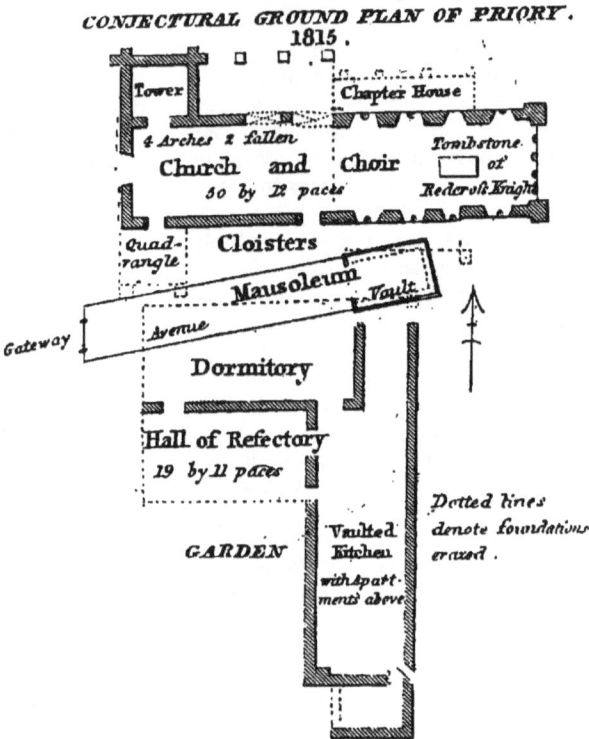

The above plan is reproduced, by permission, from the work of the Rev. W. M'Gregor Stirling. Since it was made, excavations conducted by the late Admiral Erskine have shown more accurately the foundations of the aisle and other buildings on the north side of the Church. In other respects, also, it is not perfectly accurate, but it is extremely interesting as the first attempt to delineate the ground plan of the buildings, and will serve to illustrate the references to Mr Stirling's remarks in the preceding pages.

The most striking monument is that near the centre of the choir, supposed to occupy the space in front of where the High Altar once stood. It is believed to commemorate Walter, the first Stewart Earl of Menteith, and his Countess Mary, who was the younger daughter of Maurice, the last earl of the original line of Menteith. Earl Walter Stewart died in 1294 or 1295, his Countess having predeceased him. The more ancient earls are said to have had their place of sepulture in the Church of Kippen. But in the year 1286, Earl Walter, along with his son, Alexander, and his daughter-in-law, Matilda, gave that Church to the Abbey of Cambuskenneth, in order to obtain a burial-place in the Abbey. He was not, however, buried at Cambuskenneth, but beside his wife in the choir of Inchmahome.

The monument represents a knight and lady lying side by side, their heads supported by cushions, and their feet resting on lions (or dogs). The knight has his right arm round the lady's shoulder, and his left is laid across her waist, while the lady's left arm lovingly encircles the neck of her lord. The lady is clad in a long flowing garment, the folds of which are beautifully sculptured. Her head is covered with an ample cloth falling down behind the neck and shoulders. The knight wears a suit of armour, covered with a surcoat. The round helmet which he wears on his head is encircled by something like a coronet or chaplet. The large triangular shield borne on the knight's left shoulder has for armorial bearings the well-known fess chequé, in three tracts, of the Stewarts, with a label of five points, which latter, as heraldic writers tell us, is a mark of cadency. Walter Stewart was the second son of the High Steward of Scotland. A seal of his, appended to a document, dated 1292, preserved in the Public Record Office, shows exactly the same armorial bearings, with the legend, *S. Walteri Senescalli Co̅m̅t de Menetet*. This coat of arms clearly establishes the identity of the knightly effigy. Walter Stewart was the only Earl of Menteith who bore the Stewart arms in this simple form. A seal of his son, Alexander, the sixth earl, has the three bars wavy—representing the arms of the old Menteith line (his mother's)—surmounted by the fess chequé. Earl Walter does not appear to have assumed the armorial bearings of the earldom of Menteith.

The figure is cross-legged—thus indicating a crusader, or at any rate, one who had vowed a crusade. For it was not necessary for one to have actually gone on crusade to entitle him to have his effigy represented in this sacred and symbolic attitude. It was enough if he had vowed. A substitute could be provided, or a dispensation could be obtained for a suitable sum. But it appears that Walter Stewart did really go crusading, though it is doubtful whether he reached the Holy Land. Along with his brother Alexander, the High Steward, and other Scottish knights, he joined the crusade led by Louis the Ninth of France (St. Louis). These Scottish knights —Walter among them—are said to have fought valiantly, and to have rendered valuable service to the Most Christian King in his Holy War in Egypt in the years 1248 and 1249.

The monument is seven feet in length, and the figures in very high relief. They have suffered a good deal of mutilation. The left arm of the knight has been broken off from the shoulder to the wrist, leaving only the gloved hand resting on the lady's waist. His left leg and foot have also suffered damage; and from the lady's right arm, which is bent across her chest, the hand has been rudely broken off. Whether this damage has been wanton or accidental is unknown, but one may be thankful to find the monument still so well preserved after fully six centuries of existence, and especially after an exposure of at least

Monument of Walter Stewart, Earl of Menteith, and his Countess Mary.

two hundred years to the elements. This exposure without protection to the weather has done more than actual violence to destroy the finer traits of the sculpture. These were gradually getting worn away more or less rapidly. But some years ago, Mr. Erskine of Cardross caused a canopy to be erected over the stone. This gives it protection from the rain, and may be expected to retard—it is to be hoped for a long time—the inevitable progress of decay.

Another very ancient and interesting stone is that which marks the last resting-place of Sir John Drummond—said to have been a liberal benefactor of the Priory of Inchmahome—who died about the year 1300 A.D., and was interred near the High Altar. Deeply cut on the surface of this stone, which is still in fair preservation, is a figure of Sir John. The features of the face are now rather worn, but they can still be made out, and somehow give one the impression that they have been meant for a likeness of the original. The figure is clad in chain armour, bears in the right hand a long spear, and carries on the left arm a shield with the three bars wavy—the well-known armorial bearings of the Drummonds, which they seem to have adopted from their superiors, the old Menteiths, and which this Sir John is said to have been the first Drummond to carry. On the head is a high conical covering terminating in a cross. The chest is crossed by belts which pass round the back of the neck. The waist also is girded by a broad belt, and from this are suspended two objects, one of which may be a dagger or knife, although it is not easy to make out what they may have originally represented. A long sword, depending from a hook or catch about the middle of the body, hangs to the left side. Beneath the feet, on which the spurs are plainly visible, are two lions, placed back to back, and connected by their intertwined tails. The lions underfoot, as well as the cross on the apex of the head-dress, are common enough Christian symbols.

In the vacant spaces on either side of the head of this effigy are two smaller figures. That on the right seems to represent St. Colmoc in his bishop's robes. He holds a well-defined pastoral staff in the left hand, while the right, with two fingers held up, is raised in the attitude of benediction. The figure on the other side represents Saint Michael, winged, and carrying spear and shield. The two holy men stand upon a dragon—St. Michael on the body, near the shoulder, and St. Colmoc on the tail.

A legend, in raised lettering, runs round the border of the stone on three sides. It has possibly run on to the fourth side—the top of the stone—also, but the border has scaled off at that part. What remains reads as follows:—JOHANNES DE DRUMOD FILIUS MOLQALMI DE DRUMOD VID . . . . SOLVAT ANIMAS EORUM A PENA ET ACU. If, as has been suggested, the reading—where the blank occurs —should be VIDUA UT, the translation will be:—" John of Drummond, son of Malcolm of Drummond, his widow, that she may release their souls from the penalty and the sting." If the legend was continued on the fourth side of the stone, it probably went on to say what the widow had done to release her soul and her husband's—or is it the souls of her husband and his father?—the *eorum* may be taken either way—from the pains of purgatory. Perhaps this was nothing more than interment in this place; for proximity to the High Altar in burial was supposed to ensure for the dead a safe and speedy passage to glory.

Sir William Fraser affirms that it was this Sir John Drummond or his father who gifted the lands of Cardross to the Priory of Inchmahome.[1] He gives tradition, however, as his only authority. Mr. M'Gregor Stirling, on the other

---

[1] Red Book of Menteith, vol. i. p. xli.

hand, on the authority of Malcolm's "History of the House of Drummond," names Sir Malcolm, the son and successor of Sir John, as the generous donor.[1] Malcolm's authority is perhaps not very great, but at any rate a reason for Sir Malcolm's generosity is given—as a thank-offering, namely, for his release from captivity in England, and an evidence of gratitude for the lands with which he had been endowed by King Robert the Bruce after the successful issue of the battle of Bannockburn. The Sir John here commemorated is said, in the "New Statistical Account," to have been a son-in-law of Earl Walter Stewart and his Countess, near whose monument (already described) in the Choir of Inchmahome his remains repose.

It may be regarded as a probable inference from the occurrence of St. Michael along with St Colmoc on this monumental stone—taken in conjunction with the existence of St. Michael's Fair at the Port—that there may have been a joint dedication of the Church to St. Michael and to Colmoc, the *eponymous* saint of the island.

A third old stone in the choir has the Graham arms cut in bas-relief, with the four letters very distinct, G. D. E. D. Were it not for the Graham arms, one would be tempted to read these as the initials of two members of the Drummond family. As it is, they have been ingeniously conjectured to represent the words GLORIA DEO ESTO DATA—*Let glory be given to God.*

The numerous other tombstones in the choir have less architectural and historical interest. They commemorate Grahams of every branch of the family of Menteith—

[1] Stirling's Notes on Inchmahome, p. 44.

on the left, Grahams of Gartur, Rednock, Leitchtown, Pheddal, and Soyock; on the right, Grahams of Gartmore, Glenny, and Mondhui. On the north wall appears, most appropriately, a tablet to the memory of Admiral Erskine, who loved the old place so well, and did so much to preserve the remains and to prevent the whole precincts from falling into absolute ruin.

CHAPTER V.

The Priory of Inchmahome under its early Priors, 1238 to 1528.

"I am, said he, ane Channoun regulare,
 And of my brether Pryour principall:
 My quhyte rocket my clene lyfe doith declare,
 The black bene of the death memoriall."
  —*Testament of the Papyngo.*

"Arrayed in habit black and amis thin,
 Like to an holy monck, the service to begin."
  —*Faery Queen.*

HAT there was a religious settlement on the island of Inchmahome at a very early period is obvious from the name which has carried down through the ages the memory of the saint in whose honour it was founded. In the multitude of Colmans in the hagiology,[1] it would be impossible—if we had no other indication of his identity—to determine which particular saint of the name was the *eponymus* of the island. One naturally thinks first of that St. Colman, disciple of St. Columba, who became Bishop of Lindisfarne in Northumberland, but returned to Iona in 664 A.D., in

---

[1] Baring-Gould (Lives of the Saints) says, "there were ninety-five St. Colmans in the Martyrology of Donegal alone, besides numerous other Irish saints of the name."

The Lake of Menteith. 131

consequence of being worsted by Wilfrid in the dispute regarding the observance of Easter.[1] Another Scottish St. Colmack, said to have been Bishop of Orkney, *circa* 1000, is mentioned by Innes.[2] But it is to neither of

Seal of the Priory of Inchmahome.[3]

these, but to an Irish saint, that the name of the island is due, if we are to accept the authority of the early

---

[1] Scotichronicon a Goodall, vol. i. p. 154.

[2] Innes, quoted in Chalmers' Caledonia, vol. i. p. 321, *note*. The day of this St. Colmack is given as the 6th of June.

[3] In the upper compartment of the seal is represented the Virgin Mother crowned, and seated, holding a lily in her right hand. On her left knee sits the infant Jesus, also crowned, with right hand upraised and two fingers lifted, in the attitude of benediction, and holding a globe in His left hand. In the lower compartment, under a Gothic arch, stands a figure in the vestments of a Bishop, probably intended to represent St. Colman, holding the pastoral staff in his left hand, and lifting the right with the outstretched forefingers in the act of blessing. The legend is *S. Commune de Insula Sancti Colmoci.*

ecclesiastical chroniclers. The "Breviary of Aberdeen" gives the honour to St. Colmoc (*i.e.*, Colman with the honourable suffix *-og* or *-oc*), Bishop of Dromore, County Down, Ireland. He is said to have been of a noble Scotic family, to have been born about 500 A.D., and to have founded the Monastery of Dromore, where he died and was buried. His day was the 6th of June. It is added that the Monastery of Inchemaholmock, in the diocese of Dunblane, was solemnly dedicated to him.[1] Lanigan gives many particulars of his birth and education from the Irish ecclesiastical annalists, stating that he was of a Dalriadian family, and therefore a native of the territory in which his see was situated, but giving his day as the 7th of June.[2] How he came to be honoured in Menteith is not explained, but possibly the reverence for his name may have been introduced into the west of Scotland by his kinsfolk, the Dalriadic Scots. The "Martyrology of Aberdeen"—in opposition to the statement of the "Breviary" and the Irish annalists—affirms that he was buried at "Inchmacome, where there was in after times a Monastery of Canons-Regular of the Order of St. Augustine." By the "Martyrology of Aengus" he is called *Mocholmog*[3] of Drummor in Iveagh of Ulidia. It would appear, therefore, that it is to this "Irish Pict" —as Skene calls him—that the honour of giving name

[1] Breviary of Aberdeen, foll. ci. cii.—quoted in Bishop Forbes' Kalendars of Scottish Saints, 1872, p. 304.

[2] Lanigan's Ecclesiastical History of Ireland, 1829, vol. i. p. 432.

[3] This form of the name has been explained above, p. 74. It brings us very near to the most ancient form of the island name.

to the first religious settlement on the island must be attributed.[1]

It is reasonable to infer from the only evidence that is still attainable that the early Culdee settlement on the island was under the charge of the see of Dunblane. The Culdee church at Dunblane dates back to the beginning of the seventh century, and it became a Roman see about 1160.[2] Whether the island church was Romanized at the same time, or earlier or later, it is impossible to tell. But that there was a Catholic parson there in 1210 seems likely from a reference in the Chartulary of Cambuskenneth.[3] A charter of the Abbey, of about that date, is witnessed by, among others, Malcolm, parson of the island of Macholem *(Malcolmo persona de insula Macholem)*. If Sir William Fraser is right in his identification of Macholem with Inchmahome, then there is proof sufficient that there was a Roman church here at that period; and that the parson was under the direction of the Bishop of Dunblane is inferred from the language of the Papal Instrument—to be afterwards referred to—in implement of which the Priory was erected.

The coming of the Augustinian monks to the island is variously dated by the older writers. In fact, so obscure is the early history of the settlement that it used to be

---

[1] For full accounts of the life and miracles of St. Colman, consult Lanigan's Ecclesiastical History of Ireland, 1829, vol. i. pp. 432 *et seqq.*; Reeves' Ecclesiastical Antiquities of Down, &c., 1847, pp. 104, *note,* 304, 311, 379 ; Forbes' Kalendars of Scottish Saints, 1872, pp. 304 *et seq.* ; Skene's Celtic Scotland, vol. ii. p. 32.

[2] Keith's Catalogue of the Scottish Bishops.

[3] Chartulary of Cambuskenneth, pp. 160, 161. This charter makes a gift by the Bishop, William of Dunblane, of the church of Kincardine in free alms to the Abbey of Cambuskenneth.

supposed that Inchmahome and Isle of St. Colmoc were different places.[1] Archbishop Spottiswoode affirms that the Priory of St. Colmoc's Isle in Menteith was founded by King Edgar. That must have been prior to 1107—the year of Edgar's death. But, if we are to trust Keith, or rather John Spottiswoode, there were no Augustinians in Scotland at that date. He says[2]—"The Canons-Regulars of St. Augustine were first brought into Scotland by Atelwholphus, Prior of St. Oswald of Nostel in Yorkshire, and afterwards Bishop of Carlisle; who established them at Scone, in the year 1114, at the desire of King Alexander I." An earlier authority to the same effect is Fordun :— "Scone was founded by Alexander the Fierce, who made it over to the governance of Canons-regular, called from the church at St. Oswald at Nostle (Nastlay, near Pontefract), and of the others after them who should serve God, until the end of the world."[3] John Spottiswoode further asserts that Inchmahome was an Abbey founded of old for canons of Cambuskenneth.[4] And Cambuskenneth we know was not founded till 1147. Spottiswoode also notes[5]

[1] See Spottiswoode's History of the Church of Scotland (4th ed.), vol. i.; compare app. p. 14 with p. 17; Keith's Catalogue of Scottish Bishops, with Account by John Spottiswoode of the Religious Houses in Scotland at the time of the Reformation, p. 391.; Maitland's History and Antiquities of Scotland, vol. i. pp. 255 and 259. It should be said, however, that John Spottiswoode writes—"Although this place (Inchmahome) be mentioned in most of our old lists of religious houses as a distinct monastery from that of Insula St. Colmoci, yet I am apt to believe they are one and the same." (Page 239 of Account of Religious Houses).

[2] Keith's Catalogue, &c., p. 385.

[3] Fordun's Chronicle, book v. chap. xxviii.; Skene's edition, vol. ii. p. 218. See also Liber Ecclesie de Scon (Maitland Club, 1843).

[4] Keith's Catalogue, &c., p. 319.   [5] *Ibid.*

that the Priory Insulæ Sancti Colmoci was said to have been founded by Murdach, Earl of Menteith, killed at the battle of Dupplin in 1332; although he adds that the name of Prior Adam is found in the list of those who swore fealty to Edward I. in 1296. Maitland also states that the Priory of the Isle "was founded by Murdach, Earl of Menteith, for Augustine monks,"[1] but he gives no date. The authority relied upon by both is no doubt the Scotichronicon, in which it is distinctly stated that the Augustinian monks were settled in the island by Murdach, Earl of Menteith.[2] Now, the Earl who fell at Dupplin was not the only one of that name. There was an earlier Murdach, who held the earldom from about 1180 to 1213; and it is neither impossible nor unlikely that he may have brought the Augustinians to the island. He was the father-in-law of the ascertained builder of the Priory, and it is no great assumption to suppose that the latter may have had in view the pious object of continuing the work of his father-in-law.

Whoever it may have been that was responsible for introducing the Augustinians to the island, the date of the erection of the buildings, the ruins of which still give distinction and interest to the place, and the name of the builder, are not now in doubt. These facts were settled by an authoritative document which was first published by the Rev. W. M'Gregor Stirling in his "Notes on Inch-

---

[1] Maitland's History and Antiquities of Scotland (1757), vol. i. p. 255.

[2] "*Insula Sancti Colmoci, ordinis Augustini, in Menteth; cujus fundator Murdacus, comes ejusdem.*"—Fordun's Scotichronicon, continuation by Bower (Goodall's edition), vol. ii. p. 539.

mahome" (1817).[1] This writ informs us that the Bishop of Dunblane[2] had appealed to the Pope regarding the dilapidation of his church (which seems to have been in a really lamentable condition) and the appropriation of its revenues by secular persons; and it may be inferred from the terms of the agreement come to that the Earls of Menteith and their vassals were responsible for a good deal of the spoliation of the bishopric.[2] In response to this appeal, the Pope (Gregory IX.) issued a Mandate— at Vitervi, 10th of June, 1237—to William, Bishop of Glasgow and Galfred (Geoffrey), Bishop of Dunkeld, directing them to enquire into the case and adopt suitable remedial measures. In pursuance of this mandate, the two Bishops held an investigation. The Bishop of Dun-

[1] This document was brought under Mr. Stirling's notice by Mr. Thomas Thomson, Deputy-Register of Scotland, and was printed in full, in the original Latin, in Appendix i. to the Notes, pp. 113-116. The original of this writ, it seems, cannot now be found in the General Register Office (Fraser's Red Book, vol. ii. p. 329, *note*); but its existence had been known before it was again brought to light in 1815. Mr. David Erskine, W.S., brother of the then laird of Cardross, in a letter to Captain (afterwards General) Hutton, dated 5th September, 1789, mentioned that he had in his possession an old paper entitled "The double of the apointment betwix the Bishop of Dunblain and the Pryor of Inchmahomo, Drawine out of the Auld Register." (Fragmenta Scoto-monastica, Edinburgh, 1842, app. p. 3). And in the Inventory of his Writs which was drawn up by William, seventh Earl of Menteith, about 1622, the first item set down is "ane apointment betwix Waltor Cuming, Erle of Monteith, and the Bishops of Dunkell and Dunblane, be the direction of the Pope, quhair the said Earlle gives libertie to the churchmen to build ane abbasie within his Ille of Inchmahome, of the dait 1238." (Red Book, *ut supra*). This may have been the original of which Mr. Erskine's "double" was a copy, or they may both have been copies; but at any rate they show that while the name of the builder of the Priory was quite unknown to the Scottish ecclesiastical historians, the information was in the hands of the families who were most immediately connected with the place.

[2] He is not named in the writ; but Clement was the Bishop at that time.

[3] This letter of Pope Gregory IX. to the Bishops of Glasgow and Dunkeld is to be found also in Vetera Monumenta Hibernorum et Scotorum Historiam Illustrantia, &c. (Rome, 1864), no. xci. p. 35.

blane and Walter Comyn, Earl of Menteith, appeared before them; and, having stated their respective cases, they submitted themselves to the jurisdiction of the Bishops and their Court. The result was an agreement, accepted by both parties, of which the following were the principal provisions. The Bishop was to renounce all right claimed, or that might be claimed, by the Church of Dunblane, to revenues derived from the churches of the earldom of Menteith, in which the Earl had the right of patronage, and to desist from all complaints against him. The Earl was authorised "to build a House for Religious Men of the Order of St. Augustine in the Island of Inchmaquhomok, without impediment or opposition from the said Bishop or his successors." To these religious men were assigned, "in pure and perpetual alms, the churches of Lany and of the said Island, with all the liberties and easements belonging to the said churches," reserving his episcopal rights to the Bishop. The Bishop was not to be allowed to make perpetual vicars in these two churches, but to accept proper chaplains presented to him, who should be responsible to him "in spiritual and episcopal matters." The Earl, again, was to assign the church of Kippen for a perpetual canonry in the church of Dunblane, reserving to himself and his successors the right of presentation to the canonry, and to give over to the Bishop whatever right he held in the church of Callander.

The instrument recording this agreement is dated at Perth on "the octave of John the Baptist," *i.e.*, the 16th of June, 1238; and we may assume that the building of the Priory was begun as soon as possible thereafter.

It is clear, from the terms of the writ, that there was already in the island of Inchmahome a church, over which the Bishop of Dunblane had Episcopal rights. At the same time the words "*Domum virorum religiosorum ordinis sancti Augustini in Insula de Inchmaquhomok construere*," do not make it quite clear whether there was already a body of Canons-Regular in the island, for whom merely a house was now to be built, or whether house and canons were to be placed there together. But perhaps it is not straining inference too much if we deduce from the reference to impediment and contradiction (*sine impedimento vel contradictione dicti episcopi*) on the part of the Bishop of Dunblane, a supposition that the Augustinians were in the island, and that opposition had been offered by the bishop either to their organisation or to the building of a house for them. If the Priory was connected with the Abbey of Cambuskenneth, he may have been inclined to regard it as an intrusion into his diocese.

The Augustinian Order of Monks was much favoured by the pious Scottish kings of the family of Canmore. Over a dozen communities of this Order had been established, in various parts of Scotland, by Alexander I., David I., and their nobles, previous to the erection of the Priory of Inchmahome. They had the designation of Canons-Regular from the circumstance that they were not, like other monks, confined to their monasteries, but might take charge of parish churches and discharge ecclesiastical functions wherever they might happen to be placed. The canonical dress, according to Spottiswoode (*apud* Keith) was a white robe, with a rochet (*rochetum*) of fine linen above the gown, and in the church a surplice (*superpellicium*) and an almuce (*lanutium*), formerly worn on the shoulders, thereafter on the left arm, hanging as far down as the ground. This almuce was of a fine black or grey skin, brought from foreign countries, and frequently lined with ermine, and serves to this day to distinguish the Canons-Regulars from the other religious Orders.[1] In this picturesque dress, then, we may conceive the canons of Inchmahome conducting the services in the Priory. When not so engaged the surplice and almuce were laid aside, and they appeared simply in their white tunic with gown of fine linen, over which was worn a black cloak with a hood covering the head, neck, and shoulders. So Sir David Lindsay makes the magpie in its black and white colours the ornithological representative of the Canons-Regular.[2]

The day in the convent was laid out in several divisions, marked off by the hours of prayer. These were (1) Matins and Lauds, at midnight; (2) Prime, about 6 A.M.; (3) Tierce, about 9 A.M.; (4) Sext, about noon; (5) Nones, about 2 P.M.; (6) Vespers, 4 P.M. or later; (7) Compline, 7 P.M.

---

[1] Keith's Catalogue, &c., p. 393. The following extract from Commissary Spalding's account of Charles I. at Holyrood in 1633 may be compared with the above description of the dress of the Canons-Regular :—" On Sunday, 23rd June, the King heard John Bishop of Murray teach in his *rochet*, which is a white linen or lawn drawn on above his coat, above the whilk his black gown was put on, and his arms through the gown sleeves, and above the gown sleeves is also white linen or lawn drawn on shapen like a sleeve. This is the weed of Archbishops and Bishops, and wears no surplice, but churchmen of inferior degree, in time of service, wears the samen, which is above their cloaths, a side (*i.e.*, long) linen cloth over body and arms like to a sack."— Spalding's History of the Troubles in Scotland, p. 18.

[2] Lindsay's Testament and Complaynt of our Soverane Lordis Papyngo; lines 654-657.

All the monks, with the exception of the sick and those who had dispensations of relief from the duty, rose for Matins and Lauds, after which they returned to bed till Prime. After Prime the Chapter was held. This meeting took place in a room specially designed for its purpose. The Chapter House was beside the cloisters, and during the meeting the cloisters were not allowed to be entered, so that what was going on in the Chapter House might not be overheard. It had a row of stone benches round the wall, with a reading desk, and a bench where culprits stood in the centre. There was a higher seat for the Abbot or Prior, and a crucifix. In the Chapter prayers for deceased benefactors were said, misdemeanours investigated and offenders punished by suitable discipline, and other conventual business arranged. For some time after the business of the Chapter had been completed, a period of silence and meditation was observed. Then the monks were dismissed to the cloisters till Sext—in some Orders this period was given to study, in others to manual labour. The dinner-hour was at noon. At this meal one of the brethren read aloud, while the others kept silence and listened. After dinner until the hour of Nones was the period for recreation, when the monks rambled about the grounds or otherwise amused themselves. When the Nones prayers had been said, music was practised for a while. Those who obtained permission from the Superior were allowed to go beyond the precincts of the monastery. The brothers who did not go out retired to their private chambers or "cells," to read or write or practise some manual occupation, or in some cases possibly merely to lounge away the time till Vespers. All were required to be inside the walls to sing Compline after supper. Then they withdrew to the dormitories, and were in bed by 8 P.M.[1]

The usual number of monks to a Prior was ten; and this—judging from the signatories to the deeds of the Chapter at the time when it may be reckoned to have been complete—was the number at Inchmahome.

The Priory had several chapels attached to it—one at Inchie, on the east shore of the lake, where the name of Chapel-lands still survives, the sole relic of the past; a second at Arnchly, about a mile to the west of the lake; a third at Chapel-larach (*i.e.*, chapel site or foundation), not far from Gartmore; and a fourth at Boquhapple (House of the Chapel), near Thornhill. Besides these, the churches of Leny, Port, and Kilmadock with its six dependent chapels, were under the charge of the Priory.[2] A fourth church—that of Lintrethen in Forfarshire—belonged to it at the time the lands of the Priory were secularised by Act of Parliament (9th July, 1606).[3]

Prior Adam.

No Chartulary is known to exist. Only a few charters and other documents relating to the Priory have been preserved. It is not, therefore, possible to present a continuous history of the House from its foundation to its decay, but all the properly vouched facts that have been

---

[1] This account of the conventual day is taken from Frosbrooke's British Monachism, 1817, *sub initio*; and Gordon's Monasticon, p. 8.

[2] Fasti Ecclesiæ Scoticanæ, vol. ii, pp. 724, 737.

[3] Acts of the Parliaments of Scotland, vol. iv., under date. Lintrethin was in the gift of the Prior, at least as early as 1477. See *infra*.

gathered regarding it will be set forth. The name of its earliest Prior is nowhere mentioned, nor for more than a quarter of a century after its erection does the name of the Priory occur in any extant document yet known. The earliest reference is in what was known in Scotland as Bagimont's Roll. Pope Gregory the Tenth sent to Scotland an emissary, by name Magister Boyamundus de Vitia, to collect the tenths of all ecclesiastical benefices for the Holy Land. In the account of his collections, rendered in 1275, appears the item, "De Priorie sancti Colmoti, 9 marc. 13 sol. 1 den,"[1] that is to say, the tithe received from the prior amounted to 9 merks or £6 13s 1d, from which we can readily estimate the total income of the Priory at that early period of its existence.[2] The next historical reference to the Priory—twenty years later—gives us the name of the Prior who then held office. It occurs in the Ragman Rolls,[3] where, among those who swore fealty to Edward the First of England, at Berwick, on the 21st of August, 1296, appears the name of "*Adam*, Prioure de Ile de Seint Colmoth," who took the oath for himself and his convent.

Prior Maurice.

The probable successor of Adam was *Maurice*, as his name appears (along with that of Sir John Menteith and others), as witness to a charter of Alan, seventh Earl of

---

[1] Theiner's Vetera Monumenta, no. cclxiv. p. 115. (The tithe of the Abbey of Cambuskenneth was at the same time £10 8s 11d).

[2] At this time Scots money was of equal value with English. It was not till well on in the reign of David II. that the deterioration in value began.

[3] Ragman Rolls, 117.

Menteith, which has been assigned by Sir William Fraser to the year 1305. In this charter he is designed "domino Mauricio, Priore de Insula Sancti Colmoci."[1] It seems to have been in the time of Prior Maurice that King Robert the Bruce made his three recorded visits to Inchmahome. He was here for the first time, so far as we know, at a very critical period of his life, just after his coronation at Scone, which took place on the 29th of March, 1306. Alan, Earl of Menteith, was one of his supporters, and to the quiet island in his domain came the King after his coronation, perhaps to meet his friends and consider his future course. The fact that he was on the island at that time is ascertained from a petition presented to Edward I. by Malise, Earl of Strathern, who, after the battle of Methven, had been made prisoner and sent to England. He affirmed that he had always been loyal to the English King, and, although admitting that he had on one occasion done homage to Bruce, he said that it was done only on compulsion and in fear of his life. He narrated how, deceived by a safe-conduct, he had been seized by the Earl of Athole and some others, and by them carried to "*Inchemecolmock*," where Bruce then was. On refusing to do homage—as he had twice before refused—Sir Robert Boyd advised Bruce to behead him and grant his lands away, whereupon the Earl was so frightened that he did their will, and they let him go.[2]

The second occasion on which Bruce is known to have

[1] Original in Gleneagles charter-chest : printed in the Red Book of Menteith, vol. ii. p. 223.
[2] This Petition is printed in Documents and Records illustrating the History of Scotland, edited by Sir Francis Palgrave (1837), pp. 319 and clix.

been at Inchmahome was in the autumn of 1308. By that time he had fought his romantic battles in Galloway, cleared the northern parts of his kingdom of the English enemy, and chastised his old enemy, John of Lorn, in the fastnesses of the West Highlands. On his way to Perth from this last expedition he halted at Inchmahome, probably to rest and give thanks for his victories. The fact is instructed by a charter of Malcolm, Earl of Lennox, to Sir John of Luss, which the King confirmed on the 28th of September, 1308, " apud Insulam Sancti Colmoci."[1]

The third visit of King Robert to the Priory cannot have been made for any reason of the concealment or security the place might afford, for it occurred after his power was well assured and his claim to the throne had been admitted by the people and the estates of the realm. Rather it seems to indicate that he had some liking for this sequestered retreat as a haven of rest from his warlike toils and the cares of government, and possibly also that he had acquired an affection for its Prior, Maurice. We hear no more of this Maurice as Prior of Inchmahome, but is it unreasonable to suggest that he may have been the same who, as Abbot of Inchaffray, blessed the Scottish army at the battle of Bannockburn? If that were he, then we know that he was advanced to still higher rank in the Church. He was promoted to the see of his own diocese of Dunblane in 1319.[2] The Abbot of Inchaffray, in 1314, was

[1] The original charter is preserved at Rossdhu, and was printed in Fraser's The Chiefs of Colquhoun, vol. ii. p. 276.

[2] Liber Insulæ Missarum (Bannatyne Club, 1847), p. xiv. Appointment ratified by Pope John XXII. in March, 1822.—Theiner's Vetera Monumenta, pp. 341-3.

evidently a much trusted ecclesiastical friend of the King, and if it could be proved that he was the same man as the Prior of Inchmahome in 1310, it would give an additional interest to the King's visit at that time, and would also account for Maurice's preferment in the Church. From his retreat at Inchmahome King Robert issued a writ confiscating the property of one John de Pollox, who had adhered to the enemy and plotted treason, and bestowing on the Convent and Abbot of Arbroath everything belonging to the traitor that might be found within their lands and tenements. This writ, which is dated "*apud Insulam Sancti Colmoci*, on the 15th day of April, in the year of grace 1310 and the fifth year of our reign," was first published by the Rev. W. M'Gregor Stirling from the Registrum de Aberbrothock.[1]

PRIOR CHRISTIN.

Shortly after Bannockburn, the Priory received a great addition to its possessions. Sir Malcolm Drummond—if we are to credit the historian of that house[2]—bestowed the estate of Cardross on the Convent of Inchmahome, in the year 1316, probably, it has been conjectured, as "a proof of pious gratitude for the donor's release from (a long) captivity."[3] For Malcolm had been taken prisoner by the English in 1301, and was not set free till after the

[1] Notes on Inchmahome, app. ii. p. 117 : *e Registro de Aberbrothock*, fol. xxiii. The copy was supplied to Mr. Stirling from the Panmure documents by General Hutton. The Chartulary of Arbroath has since been published by the Bannatyne Club.

[2] Malcolm's History of the House of Drummond, app.

[3] Notes on Inchmahome, p. 44.

battle of Bannockburn.[1] He was a son of the Sir John Drummond who died in 1300, and was buried in the choir of the Priory, his mother being a daughter of Walter Stewart, Earl of Menteith.[2] If we are right in conjecturing that Prior Maurice may have been translated to Inchaffray prior to the battle of Bannockburn, this donation could not have been given in his time. And indeed this is confirmed by the fact that a charter by Earl Alan[3] was witnessed by "domino Christino, Priore de Insula Sancti Colmoci." The charter is undated, but as Alan was sent as a prisoner to England after the battle of Methven in 1306,[4] and did not return, he must have died there prior to the general delivery of prisoners which followed the victory at Bannockburn.

Prior Christin is next found witnessing a charter of Earl Murdach (1318-1332) to Walter, son of Sir John of Menteith, of the lands of Thom and Lanarkins, with fishings on the Teith. This charter also is without date, but it must, of course, have been granted not later than 1332.[5] It is quite possible that Prior Christin was the hero of the next incident recorded in the history of the Priory,

---

[1] Sir Malcolm must have been regarded as rather a notable captive, for Chalmers informs us that on the 25th of July, 1301, Edward offered oblations at the shrine of St. Kentigern in the Cathedral Church of Glasgow "for the good news of Sir Malcolm de Drummond, Knight, a Scot, being taken prisoner by Sir John Segrave."—Caledonia, vol. i. p. 667.

[2] MS. addition to Notes on Inchmahome, p. 44.

[3] Of the lands of Rusky, to William de Rusky : Fragmenta Scoto-Monastica (1842), app. p. ix.

[4] Palgrave's Documents and Records, &c., p. 353.

[5] Fragmenta Scoto-Monastica, app. p. ix. Sir William Fraser, who has printed this charter in the Red Book, vol. ii. p. 225, from the original in the charter-chest at Blair Drummond, dates it *circa* 1330.

but as no name is mentioned in the record, it may have been a successor. Anyhow, the Exchequer Rolls let us know that, in the year 1358, the Prior of Inchemacolmock was accused of deforcing the representative of the Sheriff of Perth.[1] It would be interesting to have the whole story of the violence offered to the minion of the law by this holy prior, but the record gives no detailed information.[2]

In the same year that this happened there was resident at Inchmahome one who was destined some years later to become the King of Scotland. This was Robert the High Steward, the grandson of King Robert Bruce, who had just been been created Earl of Strathern by David II., and afterwards, in 1371, ascended the throne as Robert the Second. As overlord to the granter he gave his assent to the gift of certain lands, "apud Insulam Sancti Colmaci," on the 12th of November, 1358.[3] The Steward was to make a still closer connection with the district, as his son Robert, the famous Duke of Albany of a later period, in 1361 married the Lady Margaret Graham, and through that matrimonial alliance became the tenth Earl of Menteith.

By some writers the Priory is said to have witnessed a royal marriage in 1363, namely, the marriage of King David II. with Margaret Logy. The bride certainly had

---

[1] Exchequer Rolls, vol. i. p. 558.

[2] Perhaps it was in connection with the collection — by this time grown somewhat difficult — of the ransom for King David II. In consequence of this difficulty, David had been permitted by the Pope to levy, for a space of three years, a tenth of all the ecclesiastical benefices in Scotland. But the King, not content with that, compelled the churches, in addition to their tenth, to contribute in the same proportion as the barons and free tenants of the crown, for their lands and temporalities.—Fordun.

[3] Liber Insulæ Missarum, p. xlv.

a local connection, for she was the daughter of Malcolm of Drummond, the benefactor of the Priory, and the widow of Sir John Logie of Logie and Strathgartney.[1] But it was not at Inchmahome that the marriage was celebrated. The mistake has arisen from confounding the name of the place as given by Fordun,[2] Inchmurdach or Inchmachac, with Inchmahome. Inchmurdach, however, appears to have been a seat of the Bishops of St. Andrews, though its precise locality is unknown.[3]

Another donation fell to the Priory about this time. That was a grant by David II. of seven hundred shillings sterling to be paid to the prior annually—the name of the prior at the time is not stated—out of the proceeds of the Sheriff offices of Fife and Perth.[4] The grant, however, was recalled in 1367, at the time when the most strenuous efforts were being made to retrieve the dilapidation of the revenues of the Crown.

From this time onwards, for about a century, there is a blank in the annals of the Priory. Of the ecclesiastics who ruled its affairs during that period, not a name survives, nor is any document known to be extant that so much as mentions the existence of the place. It is to "The Acts of the Lords of Council in Civil Causes,"

[1] Exchequer Rolls, vol. ii., introd., pp. lv. *et seq.*
[2] Scotichronicon a Goodall (Lib. xiv. cap. xxxiv.), vol. ii. p. 379.
[3] Geographical Illustrations of Scottish History, by David Macpherson (1798), *sub voce.*
[4] Robertson's Index of Missing Charters (1798), p. 51, No. 22 : "To the Prior of Inchmahome of ane annual of 700 s. sterling furth of the Sheriff's offices of Fyfe and Perth." Mr. M'Gregor Stirling, on the authority of a MS. Index of Charters he had seen, puts the grant at *one* hundred shillings sterling.—Notes on Inchmahome, p. 119.

"The Acts of the Lords Auditors of Causes and Complaints," and, especially, the "Protocol Books of the Burgh of Stirling," that the next information regarding the Priory of Inchmahome is due.[1] It is to be hoped that the disappearance of the Priory for so long from the public records may be owing to the circumstance that the priors of that time were men of peace, and that the convent was undisturbed in any of its rights and possessions. And it may be further observed that this blank period is about co-extensive with the possession of the earldom of Menteith by the Albanies, whose powerful influence may have availed to keep the monastery quiet and secure; while the fact that their usual places of residence were in other parts of the country may explain the absence of the name of Inchmahome from the records of their public transactions.

PRIOR JOHN AND PRIOR THOMAS.

It is significant of the local disturbances that must have accompanied the fall of the Albanies, that the first notices of the monastery that occur thereafter point to disputes regarding the priorate. A *Prior John* was in office apparently about the middle of the fifteenth century. How long he held the position is not known; but he had to face a rival claimant for the Priory. This rival makes his first appearance—so far as is known to us—in the

---

[1] The record of The Acts of the Lords of Council in Civil Causes (*Acta Dominorum Concilii*) extends from 1478 to 1495; The Acts of the Lords Auditors of Causes and Complaints (*Acta Auditorum Concilii*) cover the period from 1466 to 1494; and the entries in The Protocol Books of the Burgh of Stirling begin in 1460.

Muniments of the University of Glasgow, where he is noted as one of the persons who were incorporated with that University in the rectorship of Master William Arthurle, anno 1469:—" *Thomas prior insule Sancti Colmoci ordinis Sancti Augustini.*"[1] But John claimed to be the rightful holder of the dignity. In the Stirling Protocol Book there is an entry, under date 6th of November, 1472, which informs us that in a Consistorial Court held in the Cathedral Church of Dunblane, George of Abirnethe, Provost of the Collegiate Church of Dumbertane, appeared as procurator for John, Prior of the monastery of Inchmahomok, anent certain sums due by the tenants of the said monastery and William of Edmonstoune of Duntreth, asserted procurator of Sir Thomas Dog, Prior of the said monastery.[2] Dene Thomas had thus the powerful backing of the Steward of the Lordship of Menteith, and appears for a time to have prevailed. Whether Prior John had died—as seems likely—or had been otherwise got rid of, there is no means of knowing; but the right of Prior Thomas seems to have been unchallenged for several years. His name appears as witness in Protocol entries of date 15th December, 1476;[3] 27th October, 1477;[4] and 19th December, 1477.[5] On the 14th December, 1477, " *Thomas*, Prior of Inchmahome," presented John Edmonston, M.A., to the vicarage of the Parish Church of Luntrethyn, and on the same day he took instruments that William Edmonston of

[1] Munimenta Alme Universitatis Glasguensis (Maitland Club, 1854), vol. ii. p. 76.
[2] Abstract of the Protocol Book of the Burgh of Stirling, 1896, p. 13, No. 63.
[3] *Ibid*, p. 32.   [4] *Ibid*, p. 35.
[5] *Ibid*, p. 36.   Prior Thomas' name as witness to these deeds has been supplied from the MS. Protocols by Mr. W. B. Cook.

Duntreth had promised to defend the honour of the said Prior.[1] This looks to trouble. The fact is, there was another claimant of the priorate in the person of Sir Alexander Ruch, who ultimately prevailed in the Ecclesiastical Courts, and the usurpation of Prior Thomas came to an end immediately after the transactions referred to.

PRIOR ALEXANDER.

In an Act of the Lords of Council,[2] dated 22nd March, 1478, they gave decree "in an action and cause persewit be Dene David Ruch, as procurator for *Dene Alexander Ruch, Prior of Inchmaquholmok*," against Matthew Forester,[3] burgess of Stirling, for wrongously intermitting with the teinds of Row. Forester, it seems, had got a lease of these teinds from Prior Thomas, but the Lords decided that the tack was of no avail to him, "because the Priory of Inchmaquhomock *was opteinit and wounyn fra the said dene Thomas dog be twa sentence definitive in the Court of Rome* befor that he maid the said tak to the said Mathow." He was therefore ordered to restore the teinds, or the value of them, to the Prior or his procurator. After the right to the teinds of Row had been thus vindicated, it is satisfactory to learn that an amicable arrangement was come to between the litigants. Procurator David Ruch agreed to discharge all claims against Matthew Forester, and to let him the teinds on the same terms on

---

[1] Abstract of the Protocol Book of the Burgh of Stirling, 1896, p. 36, No. 193.
[2] Acta Dominorum Concilii, p. 24.
[3] Matthew Forrester was Provost of Stirling in 1470-1, and again in 1478-9. —Extracts from Stirling Records, vol. i. pp. 272, 273.

which he had hold them from Sir Thomas Dog. Moreover, for the good deeds done to the Convent by the said Matthew, it was resolved to pay him the sum of forty marks—twenty in money, and the other twenty in the form of a grant of teinds free of rent for one year.

This Prior Alexander is evidently the same as appears in the printed Fragments of Stirling Protocols as Sir Alexander *Ruth*—most probably from an error on the part of the transcriber. The forms of the letters *c* and *t* in the old writing are very easy to be mistaken, the one for the other. And Ruch (now spelled *Rough)* is a good Scotch name; whereas Ruth is, if not unknown, at least uncommon in Scotland. The reference in this Protocol entry is also to tithes belonging to the Priory. It is dated 29th April, 1479, and the abstract sets forth that " Mr John Ruth, vicar of Garreoch, and Sir David Ruth, monk of Dunfermlyne, procurator for Sir Alexander Ruth, Prior of the Isle of St. Colmoc, of Dunblane diocese, confessed them paid by Sir James Ogilvy of Ernby, knight, of the sum of £30 Scots, for lease of the tiend sheaves of the Parish Church of Leuchris, for two terms bypast and one term to come."[1] Here Dene David again appears as procurator for the Prior, in conjunction with John Ruch, who had attained the degree of Master. We may conclude that in all likelihood they were brothers, or perhaps nephews, of Prior Alexander.

In the sederunt of the Parliament which met on the

[1] Extracts from Stirling Records, 1519-1666, app. i. p. 264. The Abstract of Protocols, which has been printed since the publication of the "Extracts," gives the name as Rucht, thus confirming the Act of Parliament.

The Lake of Menteith. 153

13th April, 1481,[1] in order to concert measures for putting the country in a posture of defence against the "auld enemy," appears a Prior of Inchmahome *(Priore de Inchmaquholmo)*, along with the Earl of Menteith. Considering the closeness of the date, this was most probably Prior Alexander. But as the name is not mentioned in the record, room is left for the possibility that it may have been his successor, whose name appears to have been David.

PRIOR DAVID.

Prior David was certainly in office in 1483, for he is mentioned in the Protocols on the 8th of June of that year as requiring from one Duncan Forestar, burgess of Stirling, a certain some of money from the goods of the Prior then in Forestar's hands.[2] In his time, litigation regarding the revenues and possessions of the monastery was continued, and became rather intricate. The first of these lawsuits was decided by the Lords of Council on the 18th of March, 1490.[3] The opponent of the Prior in this case was John Haldane of Gleneagles. Haldane had married (1460) Agnes, the heiress of the Menteiths of Rusky, and had thus acquired an interest in lands in the district.[4] The dispute was about the teinds of the kirks

---

[1] Acts of the Parliaments of Scotland, vol. ii. p. 134.
[2] Duncan Forestare was Provost of Stirling in 1477-8, 1479-81, 1487-90. —Extracts from Records of the Burgh of Stirling, 1619-1666, app. ii. p. 273.
[3] Acta Dominorum Concilii, p. 184.
[4] John Haldane and his spouse had before this afforded much employment to the Law Courts: see various entries in the Protocol Books of Stirling from 1476 onwards.—Extracts from Stirling Records, vol. i. app. i. pp. 256, 260, 261, 262, 264.

of Leny and Kilmadock. The Prior claimed, in name of these teinds, thirteen chalders of meal, which Haldane affirmed he had already paid to Henry,[1] Abbot of Cambuskenneth, factor for the Prior of Inchmahome—with the exception of five chalders and thirteen bolls, which the Abbot had assigned to Dene Gilbert Buchanan, a canon of Inchmahome, who was in charge of the Church of Leny. Haldane's contention was upheld by the Court. He was ordained to pay the proportion assigned to the parson of Leny, and discharged of what was already paid, for which the Prior, if he thought proper, might have recourse against the Abbot, his factor.

The next action was in defence of the property of the monastery. On the 20th of June, 1491, the Prior and Convent complained against Robert Buchanan of Leny for purchasing the King's letter to eject the above-mentioned Dene Gilbert Buchanan from part of the lands of Leny, lying beside the church, of which they alleged they had long been in possession. The Lords decided that the King's letter had been improperly procured, and was of no effect, and that Dene Gilbert and the Convent were to remain in possession until, at any rate, the case was settled in the next Justice-ayre to be held at Stirling.[2]

Before this case was settled, a dispute arose with John

---

[1] Abbot Henry of Cambuskenneth appears to have been himself rather a litigious person. He had a long dispute with the community of Stirling concerning their respective rights to fishings in the Forth.—Stirling Charters and other Records, 1124-1705, p. 54, &c.

[2] Acta Dominorum Concilii, p. 201. Dean Gilbert Buchanan, vicar of Leny and canon of Inchmahome, was the sixth son of Andrew Buchanan, second laird of Leny, and uncle of the above-mentioned Robert, who was the fourth laird.

Lord Drummond, who was bailie on some of the Priory lands. He claimed the rents of certain lands which had been assigned to him as his bailie-fee, and this claim the Convent resisted. It would appear that he was receiving more from the tithes of these lands than the Prior and Convent thought he was entitled to, and to get even with him, they let a portion of them to John Haldane of Gleneagles. Thus the quarrel first came before the Lords Auditors, on the 5th of May, 1491,[1] as a complaint by John Haldane against John Lord Drummond, for withholding from him the tithes of Collouth, Borrowbanks, Lochfield, Wat Dog's toune, Wat Smith's toune, and the Spittals—all in the parish of Kilmadock—which he had received in assedation from David, Prior of Inchmaholmo, for three years, the value of these tithes being equal to one chalder of meal and two bolls of bere yearly. It was found that Haldane had no claim, as Lord Drummond held these teinds in his fee for nineteen years, and his grant preceded the tack to Haldane.

Driven thus into the open, the Prior next took action directly against Lord Drummond himself. The feeling became very bitter, if we may draw such a conclusion from the fact that on the 19th of January, 1492, the Prior of Inchmaholmo, in presence of the Lords of Council, took instruments that Lord Drummond produced an instrument in the form of excommunication upon the said Prior and Convent.[2] What that meant or how it was procured is not easy to say, but it certainly has a serious look about it.

[1] Acta Auditorum Concilii, p. 147.   [2] Acta Dominorum Concilii, p. 226.

On the 25th of January, 1492, the dispute came before the Lords of Council[1] in the form of an "action of the Prior and Convent of Inchmaquholmo against John Lord Drummond, for the wrangous uptaking of the teinds and frottis (fruits) of their lands of the Lochfield, the Banks, Calquhollat, the twa Collatts, and the Spittale tounis of the last year bygane"—amounting to five chalders of meal and a chalder of bere.[2] The bailie-fee of Lord Drummond, it appears, was four chalders of meal, and in payment of it the Prior and Convent, by letters under their common seal, had assigned to him these teinds, which were supposed to be of the same value. Lord Drummond, however, by careful management, or by a stricter exaction of the dues, had increased the value of the teinds to the amount above stated. The Convent now wished to recall the grant. But the Lords decided that Lord Drummond had "done na wrang," but they added that when the teinds of these places amounted to more than the value of his fee of baliary, he should pay the surplus to the Convent.

Once more Prior David appears before the Lords Auditors, when, on the 21st June, 1493, he "granted that he had in fermance and keeping Dene Patrick Menteth, channone of the said place (Inchmahome) as ordinary to him, quhare apone Maister David Menteth, allegeand him procurator for the said Dene Patrick, askit a not and of the privilege of law."[3]

[1] Acta Dominorum Concilii, p. 265.
[2] The names of these places and others before mentioned are interesting as showing some of the possessions of the monastery at that time.
[3] Acta Auditorum Concilii, p. 181.

With that case this litigious Prior disappears from the public records. Whether he died shortly after, or, tired of his legal encounters, thenceforth cultivated a meeker spirit, there is no means of knowing. We do not meet with the name of a successor till 1526.

Prior Andrew.

This successor, whose name is *Andrew*, may have been in office for a good many years previous to 1526. From the fact that he held office for less than three years after that date, we may be justified in assuming that it was so. But even on the supposition that the transaction in which Andrew is introduced to us was at or near the beginning of his priorate, the length of time between that and the last recorded lawsuit of Prior David, does not make it impossible that the latter may have lived to be succeeded by the former. In all the circumstances, therefore, it is likely that there is no break here in the continuity of the Priors, and that Andrew was the immediate successor of David.

On the 16th of April, 1526, "Andro, be the permissioun of God, Prior of Inchemahomo, with full consent and assent of all our Convent cheptourlie gadderit, granted a lease to 'Andro Stewart and Elezabetht Maistertoun his spous' of the lands of Drumlanniklocht, with twenty shillings' worth of the lands of Arniclerycht, in their barony of Cardross, for the term of nineteen years, at an annual rent of fifty shillings, 'gud and usuall mony of Scotland.'"[1] This

---

[1] Lease printed in the Red Book of Menteith, vol. ii. p. 329, from the original in H.M. General Register House, Edinburgh.

lease, to which the common seal of the Chapter was
"affixit and hungyn," is signed by the Prior and ten
canons—presumably the whole Chapter. Their names
are as follows:—

ANDREW, PRIOR OF INCHEMAHOMO.

DENE JAMES BAD, SUB-PRIOR.   DENE JAMES THOMSOUN.
DENE JOHN HUTOUN.   DENE THOMAS MAKCLELLANE.
DENE DUNCANE PRYNGVLL.   DENE ADAM CRISTESON.
DENE JHON YONGMAN.   DENE JAMES BRADFUT.
DENE ADAM PEBLIS.   DENE JHONE MONT.

Prior Andrew must have died in 1528, or very early
in 1529. He was the last of the strictly ecclesiastical
priors. On his death the Priory was given *in commendam*,
and the list of the Commendators is complete. They were
all but one members of the same family, and that one held
his office for so short a time that the family possession
of the Erskines can hardly be said to have been interrupted.

CHAPTER VI.

**The Priory under Commendators—
1529 to 1628.**

"For holy offices I have a time: a time
To think upon the part of business which
I bear i' the State."

COMMENDATOR ROBERT ERSKINE.

ROBERT ERSKINE, the first of the Commendator-Priors, is dated by Sir William Fraser 1531-1547.[1] The first of these dates is certainly wrong: the second is probably also incorrect. The same writer further assumes that this Commendator was that Robert, Master of Erskine, who fell on the field of Pinkie-cleuch in 1547, and who was said to have been beloved of the Queen Dowager, Mary of Lorraine.[2] The

---

[1] Red Book, vol. i. p. 522. Fraser's authority is the Fragmenta Scoto-Monastica, app. p. viii. The statement founded on is contained in a letter from David Erskine, W.S., to Captain Hutton. All that the writer says, however, is merely that *Robert was Commendator in September 1531*.

[2] "In that same battel," says John Knox, "was slayne the Maister of Erskin, deirlie belovit of the Quein; for quhome sche maid grit Lamentatioun and bure his deythe mony Dayis in Mynd."—Knox's History of the Reformation, edit. 1732, p. 79. See also the poem of Alexander Scott, entitled "Lament of the Maister of Erskyn," which depicts a lover's feelings on parting with his mistress in a state of uncertainty whether they shall ever meet again, and is believed to have been written with reference to the last parting of Erskine and the Queen Dowager.—The Poems of Alexander Scott (Scottish Text Society, ed. 1896), p. 51.

ground for this assumption appears to be that there is no extant record in which John Erskine, the second Commendator, is mentioned as such, until the visit of the young Queen Mary to the island; and, as that was immediately after the death of Robert, it is inferred that John stepped at once into an office which had been, up till that time, held by his brother. It must be noted, however—and this Sir William Fraser himself observes—that, while several writs are extant in which Robert, Master of Erskine, is mentioned, there is not one in which he is at the same time designated Prior of Inchmahome.[1]

The assumption of identity with the Master of Erskine cannot be held as anything more than a guess, and indeed there is ground for believing that it is an incorrect one. The Robert Erskine who became Commendator of Inchmahome was previously rector of Glenbervy in the Mearns, and received his appointment to Inchmahome early in the year 1529. In one of the Protocol Books of Stirling the following record of his induction is found under date 15th of March of that year:—

"Robert, rector of Gilbervy and perpetual Commendator of the Priory of the Isle of St. Colmoc, of Dunblane diocese, holding in his hands certain Apostolic letters or bulls [of Clement the Seventh], past to the presence of Mr. Robert

[1] On the 20th of May, 1536, King James V. granted to Robert, Master of Erskine, and his wife, Margaret Graham, the lands of the barony of Kelle, which his father, John Lord Erskine, had resigned—perhaps as a marriage provision for his son. (Reg. Mag. Sig., vol. iii., No. 1584, p. 353). Again, on the 23rd February, 1541-2, the King granted him, for himself and his heirs, a charter of the lands of Schirgartane, Drumb de Kippan, and Arnebeg, with the mill of the same. These lands were in the neighbourhood of the Priory possessions; but in this charter, as in the former, he is designated only Master of Erskine. (Reg. Mag. Sig., vol. iii., No. 2602, p. 598.)

Graham, vicar of Drummond (Drymen), and required him to put the said letters to due execution, who, receiving them with the reverence that became them, past to the high altar of the church of the said Priory, and gave institution and investiture of the said Priory and monastery thereof, with fruits, rents, provents and emoluments, lands, baronies, &c., by delivery of a silver chalice gilt, missal book, and sacred ornaments of the said high altar, as use is, to the said Robert Erskine, rector of Gilbervy, and invested him in possession thereof; in presence of Alexander, Earl of Menteith, &c."[1]

The question, therefore, is, who was this Master Robert Erskine, rector of Glenbervy? It is scarcely likely that the Master of Erskine—the eldest son and heir-apparent of an illustrious noble—would have held so small an ecclesiastical benefice as this rural parsonage. But beyond this general consideration, and the fact that the Master of Erskine is never in any writ styled Prior of Inchmahome, we have some independent information regarding the rector of Glenbervy. He is met with frequently in the Public Records, and almost invariably in the company of Sir Thomas Erskine of Haltoun, lord of Brechin, who became Secretary to King James the Fifth in 1524.

The first occurrence of his name is in the Register of the Great Seal, when he witnesses a deed executed on the 31st of March, 1525, and confirmed by the King on the 30th of April following—other two witnesses being Master Thomas Erskine de Haltoun and George Arrot

[1] Extracts from Stirling Burgh Records, vol. ii. p. 265.

de eodem.[1] The next document is still more conclusive of his near relation to Sir Thomas of Haltoun and the family of Dun to which Sir Thomas belonged. It is quoted by Mr. A. H. Millar, apparently from the family papers preserved at Dun House. "In 1526," he says, "an instrument of sasine was executed in favour of the Provost and Canons of St. Salvator's College, St. Andrews, on precept of John Erskine of Dun, who was represented by 'the noble lady Margarete, Countess of Buchquhan, *the venerable Mr. Robert Erskine, rector of Glenbervy*, and that honourable man Richard Mailuil de Baldouy.'"[2] This John Erskine of Dun was the afterwards famous Superintendent. He was at this time in his seventeenth year. Sir Thomas Erskine of Haltoun was his uncle and legal tutor. The Countess of Buchan was his mother, and she is here associated with the parson of Glenbervy as one of the youth's representatives in a way that seems to argue near relationship. The Melvilles we know were neighbours and close friends of the family.

The most common names in the Erskine family appear to have been John, Robert, Thomas, and Alexander. John Erskine of Dun, who fell at Flodden, is said to have had several sons—the exact number is not by any genealogical writer stated. Two of these, John and Alexander, were slain along with their father in the battle; Thomas of

---

[1] Reg. Mag. Sig., No. 306, p. 306. In the print of this deed Master Robert's name is given as *Ersly*—an apparent mistake for Erskine. Arrot was held in vassalage of the lordship of Brechin, and lies in that parish. The Arrots were superseded in the possession of their property by the Erskines of Dun. (Jervise's Memorials of Angus and Mearns, vol. ii. p. 60.)

[2] Millar's Castles and Mansions of Scotland, 1890, p. 348.

Haltoun, the King's Secretary, was a third; and if there was a fourth son, his name is likely to have been Robert, and we are at liberty to conjecture that he may have been this very rector of Glenbervy. At any rate, his close connection with the family of Dun, and with Sir Thomas Erskine in particular, is made clear by the association of the two names in no fewer than eight deeds recorded under the Great Seal between 1541 and 1544.[1] In these deeds it is to be observed that he is not styled Prior of Inchmahome, but Dean of Aberdeen, and that continued to be his designation to the end of his life. In July, 1547, he was instructed by the Bishop of Aberdeen to receive, in his capacity as head of the Chapter, a new canon;[2] and in an inventory of the ornaments of the altar of St. Maurice, made in 1549, occurs the following note of a gift made by him — "cum duobus antependiis, quorum unum ex dono venerabilis viri magistri *Roberti Erskyne, decani Aberdonensis moderni.*"[3] In 1552, he subscribes an assedation made by the Bishop as decanus Aberdonensis.[4] He still, however, held his old rectory, for he appears in the Register of Brechin as "Prebendary of Glenbervy" in 1556.[5] On the eve of the Reformation, the Chapter of the Cathedral of Aberdeen directed a memorial of advice to the Bishop, making certain recommendations of reforms which they thought might avail to stay or avert the

---

[1] Reg. Mag. Sig., vol. iii., No. 2430, p. 556 (anno 1541); No. 2347, p. 536 (1541); No. 2432, p. 557 (1541); No. 2433, p. 557 (1541); No. 2439, p. 558 (1541); No. 2678, p. 618 (1542); No. 2973, p. 296 (1543); No. 3050, p. 74 (1544).
[2] Registrum Episcopatus Aberdonensis (Spalding Club, 1845), vol. ii. p. 318.
[3] *Ibid*, vol. ii. p. 199. [4] *Ibid*, vol. i. p. 456.
[5] Registrum Episcopatus Brechinensis (Bannatyne Club, 1856), vol. ii. p. 204.

storm which they clearly saw was approaching. The first signature to this important document—dated 5th January, 1558—is that of Robert Erskyne, "decanus Aberdonensis."[1] Not improbably it was drawn up by Erskine himself; and the fact that it has been preserved among the collections at the House of Dun may be another proof of his near relationship to that family.[2] His name is last met with in the Brechin Register in April, 1585, where he is spoken of as *quondam* Master Robert Erskine, Dean of Aberdeen, from which we may conclude that he was dead before that time.[3]

The inference from these facts seems to be this, that the Lord Erskine to whom James the Fifth is said to have given the patronage of the Priory of Inchmahome, put the rector of Glenbervy into the Commendatorship to keep the place warm for his third son, John, who—as a younger son, with two elder brothers between him and the succession to his father—was being educated for the Church; and that, when John Erskine was ripe for the position, Robert retired in his favour, or was superseded, and probably received the Deanery of Aberdeen in com-

---

[1] Reg. Epis. Aberd., vol. i. p. lxi.

[2] Jervise states distinctly that Robert Erskine, rector of Glenbervy, "*belonged to the family of Dun*" (Memorials of Angus and Mearns, vol. i., p. 147). He adds that he held in addition the provostry of the Collegiate Church of the Holy Trinity, near Edinburgh, and was also apparently Dean of Aberdeen. The latter part of this statement is sufficiently proved by the references to the Records given above. Another document may be quoted in which Robert Erskine is brought into connection with Dun. This is a lease of the fruits of the parsonage and vicarage of Arbuthnott for three years by Wilzem Rynd, parson of Arbuthnott, and Robert Erskine, Dean of Aberdeen, in favour of John Erskine of Dun. The lease is dated at Brechin, 23rd April, 1552, and is in the Dun collection. (Historical Manuscripts Commission, Fifth Report, p. 640).

[3] Regist. Episc. Brech., vol. ii. p. 348.

pensation for the loss of Inchmahome. This would date Robert's tenure of the office from 1529 to about 1540 or 1541.

There are but few indications of what was going on at the Priory during the time of this Commendator. Of the canons who witnessed the lease already referred to as granted by Prior Andrew,[1] one is mentioned as witness to a precept of sasine by Alexander, Earl of Menteith, to William, Master of Menteith, and Margaret Mowbry, his spouse, of certain lands specified. The precept was dated "at Inchmaquhomok, 5th May, 1533, before Walter Graham, the earl's son, *John Hutoun, Canon professed of the said monastery*, and others":—sasine recorded on 16th and 17th July, 1533.[2] Two others, John Youngman and James Thomsoun, witnessed a deed of Earl Alexander, on the 21st of August, 1534, in the court of the monastery of St. Colmoc, on the island called Inchmoquhomok.[3]

A statement regarding George Buchanan's connection with Cardross in the time of Commendator Robert Erskine, made originally by Dr. Robert Anderson, is only partially correct. As it refers to the foremost literary Scotchman of his time, and has been repeated with several aggravations by Mr. M'Gregor Stirling and Sir William Fraser, it may be of interest to examine it. Anderson, in the "Life of Smollett," which takes up the first volume of his edition (first published in 1796) of that author's works, after stating that Buchanan was born at Moss in the parish of Killearn, goes on to say that "having lost his

[1] *Supra*, p. 157.   [2] Extracts from Stirling Records, vol. i. app. i. p. 268.
[3] Fraser's Red Book of Menteith, vol. i. p. 523.

parents in infancy" (his father only; his mother long survived), "he was educated by James Heriot, his maternal uncle. It is not generally known that his family was bred on a lease of two farms hard by Cardross, granted by Robert Erskine, Commendator of Dryburgh and Inchmahome, to Agnes Heriot and her sons Patrick, Alexander, and George Buchanan, in 1531."[1] Dr. David Irving, whose "Memoirs of George Buchanan" were first published in 1807, makes the same statement—expressly on Anderson's authority:—"In the year 1531, a lease of two farms near Cardross was granted by Robert Erskine, Commendator of Dryburgh and Inchmahome, to Agnes Heriot and three of her sons, Patrick, Alexander, and George."[2] M'Gregor Stirling quotes Anderson, but gives the date as 1581.[3] Sir William Fraser follows, and although he puts Anderson's date (1531) in brackets, he seems to take M'Gregor Stirling's 1581 as correct, for he adds in a note that Robert "is evidently a mistake for David, the writer being misled by the wrong year."[4] David certainly was Commendator in 1581, but by that time Agnes Heriot was far away from any region where leases are granted, and her son, George Buchanan, was very near the end of his earthly tenure. He died in 1582. Notwithstanding this dreadful confusion of date, Stirling thinks it was to his early connection with Cardross and the Erskines that Buchanan was probably indebted for the positions he

[1] Works of Smollett, ed. by Robert Anderson, M.D., 6th edit., 1820, p. 10, *note*.
[2] Irving's Memoirs of George Buchanan, ed. 1837, p. 4.
[3] Notes on the Priory of Inchmahome, p. 59.
[4] Red Book, vol. i. p. 522, *note*.

subsequently held as professional scholar to Queen Mary, and tutor to her son, James the Sixth; while Fraser introduces the quotation from the "Life of Smollett" with the remark, " this Commendator (Robert) has received from the biographer of the great scholar the credit of having materially assisted in the education of Buchanan and his family." Dr. Irving, who appears to be referred to, does not—and neither does Dr. Anderson—make any such remark. He could not have done so in the face of his own dates. In 1531—the date of the lease referred to— George Buchanan was twenty-five years of age; he had been, for some years before that date, a professor in the College of St. Barbe at Paris, and at that very time was engaged as tutor to the Earl of Cassilis. Anderson merely says that *the family* was bred on a lease at Cardross. But notwithstanding the errors which the later writers have introduced into the account, Anderson's statement is, so far as it goes, correct enough. He does not seem, however, to have been aware that part of Buchanan's infancy really was spent at Cardross. The lease of 1531 was merely a renewal of one previously existing. George's name appears on the later lease with the prefix of Maister —he was then a graduate; and he certainly was not living at Cardross at that time. Whether he ever revisited it we have no information to show. The original lease was granted in 1513,[1] long before Commendator Robert's time,

---

[1] These leases are in the possession of H. D. Erskine, Esq., of Cardross. In the earlier lease the principal farm is called Gartladerland, *alias* Hill: in the renewal, Offerone of Gartladernick. This, with the Mill of Arnprior, constituted the farm of the Buchanans. Gartladernick appears to be the same place as, in a charter by Commendator David to John Lord Erskine (5th August, 1562),

and the name of George—although he was then a child of only seven years of age—appears on it, along with those of his mother and brothers. There is thus every probability that the childhood of Buchanan, until he went to Paris in 1520, that is, from his seventh to his fourteenth year, was spent at Hill of Cardross. It is quite possible, therefore, that he may have received at least part of his early education in some school under the superintendence of the monks of Inchmahome—perhaps at Port, where there was a Church. Biographers in general say that he was educated in the schools of Killearn and Dumbarton. But there is no reputable authority for the statement. Killearn was unlikely, after the removal to Cardross, and for a more advanced school, Stirling was more accessible than Dumbarton. He himself gives no information on the subject. In the somewhat meagre autobiography written two years before his death, he merely says that he was brought up *in scholis patriis*—in the schools of his country—until, at the age of fourteen, he was sent to Paris by his uncle, James Heriot.[1] It was to Cardross, no doubt, that he returned, broken down in health, in 1522, and here, after this short campaign in England with the French auxiliaries, he spent the winter of 1523 confined to his bed. Hither, also, he might occasionally come when studying at St. Andrews. But he left for the Continent

---

is denominated Gartcledeny—*terrarum de Gartcledeny cum molendino de Arnepriour*. The name appears now to be lost, but the *alias* Hill survives in Hilltown of Cardross. In the Rental of the Feu-duties of Inchmahome—October, 1646: Retour by David Lord Cardross, appears the *item*—" The landis off Gartledenye, *alias* Hiltoun."

[1] Buchanani Opera a Ruddiman, vol. i. p. 1.

in the summer of 1525, and there is nothing to indicate that he ever saw the place again.

In the passages quoted from Anderson and Irving, Robert Erskine is styled Commendator of Dryburgh as well as Inchmahome. But that is a mistake. The Commendator of Dryburgh in 1531 was James Stewart.[1] Thomas Erskine, however—who may have been the immediately younger brother of Robert, and who became Master of Erskine on the death of the latter at Pinkie—was made Commendator of that Abbey in 1541:[2] and from his time onwards, the Abbey was held, almost without interruption, by members of the same Erskine family.

COMMENDATOR JOHN ERSKINE.

Robert Erskine was succeeded in the Commendatorship of Inchmahome by John, the third son of John, fourth Lord Erskine. He seems also to have succeeded Thomas in the Abbey of Dryburgh in 1548;[3] and along with these two ecclesiastical offices, he held also that of Commendator of the Abbey of Cambuskenneth. By the death of his brother Thomas, he became Master of Erskine in 1551, and in the year following succeeded his father as fifth Lord Erskine. Afterwards as Earl of Mar—created

---

[1] Liber S. Marie de Dryburgh, Bannatyne Club ed., 1847, p. xxii.

[2] *Ibid*, p. xxii. In Theiner's Vetera Monumenta, Nos. 1057 and 1059, p. 612, are two letters from James V. asking Pope Paul III. to sanction the appointment as Commendator of Dryburgh of Thomas Erskine, who is described as a member of an illustrious family, and *adolescentem nobilem, animi et corporis viribus pollentem*, qualities very necessary for the defence of a place so exposed to incursions from across the borders. And, indeed, Thomas had his troubles with the English marauders, who plundered and burned his Abbey in 1544.

[3] Liber S. Marie de Dryburgh, p. xxiv.

in 1565—and Regent of the Kingdom, he made a great figure in the politics of the country. It is not, however, the purpose of this history to follow his distinguished career in statesmanship, but merely to note the facts of his connection with Inchmahome.

It has already been mentioned that he was educated in his youth for the Church, so that he may be said to have had a professional training for his pluralities. He held the office of Commendator till 1555—three years after he had become Lord Erskine—when he resigned it to his nephew David.

Signature of Commendator John Erskine.

In 1541 the Priory was the scene of the marriage of Margaret Grahame, daughter of William, Earl of Menteith, to Archibald, Earl of Argyle, which, according to the Stirling Protocol Book, was solemnized at the church of Inchmahome on the 21st of April of that year, after proclamation three times made at the churches of Port and Dollar (?—apud Ecclesiam de Port et Dolarie), the celebrant being Sir John Youngman, canon of Inchmahome.[1]

But by far the most interesting incident in the history of the Priory during the time it was held by John Erskine —if not the most interesting in the whole of its history—

[1] Red Book, vol. i. p. 523.

was the residence, for a short period, within its walls of the youthful Mary, Queen of Scots.

At the time of the battle of Pinkie (10th September, 1547), Mary was in Stirling Castle, under the guardianship of Lords Erskine and Livingston, who had been entrusted with "the keiping of our Sovrane Ladies persoun, in cumpany with the Quenis Grace hir moder," rather more than two years previously.[1] After that disastrous battle, Stirling was no longer deemed a safe residence for the royal child, and she was removed to the island of Inchmahome. This was done most probably on the suggestion of her devoted "keeper," Lord Erskine, that she might be surrounded and protected by his own family and friends. Otherwise, it is not quite easy to see why Inchmahome should have been reckoned a more secure refuge than the Castle of Stirling. Hill Burton endeavours to explain it by saying—"The place selected as of greater security was a flat island called Inchmahome, in the Lake of Monteith, half-way between Stirling and the Highlands. From such a spot no enemy could be assailed as from a fortress; yet, on the principle of the lake-dwellings of older ages, it was deemed less assailable than a fortress on land or an island approachable by sea."[2] But, indeed, it could have offered only a slight resistance to any army that would have been thought strong enough to assault the fortress of Stirling. Lord Erskine, as responsible for the safe keeping of the infant Queen, most probably brought her

[1] Acts of the Parliaments of Scotland, vol. ii. p. 463. Register of the Privy Council, vol. i. p. 11.
[2] Hill Burton's History of Scotland, vol. iii. p. 275.

here that she might be free from the discomfort and danger of a possible siege of Stirling, and at the same time within easy reach of the Highland hills, into whose fastnesses she could readily be conveyed from her island retreat.

Much fable of a romantic and poetical kind has gathered round Mary's residence on Inchmahome. Imagination has revelled in pictures of the youthful Queen wandering among the island groves with her four little Maries, romping on the shores of the lake, planting bowers, or diligently conning her lessons in the Prior's lodging. An eloquent French writer,[1] who seems to think that she frequented Inchmahome during the whole period of her residence at Stirling, attributes to the open-air and hardy upbringing she there received her health and glowing colour, her well-developed yet slender and supple waist *(taille svelte et souple)* so much admired, and that "peasant appetite" which afterwards at the court of Henry II. required to be kept in check. He describes her as rising at daybreak and rushing out, scarcely dressed, to run merrily over the gravel paths, the heath, and the rocks; then, recalled with difficulty to the *chateau*, applying herself listlessly to her English and French lessons, to be by-and-bye thrown aside for music and dancing, which she pursued with such passionate ardour that it was necessary to use authority to detach her from them. She was delighted with the singing of ancient ballads, the recital of the old national legends, and the varied strains of the pibroch. She made a charming picture at this Monastery of Inch-Mahome, "with her snood of rose satin, her plaid

[1] Histoire de Marie Stuart, par J. M. Dargaud, Paris, 1850; vol. i. p. 31.

of black silk fastened with a golden clasp, with the arms of Lorraine and of Scotland." Even at this early age she had the gift of charming every heart. She was adored by her governors, her officers, her women, her teachers, and all who chanced to come into contact with her, citizens or gentlemen, tradesmen of the Lowlands, fishers, and Highlanders.

Miss Strickland follows, in some details, the imaginative Frenchman, but is more careful to restrict the period of Mary's stay on the island to " several months," during which time "she pursued her studies quietly and steadily with her four Maries in the cloister shades of Inchmahome."[1] She was there taught, says Miss Strickland, in addition to French, which was literally her mother tongue, history, geography, Latin, tapestry work, and embroidery. Dr. John Brown, in his charming paper, "Queen Mary's Child Garden,"[2] employs the infant Queen in tending the plots in the curious little enclosure on the island known as Queen Mary's Bower.[3] Chalmers, who is Miss Strickland's authority for the length of time Mary spent at Inchmahome, says she remained there until she was taken to Dumbarton in February of 1548.[4]

Sheriff Glassford Bell affirms that she was upwards of two years on the island;[5] and in this he is followed by Charles Mackie, who asserts that here "the young Queen

[1] Strickland's Lives of the Queens of Scotland, 1852, vol. iii. p. 20.
[2] Horæ Subsecivæ, 2nd series, 1861, p. 172.
[3] See *supra*, p. 87.
[4] Chalmers' Life of Mary, 1818, vol. i. p. 5. Miss Strickland refers to Chalmers' Caledonia.
[5] Life of Mary Queen of Scots, by Henry Glassford Bell, 2nd ed., 1831, p. 44.

experienced for two years the most unalloyed tranquillity which she enjoyed during her eventful life "—and then goes on to imagine all the delights of that happy time.[1]

But it is not only these comparatively recent writers who have allowed their imagination to attribute much of Mary's accomplishments to her residence at Inchmahome: older authors have done the same. An early Life, written in Latin, states that she was taken to the island specially for the purpose of her education, which was conducted by her mother with peculiar strictness; that there her mind was cultivated with the principles of the Catholic faith and many suitable accomplishments; that her time was wholly taken up with study—no room being left for idleness or useless amusements; and that to instruction in her native language, in which even then she was proficient, were added Latin and French and the rudiments of Italian and Spanish.[2]

Now, the real facts of the case are unfortunately against all these suppositions. The little Queen was only four years and nine months old when she was conveyed to Inchmahome, and her stay there was limited to about three weeks—a period too short to permit of much practice in gardening, and altogether inadequate for the acquirement of Latin, French, Italian, Spanish, and the other accomplishments mentioned, even if she had been of an

[1] The Castles, Palaces, and Prisons of Mary Queen of Scots, by Charles Mackie, 1853, p. 95.
[2] De Vita et Rebus Gestis Mariae, &c., a Samuele Jebb, 1725, vol. ii. p. 13. The writer of the Latin Life is described as Georgius Conaeus, a Scotsman, of the Order of Friars Preachers, legate of the Roman Pontiff to the most serene Queen of England, Henrietta Maria.

age fit for studying them. Besides, although she was attended by her nurse and her governess—as well as by her mother and certain Lords of Council—it may well be supposed that it was too agitated a time to admit of much attention being paid to lessons.

That the short space of three weeks was the whole time spent by Mary at Inchmahome has been proved by Dr. Hay Fleming in his recent careful and accurate biography of the Queen.[1] The authorities on which he relies are indisputable, and are here indicated. First of all, the statement of Bishop Lesley is distinct and definite. He says:—" During the tyme of the Inglismennis byding at Leith the Governour being in Striveling, be the counsell of the Quene Dowarier, the Erlis of Angus, Argyle, Rothes, Cassillis and utheris lordis, caused suddantlie convoye the Quene to the yle and abbay of Inchemahomo within the countrey of Menteith, quhair she was keped with the Quene hir moder, be the Lordis Erskyn and Levingstoun her keparis, *till the Inglismen was departed furth of Scotland, and than returned to Striveling.*"[2] Now, the Englishmen were at Leith from the 11th to the 18th of September, 1547, and they crossed the Tweed on their return home on the 29th of the same month.[3] It has generally been believed that the Queen was taken directly to Dumbarton from the island of Inchmahome; but Lesley's statements,

---

[1] Hay Fleming's Mary Queen of Scots, 1897, vol. i. p. 12 and *notes*—a work of thorough research and extreme accuracy.

[2] Lesley's Historie of Scotland (Bannatyne Club ed.), p. 200.

[3] " My Lordes Grace (*i.e.* Somerset) this morening (Thursday, 29th September) soon after vii of the clok was passed over the Twede here."—Expedicion in Scotlande, &c., by W. Patten, Londoner, p. 94.

both regarding the time of her coming and as to her returning to Stirling, are confirmed by official documents. The Discharge granted to her "keepers," Lords Erskine and Livingston, tells us that she was taken to Inchmahome "in the monethe of September last bypast, sone eftir the feild of Pynkyne Clewiche."[1] That she went back to Stirling is proved by a letter in the State-Paper Office— Lord Grey to the Duke of Somerset—dated 22nd February, 1548, in which Grey informs the Protector that he has learned that the Queen has been removed *from Stirling to Dumbarton.*[2] Thus the utmost limits of the time that Mary could have spent at Inchmahome are from the 11th of September to the end of the month.

The only other transactions in connection with the Convent during the period of John Erskine's commendatorship, of which a record has been preserved, are two leases. The first, dated 29th of July, 1548, grants a nineteen years' tack of the lands of Lochend, extending to forty shillings' worth in the rental of the Priory "of old extent" to Alexander Menteith in Polmont mill and his four sons. It is subscribed by the Commendator, the sub-Prior Dene James Bradfute, and seven other members of the Chapter —Dene Jhone Huten, Dene James Bad, Dene Johen Youngar, Dene Adam Peblis, Dene Thomas M'Lellen, Dene Adam Cristesone, Dene Jhonne Mont.[3]

It is interesting to compare these names with those

---

[1] This Discharge, granted on the 20th July, 1548, is preserved in Lord Elphinstone's charter-chest, and has been printed in the Red Book, vol. ii. pp. 331-3.

[2] Thorpe's Calendar of State Papers relating to Scotland, p. 79, No. 49.

[3] Preserved at Cardross. Printed in the Red Book, vol. ii. pp. 333-5.

attached to the lease granted by Prior Andrew in 1526.[1] The Chapter has changed but little since that time. In addition to the Prior, Duncan Pringle and James Thomson have disappeared from the list, and instead of John Youngman there is John Youngar, which may possibly be the same person with name differently written. With these exceptions the names of the Chapter are the same as those of twenty-two years before. No new name has been added. The monks of Inchmahome apparently enjoyed good health and long life.

The second lease is mentioned in a manuscript addition by Mr. M'Gregor Stirling to his "Notes on Inchmahome," as having been found by him in an old collection of writs, made by Laurence Mercer of Meikleour in 1612.[2] It is a tack granted by John Erskine, Commendator of the Abbacie of Inchmahomo and the Convent "chapterly gaddered," to William Sinclair of The Banks, of the lands of the Banks of Cragannet, &c., dated at the Abbey of Inchmahomo, 25th of April, 1555. The seal of the Convent is appended, and the tack is subscribed by the Commendator, Den James Bradfut, sub-Prior, Den Adam Peblis, Den Thomas M'Clellan, Den Adam Cirstesone, and Den Jhone Monet. Three of the former canons—John Hutton, James Bad, and John Youngar—have now dropped from the list, and no new name has been added to it.

John Erskine had succeeded to the title of Lord Erskine on the death of his father in 1552, but continued to hold

[1] See *supra*, p. 158.
[2] He adds—"This curious collection, consisting of fifty-three folio leaves closely written, is now (5th June, 1818) in the possession of Sir John M'Gregor Murray, Bart."

the office of Commendator for three years beyond that time. In 1565, on the occasion of the marriage of Queen Mary with Darnley, he was made Earl of Mar. Next year, the infant Prince James was committed to his charge. On the 6th of September, 1571, he was chosen Regent of the Kingdom in succession to the murdered Regent Lennox. But he did not long hold that high office; he died at Stirling on the 28th of October, 1572. According to Sir William Drury, he was "one of the best nature in Scotland, and wholly given to quietness and peace."[1]

COMMENDATOR DAVID ERSKINE.

In 1555, Lord Erskine—as his title then was—transferred the ecclesiastical benefices he then held to his nephew David, the natural son of his elder brother Robert. Thus David Erskine became Commendator of Dryburgh and of Inchmahome, as well as Archdean of Brechin. As he lived for fifty-six years after, he must have been comparatively young at this time. The bull of Pope Paul IV. appointing him Commendator-Prior of Inchmahome for life is dated 10th of January, 1555; and he took the oath and was formally inducted in the beginning of the following year. A second bull, dated 17th of July, 1556, gave him the authority of the Pope for holding the Abbey of Dryburgh *in commendam*, along with the Priorate of Inchmahome.[2] In these documents, the Priorate is styled "of the

[1] Letter from Drury to Lord Burghley, 14th September, 1571, in the State-Paper Office; quoted by Tytler in the History of Scotland, vol. iii. p. 342, *note*. (Ed. 1864).

[2] These papal writs are preserved in the charter-chest of the Earl of Mar and Kellie, and have been printed in the Red Book, vol. ii. pp. 335-349.

The Lake of Menteith. 179

monastery of the island of Saint Colmocius of Inchmahomo," and David Erskine is described as "a venerable man, Sir David Erskine, Clerk of the Diocese of St. Andrews." From this description it is permissible to infer that he had been trained for the Church. He is characterised by Father Hay as "an exceeding modest, honest, and shame-faced man."[1]

Signature of Commendator David Erskine.

Although he took the oath requiring obedience to the Pope and the defence of the Church against heretics and schismatics, he did not long remain bound by it. The Reformation, then in progress, was consummated in 1560, and David Erskine, in common with the family of which he was a member, cast in his lot with the reformers. In his time, therefore, began the dilapidation of the revenues of the Convent, by which his relatives, and especially his uncle, the Earl of Mar, greatly profited. Sir William Fraser has suggested that, when Lord Erskine resigned the office of Prior to his nephew, it was on the understanding that he should obtain the grants of Priory lands which were eventually assigned to him.

Whether there was any understanding of that kind or not, the Commendator, on the 8th of August, 1562, granted two deeds by which the lands of Borland, called the dominical lands or Mains of Cardross, and the office of

[1] Quoted in Introduction to Liber S. Marie de Dryburgh, p. xxvii.

bailie of the barony of Cardross, and of all other lands belonging to the Convent, with the feu-farms and duties of certain lands in the barony, were assigned to his Lordship.[1] The office of bailie belonged heritably to James Erskine of Little Sauchie, the uncle of John Lord Erskine, but he was induced to resign it to the Commendator in favour of his nephew. On the 31st of December of the same year, the Commendator and Convents of Dryburgh and Inchmahome granted Lord Erskine a yearly pension of five hundred merks, in recompense of his many good deeds and his protection of their interests in the troublous times, and in consideration of the expenses he had incurred in their service. The proportion of this pension payable by Inchmahome was to come out of the fruits of the kirk of Lintrethin and the lands of Borland, both belonging to the Convent.

Earlier in the year 1562, two tacks had been granted, which are interesting as giving the names of the then existing Chapter. The first, dated 16th of January, is a tack by the Commendator, with consent of the Convent, in favour of Allan Oliphant, his servitor, of the teinds of Newton of Doune and Wester Row. It is signed by the Commendator, the sub-Prior Den Thomas Maclellan, Den James Bradfut, Den Robert Schortus, Den Alane Baxter, Den Vellem Stirleng, and Den Johin Baxter.[2] Of

[1] Red Book of Menteith, vol. i. p. 529. The names of these lands are interesting—Arnprior, Cardene, Kepe, Wester and Easter Poldoir, Gartcledeny with Mill of Arnprior, Arnevicar, Gartours Over and Nether, Lochend, Mill of Cardross, Ardenclericht, Drummanikloche, Blairsessenoche, Ballingrew, Hornahic, Waird of Guddy—with the astricted multures of said lands, and the lands of Boirland, called the dominical lands of Cardross.

[2] Liber S. Marie de Dryburgh, p. xxvi. Original of tack at Cardross.

these, only Bradfut and Maclellan have survived from the Chapter of 1555. The other document was found by M'Gregor Stirling among the Mercer writs already referred to.[1] It is a lease of three glebes in the neighbourhood of the Kirk of Leny, "infra prioratum monasterii sancti Colmoci Dunblanen diocesis vocatum vulgo Inchmahomock,"[2] and is signed by David, the Commendator, Mr Alexander Drysdail, vicar of Lany, and Denes James Bradfut, Robert Short, John Baxter, and Thomas M'Clellan. These names are identical with those of the subscribers of the previous tack, except that Allan Baxter and William Stirling do not now appear. William Stirling, however— or another of the same name—appears in connection with documents of later date. This lease purports to bear the seals of the monastery and the vicar of Leny, "appended at the said monastery and burgh of Stirling, 2nd February, 1562." From this Mr. Stirling infers that "the Convent had moved to Stirling before the 2nd of February, 1562, a circumstance which renders it not improbable that the church and refectory had been attacked by the populace at the Reformation about two years before."[3] That the Priory possessed a house in the burgh of Stirling is certain. In the Act of 1606, erecting the temporal lordship of Cardross, in the enumeration of the properties of the Priory is included "the Prior's Manse or Tenement, with the yaird and pertinentis thairof, in Stirling."[4] The "Rental of the Feu-duties of Inchmahome, 1696," also mentions "ane tenement off land in the town of Striviling

[1] See *supra*, p. 177.   [2] MS. addition to Notes on Inchmahome.
[3] *Ibid.*   [4] Acts of the Parliaments of Scotland, vol. iv. p. 343.

and yarde callit the Priouris Manse."[1] At the same time, it is not very probable that the Chapter had moved to Stirling because of the destruction of their buildings on Inchmahome. The documents issued by them in the later months of the year were subscribed at the island. The explanation seems rather to be that while the seal of the Convent was appended at Inchmahome, that of the vicar of Leny, for some reason of convenience, was "to-hung" at Stirling.

It is satisfactory to be able to add further that, through the researches of Mr. W. B. Cook of Stirling, the site of this old Prior's Manse has now been definitely ascertained.[2] He has found in the Protocol Book of Robert Ramsay, under date 1st February, 1568-9, a registered deed, of which the following is an abstract :—

"John Lechman, one of the bailies of Stirling, by command of the provost and other bailies, proceeded to that tenement of houses and stables, with garden and pertinents, *lying in the Castle Wynd on the south side* of the same, between the late Malcolm Kinross's tenement on the south, the late John Kinloch's tenement on the west, and the said Wynd on the north and east, and there gave sasine of same to *David Erskine, Commendator of Dryburgh and Inchmahome: reddendo*, 40 shillings per annum to the treasurer of the burgh."

[1] In the second edition of Nimmo's History of Stirlingshire, vol. i. p. 378, the editor (M'Gregor Stirling) says—"In a *retour* of David, second Lord of Cardross, we find that the lordship and barony of Cardross comprehended, amongst other things, the mansion of the Priory of Inchmahome in the borough of Stirling. We cannot pretend to point out even the probable site."

[2] Mr. Cook's intimate acquaintance with the old protocols and sasines of the burgh makes him the highest authority on the situations of old houses in Stirling.

Manse of the Prior of Inchmahome (George Buchanan's House), in the Castle Wynd of Stirling.

Mr. Cook supposes that while the Commendator was already in possession of the manse by virtue of his office, legal sasine had been delayed by reason generally of the troubles of the time, and specially because of the disputes between the Town Council and the Erskines, which had arisen from the seizure by the latter of the mills that had belonged to the Dominican friars and were claimed by the town. He has traced the history of this tenement, with the neighbouring properties, through sasines and titles, down to the present time; and he identifies it with an old house, with turreted chamber in the front, that used to be known, at a later period, as George Buchanan's House. It stood on the left hand side of the Castle Wynd—as one goes towards the Castle—nearly opposite to the house of the Abbot of Cambuskenneth. This old house was taken down in 1835, but its appearance is preserved in a drawing, which is here reproduced. It is rather ornate in style, and certainly picturesque. Its apparent size and its possession of stables—which in a deed of 1702 are described as then in ruins *(nunc vasto seu demolito)*—prove its importance as a town-house. Considering the position that the Commendator held in the upbringing of the King as one of the four friends of the House of Erskine, who in turns were to be always with the King and attend to his education, it is not difficult to understand how the Prior's Manse—or a portion of it—should have been assigned as a residence to his Majesty's preceptor. Neither is it to be wondered at that the house should have come down to later times with the name of its most distinguished inhabitant attached to it, rather than that of the Priory which had been abolished and forgotten. Here Buchanan dwelt for about ten years (1570-1580). The circumstance makes another interesting link in his connection with Cardross and the Priory of Inchmahome.

Canons Allan Baxter and Robert Short have dropped out of the Chapter in the latter half of 1562, and William Stirling has come in. Stirling was probably the last addition to the canons of Inchmahome. M'Lellan, who made his first appearance as signatory to a deed of Prior Andrew in 1526, is not found after 12th August, 1562. Bradfute, John Baxter, and Stirling are co-signatories to deeds of 1573 and 1583; and the last lease granted by Commendator David Erskine and the Convent "togidder convenit" is in 1587, and bears only two names in addition to his own—those of Dene James Bredfute and Dene Wellem Sterleng. These appear to have been the last of the old monks of Inchmahome. Whether they continued to hold by the old religion, or, like their Commendator, became Protestants, cannot be said. There was a William Stirling who was Reader in the Church of Port up to 1589, but beyond the name there is nothing to identify him with the erewhile canon of Inchmahome. The venerable sub-Prior could not have long survived this last appearance of his name. He must then have been a very aged man, for—as the first occurrence of his name as a member of the Chapter was in 1526—he had over sixty years of service behind him. In a lease granted by David Erskine, as Commendator of Dryburgh, in the year 1600, he explains that all the members of that Convent were then deceased;[1]

[1] Liber S. Marie de Dryburgh, p. xxix.

and that probably was also the case of Inchmahome at the same or an earlier period.

The Commendator was one of the "four friends of the House of Erskine" who were appointed by the Parliament of November, 1572, to assist the Countess Dowager and the young Earl of Mar in the charge of James VI.[1] Two of these were always to be with the King in the Castle of Stirling, to look to his personal comfort and the management of his household. It was perhaps in pursuance of this duty that David Erskine was in Stirling Castle on the 7th of September, 1573, when he granted a lease of the lands of the Camp of Ardoch to William Sinclair of the Camp and Elizabeth Striveling, his spouse. This lease reveals the curious fact that the Chapel, which had been built within the old Roman Camp, and the Camp itself, belonged to the Priory. How and when it came into this possession is as yet unknown. The tack is granted with consent of the Convent chapterly gathered, and bears the signatures of James Braidfut, William Stirling, and John Baxter. One of the witnesses is David Hume of Argaty, who afterwards (in 1584) suffered death for communicating with his friend the Commendator, when the latter was in exile.[2]

At this time the Commendator was in difficulty about his Thirds. These Thirds were the proportion of their revenues which, after the Reformation, the holders of the

---

[1] Acts of the Parliaments of Scotland, vol. ii. p. 81.

[2] Laurence Mercer's Writs, as quoted in the MS. of M'Gregor Stirling. The Camp, at a later date, was called Raith, and also Chapel-lands (Retour of Sir William Stirling, Bart., 1670); in the Old Statistical Account it is called Chapel Hill.—MS. addition to Notes on Inchmahome.

old benefices were ordained by Act of Parliament to pay for the support of the Protestant ministry.[1] They had not been well paid; and, by Acts of 1567, the collection of them was put into the hands of the ministers themselves.[2] David Erskine had never been asked for the Thirds of his benefices (Abbey of Dryburgh, Priory of Inchmahome, Archdeanery of Brechin) during the time of Queen Mary; and up till 1573, as he set forth in his petition, he had been "owerlukit and not pressit with payment thairof." Relying on this immunity he had spent not only the whole revenues of his benefices, but other large sums on his own credit, which made it impossible for him to pay the great amount now demanded as arrears. He therefore petitioned the General Assembly for a remission, affirming that though he had the titles of the benefices, he had "litill of the profeit thairof."[3] The Privy Council, on the 20th of March, 1574, granted him a discharge of all the dues up to 1573, and relaxed him of horning.[4]

David Erskine was made a member of the Privy Council in 1579, although he had previously been a frequent attender at meetings of that body as a Councillor Extraordinary appointed by the King. In 1583 a lease of the teind sheaves, fruits, rents, profits, emoluments, and duties of the parsonage of the Kirk of Leny was given to James Seton of Tullibody and his son John, for the sum of eighty merks yearly. The deed was granted at Cardross,

[1] Acts of the Parliaments of Scotland, vol. ii. pp. 81 and 607.
[2] *Ibid*, vol. iii. pp. 24 and 37.
[3] This is likely enough to have been true. The greater part of the "profeit thairof" doubtless went to the Earl of Mar.
[4] Register of the Privy Council of Scotland, vol. ii. p. 347.

The Lake of Menteith.

and the co-signatories with the Commendator were James Bradfut, sub-Prior, Dene Wellem Steruiling, and Dene Johin Baxter.[1] But his lease-granting was now destined to suffer interruption for a time. Trouble was brewing for the House of Erskine. For their share in the raid of Ruthven in 1582, and in the confused and troubled proceedings which followed that event, the Erskines were obliged to flee from the country; and on the 21st of August, 1584, Parliament found them guilty of treason, and declared their estates and offices confiscated.[2]

Commendator Henry Stewart.

The Commendator's post did not remain unoccupied. Two days after the confiscation of David Erskine, King James the Sixth gave the Priory of Inchmahome for life to Henry Stewart,[3] the second son of James Lord Doune, and brother of the "bonnie Earl of Moray." No document signed by Henry Stewart as Commendator seems to be extant; but, on the 4th of June, 1585, the King himself ratified a grant, formerly made by Commendator David, in favour of Patrick Bathok, of a yearly pension of nine merks out of the lands of Gartavertyne in the Stewartry of Menteith. And, in this ratification, David is designed "sumtyme Commendator of Dryburght and Inchmahom."[4]

[1] Printed in the Red Book, vol. ii. p. 364, from the original in the charter-chest of the Earl of Mar and Kellie.
[2] Acts of the Parliaments of Scotland, vol. iii. p. 344.
[3] Registrum Magni Sigilli, Lib. xxxvi. No. 10.
[4] Liber S. Marie de Dryburgh, p. xxviii. Original at Cardross.

COMMENDATOR DAVID ERSKINE REPONED.

The absence of the Erskines was not of long continuance. In 1585, the banished lords returned to Scotland, and succeeded in depriving Arran of his power. An Act of Parliament was passed in December,[1] reversing the sentences of forfeiture. David Erskine was consequently reponed in his offices. After this, till the end of his life, he seems to have resided at Cardross. He possibly enlarged the old house for his residence, as his initials, with those of his wife, are cut on it. All the remaining leases granted by him—whether as Commendator of Dryburgh or of Inchmahome—are dated thence. He showed his interest in education by granting, on the 4th of March, 1586, a tack of the teinds of Wester Lanark to Mr. Duncan Neven, schoolmaster at Dunblane, "for teaching of the youth."[2] The last lease signed by the remanent members of the Convent was granted on the 20th of April, 1587, in consideration of "certane sowmes of money, gratitudes, guid deidis and pleasouris thankfullie payit and done to us be oure weilbelovit cousing Michaell Elphingstoun, servitoure domestik to oure soverane lord," to the said Michael of the teind sheaves of Gartincaber, Wester Spittiltoune, Murdochstoun, Ballintoun, M'Corranestoun, in the parish of Kilmadock, for his lifetime and nineteen years thereafter, at a rent of nine pounds, six shillings and eightpence. The lease is signed by David, Commendator of Inchmahomo, Dene James Bredfut, and Dene

---

[1] Acts of the Parliaments of Scotland, vol. iii. p. 383.
[2] Liber S. Marie de Dryburgh, p. xxviii. Copy, authenticated by Neven in 1617, said to be in possession of the Earl of Mar and Kellie.

Wellem Sterleng.[1] Later leases—one of them on the day before his demission of office, 30th May, 1608—in connection with the lands of the Abbey of Dryburgh are extant;[2] but this is the last of his recorded transactions with the property of Inchmahome. He lived for three years after his demission, dying at Cardross on the 28th of May, 1611. He left a widow, named Margaret Haldane, and known as Lady Cardross and Lady Dryburgh,[3] whom, in his will, he earnestly recommended to the protecting care of the Earl of Mar. It appears that he had a son whose name was James, and who must have predeceased his father, as no mention is made of him in the will.

COMMENDATOR HENRY ERSKINE.

By this time the Chapter of Inchmahome was extinct, the "monastery and superstitions thereof" had been abolished, and the church lands annexed to the Crown.[4] The history of the Priory might therefore be said to terminate with David Erskine. But, by the grace of King James the Sixth, there was still another Commendator appointed to enjoy the revenues of Dryburgh and Inchmahome. This was Henry Erskine, the second son of John, second Earl of Mar, by his marriage with Lady Mary Stewart, daughter of the first Duke of Lennox. Both the father and mother of the new Commendator were high in the favour and friendship of the King. The Earl of Mar had been educated along with King James under the rigorous

---

[1] Printed in the Red Book, vol. ii. pp. 365-7, from the original in the charter-chest of the Earl of Mar and Kellie.
[2] Liber S. Marie de Dryburgh, pp. 316 and 319.   [3] *Ibid*, p. xxix.
[4] Acts of the Parliaments of Scotland, vol. iv. p. 345.

rule of George Buchanan, was his early playfellow—the "Jock Sclaitis" of his familiar letters—and for a while his Governor; while Lady Mary was the daughter of Esme Stewart, the King's cousin and prime favourite. It was to make provision for this younger son of the Mar family that David Erskine was induced to resign his offices into the hands of his Majesty. Immediately thereafter, on the 31st of May, 1608, the King granted a deed providing the Abbey of Dryburgh and the Priory of Inchmahome to Henry Erskine for his lifetime, along with a seat and vote in Parliament. For twenty years he continued to enjoy the fruits of these estates, but of course all pretence of ecclesiastical function had ceased. Henry Erskine was simply a country gentleman—of an unusually good type, it may be hoped—who attended to his own affairs and faithfully discharged his Parliamentary duties. His portrait by Jameson exhibits a remarkably sweet and pleasant countenance. If he were as good as he looks, everything must have gone well and pleasantly with the tenants of the old kirk lands in his time. In 1617, the Earl of Mar assigned the lordship and peerage of Cardross—which had been erected a temporal barony in his favour in 1604—to his son Henry Erskine in fee. Hence he was known as the Fiar of Cardross. He did not, however, enjoy the dignity of the peerage, as he died in 1628, predeceasing his father by about six years.

Signature of Commendator Henry Erskine.

APPENDIX.

Subsequent History of the Priory Lands.

The transference of the lands of the Priory to the House of Erskine began in 1562, when Commendator David, with the assent of the Convent, assigned (8th August, 1562) to John Lord Erskine and his heirs-male, the lands of Boirland, commonly called the dominical lands of Cardross,[1] as also the bailieship of their barony of Cardross, and of all other lands belonging to them, with the feu-farms and duties of certain lands specified as his bailie-fee.[2] This was the beginning of many complicated transactions in connection with the Priory lands between the Convent and members of the Erskine family. For example, the Stirling Protocol Books[3] contain notice of a charter granted by the Earl of Mar to Commendator David Erskine, of Shirgarton, Drums of Kippen, and Arnbeg, under date 19th March, 1571-2; and on the same day, a charter granted by John Master of Mar, with consent of John Earl of Mar, his father, to David the Commendator, of Bordland, called the dominical lands of Cardross, and Ballingrew.

It is rather difficult to follow these various transactions and explain their significance; but the next great step in

---

[1] "Totas et integras terras nostras de Boirland, vulgo nuncupatas terras dominicales de Cardross."

[2] See *supra*, p. 180.

[3] Protocol Book of Robert Ramsay, 1566-1573: extracts furnished by Mr W. B. Cook, Stirling.

the alienation of the ecclesiastical lands is clear enough. This was accomplished by a charter which King James the Sixth granted to John, second Earl of Mar, on the 27th of March, 1604, assigning to him the lordship and barony of Cardross. Infeftment followed, and the charter was ratified in a Parliament held at Perth on the 9th of July, 1606.[1] By an Act of this Parliament, the Abbacies of Dryburgh and Cambuskenneth, and the Priory of Inchmahome, were erected into a temporal lordship in favour of the Earl of Mar. The Act, after reciting the good deeds of the earl and his father—their care of the upbringing and education of the King, and their various labours for the good of the State—and declaring that the said "monasteries and superstitiounis had now been abolishit, and the kirklandis of the samin now annexit to his Hienes Crowne," ratifies, approves, and confirms the charter of 1604, dissolves these lands from the Act of Annexation to the Crown, and suppresses, abolishes, and extinguishes for ever the said Abbeys and Priory. The properties of the Priory are enumerated as follows:—The place and mansion of Inchmahomo, the lands and barony of Cardross, viz., Arnprior, East Garden, Kepe, West Polder, East Polder, Gairtledernick, and Hilltoun mylne, Mill of Arnprior, lands of Arnevicar, Clerkum, Garturs Over and Nether, Lochend, Mill of Cardross, Ardinclerich, Drummanikcloch, Blaircessnock, Ballingrew, Hornehaick, Ward of Gudie, Bordland or Mains, the loch and isles of Inchmahomo with salmon fishings in the Forth and Gudie, Priors Meadow, Armavak, kirklands of Port and Leny, the

[1] Acts of the Parliaments of Scotland, vol. iv. p. 344.

Prior's Manse or tenement with the yaird and pertinents thereof in Stirling, house and yard in Dumbarton, Row, the Kirkis of Kilmadock, Port, Leny, and Lintrethin, [Leny] pertaining to Inchmahome. These lands—"estimat to £100 land of auld extent"—are declared secular land, free from ecclesiastical burdens, and the Manor-place of Cardross is ordained to be the principal messuage thereof.

It has already been mentioned that the purpose of these grants to the Earl of Mar is generally stated to have been to enable him to make provision for his younger sons by his second wife, Lady Mary Stewart. His son by the first wife was, of course, destined to succeed his father as Earl of Mar. The eldest son of Lady Mary became Earl of Buchan by his marriage with the heiress of that earldom. The Countess is said, by the family tradition, to have complained to the King that her younger sons, Henry and Alexander, were unprovided for, and the King promised to look after their interests. This he did by granting to the Earl of Mar the lordship of Cardross, with the right of assignation to any of his heirs-male.[1]

The curious story related by David Earl of Buchan regarding the marriage of the Earl of Mar and Lady Mary Stewart will bear repetition. "Mar," he says, "as was the superstitious custom of the times, had listened to the nonsense of an Italian conjurer, who showed him a limning of a lady whom he said Mar's future sweetheart and wife resembled; and Mar thought he observed these features in the lovely daughter of Lennox. He had heard she was destined by the King for another, and wrote a plaintive

[1] Alexander Erskine received the benefice of Cambuskenneth in 1608.

letter to James, saying that his health had even begun to suffer from the fear of disappointment. The King visited Mar, his old class-fellow, and said, 'Ye shanna dee, Jock, for ony lass in a' the land.' The King accordingly secured for Mar the object of his attachment, Lady Mary Stewart, second daughter of Esme, Duke of Lennox, the King's kinsman."[1] This story is, at any rate, characteristic of the homely humour of King James the Sixth.

Whether the meeting with the Italian conjurer was prior to his first marriage, or after it, does not appear from the narrative. But that it was subsequent to the death of his first wife may be inferred from the circumstances, and from a pendant to the story which M'Gregor Stirling relates on the authority of the then Countess of Buchan. Mar, it seems, had obtained from the Italian the portrait of the lady, and kept it in his residence at Alloa Tower. When he first saw the Lady Mary Stewart—at Stirling, it is said—and was struck by her resemblance to the carefully cherished picture, he sent a servant to Alloa to fetch it for a more careful comparison. Unfortunately, however, the servant, by awkward handling, let the picture fall on the muddy road. Anxious to conceal his carelessness, he tried to clean off the mud, with the result that he succeeded only in obliterating the features of the portrait. But, adds the narrator, "it was a consolation to the love-sick peer that the loss of the picture was supplied by the possession of the fair original."[2]

[1] Earl of Buchan's Anonymous and Fugitive Essays, 1812, vol. i. pp. 288, *et seq.*
[2] Notes on Inchmahome, p. 60.

On the 30th of May, 1608, David Erskine, Commendator of Dryburgh and Inchmahome, resigned his benefices into the hands of the King, and so, at the same time, did Adam Erskine, the Commendator of Cambuskenneth. Next day, at Greenwich, a royal charter gave the first to Henry, and the second to Alexander, the two younger sons of the Earl of Mar. A charter was granted, dated at Greenwich, 10th June, 1610, by King James, whereby the Earl of Mar, his heirs-male, assigns, and successors were made free lords and barons of Cardross, with the title and dignity and a right to sit and vote in Parliament; and another followed on the 10th April, 1615, to the same effect. Next the Earl, by a charter dated at Holyrood, 31st January, 1617, and confirmed by the King on the 13th of March the same year, assigned the fie of the barony and lordship of Cardross—reserving his life-rent—to his son Henry.

It was in the summer of this year that Cardross welcomed a royal visitor. King James the Sixth, impelled by "a natural and salmon-like affection," revisited his native land, where he was regaled, much to his satisfaction, with addresses of welcome at all the principal towns, and had opportunities of showing off his learning and wit and dialectic skill in the conferences and disputations of the most learned professors of the Scottish Universities. Mindful of his old school-fellow and friend, he paid him a visit at Cardross. Great preparations were made for his reception. The old tower, the most ancient part of the building, had probably served for the residence of the Commendators, although it is said to have been considerably enlarged by Commendator David in 1598. But on this occasion the

Earl of Mar made a large and splendid addition to the house for the express purpose of entertaining the King with a magnificence worthy of his royal state.

Henry Erskine, Commendator of Dryburgh and Inchmahome, with a seat in Parliament, and Fiar of Cardross by the charter of his father, did not attain the dignity of the peerage, as he died in 1628, during his father's life-time. His son and heir was David, a child of eighteen months at the time of his father's death. He was served heir to the estates on the 11th of January, 1637. His grandfather, before his death, had granted a charter conferring on him the peerage of Cardross, and this charter was ratified by an Act of Parliament at Edinburgh, 17th November, 1641.[1] Thus David is known as the second Lord Cardross.

In Lord David's time Cardross was garrisoned by the troops of the Commonwealth. It was from the house of Cardross that General Monck addressed his letter of 17th May, 1654, to the Earl of Airth, ordering him to cut down the woods of Milton and Glegait in Aberfoyle, "that soe they may nott any longer bee a harbour or shelter for loose, idle, and desperate persons."[2] Possibly this occupation of his house by the Parliamentary forces may have been intended as some sort of punishment for Lord Cardross's political opinions and actions. He had protested against the delivery of Charles I. to the Parliamentary army, and he had joined the "Engagement" of the Duke of Hamilton in 1648. In consequence of this latter performance of his he was fined in £1000, and debarred from taking his seat

[1] Acts of the Parliaments of Scotland, vol. v. p. 547.
[2] Letter printed in Red Book, vol. ii. p. 158.

in the Parliament of 1649. David had a new charter of Cardross in 1664, and died in 1671.

The house of Cardross may have suffered somewhat from its Parliamentary garrison, although it is not likely that there was any oppression of the tenantry or much damage done to the estate. The same, however, cannot be said regarding its next occupancy by the Government troops, during the time of the religious persecutions in Scotland that marked the reign of Charles the Second.

Henry, the third Lord Cardross, was a steadfast Presbyterian and Covenanter, and in consequence suffered severely, in person and property, at the hands of the unprincipled gang who then ruled Scottish affairs. A full account of the persecutions to which he was subjected is given by Wodrow.[1] They began in 1674 with a fine of £5000 for listening to his own chaplain preaching in his own house of Cardross. He paid £1000 of this fine, and made efforts to procure a remission of the remainder; but this was refused, and he was ordered to be imprisoned for four years in Edinburgh Castle. A party of guards, under one Sir Mungo Murray, were sent to occupy Cardross. They grossly ill-treated his lady, broke open his repositories, and did much damage to the house, which had been recently repaired and refurnished. While he was in prison, his lady had had a child baptized at Cardross. On the ground that the rite of baptism had been performed by a clergyman who was not the minister of the parish, Lord Cardross was again fined. He was only released from prison in 1679 on giving a bond for the amount of his fines. He then

[1] Wodrow's Sufferings of the Church of Scotland, 1721, vol. ii. p. 122, *et passim*.

went to London in the hope of obtaining redress, but was repulsed with something more than insult. Despairing of further relief at home, he set sail for America, where he endeavoured to found a colony in Carolina. Misfortune pursued him here also, for his colony was attacked and destroyed by the Spaniards. As a consequence of his accumulated fines and other misfortunes he became insolvent, and the property of Cardross had to be given up to others in security for his debts.

That portion of the Lordship of Cardross called the "Abbacie of Dryburgh" had been sold by him to Sir Patrick Scott, younger of Ancrum,[1] in 1682; so that the estate was now again reduced pretty much to the original Priory lands. But somewhat better times were coming. He left America, and proceeding to Holland, entered the service of William of Orange. He accompanied that prince to England in 1688, and was instrumental in raising a regiment of dragoons in 1689. With these dragoons he did good service in the war with the Highland partizans of the exiled King.[2] Under William III., he enjoyed a few years of peace and comparative prosperity; but his numerous troubles and hardships had undermined his constitution, and he died at Edinburgh on the 21st of May, 1693, in the forty-fourth year of his age.

Two years before his death, the house of Cardross was again garrisoned by soldiers, but this time in a friendly way. On the 2nd June, 1691, the Privy Council granted

[1] Liber S. Marie de Dryburgh, p. xxxiii. The "disposition and rental," dated 24th June, 1682, are at Cardross.
[2] Hill Burton's History of Scotland, ed. 1897, vol. vii. p. 388.

warrant to Sir Thomas Livingston, Commander-in-Chief, to send forces to defend the house of Cardross against the Highland rebels.

Henry's eldest son David succeeded his father in the Lordship of Cardross. In 1695 he became Earl of Buchan, and the peerage of Cardross has since that time remained with that earldom. The lands of Cardross—the ancient property of the Priory of Inchmahome—had been disponed by Lord Henry, in 1683, to the Earl of Mar and others, for behoof of his creditors. Colonel the Hon. John Erskine —the "Black Colonel"—a younger brother of Lord Henry, set himself to clear off the burdens on the property, and succeeded so far that, in 1699, David, Earl of Buchan, disponed to him the estate of Cardross. Apparently all the bonds had not been redeemed, for in 1739 the Colonel began a litigation with his nephew the Earl, which had not been settled at the death of the former in 1743. The process was continued by his son and heir, John Erskine of Carnock, the well-known Professor of Scots Law in the University of Edinburgh, and author of "The Institutes of the Laws of Scotland"; and on the 25th of July, 1746, decree was given in his favour, and he was adjudged purchaser of the estate of Cardross. His eldest son, John Erskine, D.D., succeeded him in Carnock, while the estate of Cardross went to the second son, James Erskine, in 1768. From James Erskine, Cardross has descended in regular succession of the same family to the present proprietor, Henry David Erskine. The estate is now of greater extent than the lands held by the old Priory. Additions have been made by successive lairds. The property, also, has been greatly improved and adorned by several of them—by none more so than the present highly esteemed proprietor. At the same time some small parts of the original lands—such as the ancient Priory itself, with its demesne on the island of Inchmahome—have left the estate, it is not very well known how.

CHAPTER VII.

The Castle of Inchtalla: the old House and its Furnishings.

"I looked and saw between us and the sun
A building on an island,
With floating water-lilies, broad and bright."
"Here desolation holds her dreary court."

ALMOST the whole surface of the island, Inchtalla, is covered with the ruins of the old Castle buildings and their central court-yard. The date of erection of these is not mentioned in any extant writing, and can therefore only be inferred from the character of the buildings themselves. It is known that the principal residence of some of the earlier Earls of Menteith was Doune Castle. But after the extermination of the Albany family, and when a portion of their old domain had been erected into a new earldom in favour of Malise, formerly Earl of Strathern, by James I., in 1427, the Castle of Doune was retained by the King. Malise therefore—as is shown by his writs dated from the place—made Inchtalla his chief seat; and if, as has been with probability conjectured, there was already a keep or strong building of some sort on the island, it is equally probable that Malise considerably enlarged it, or even rebuilt it, in order to make it a suitable residence.

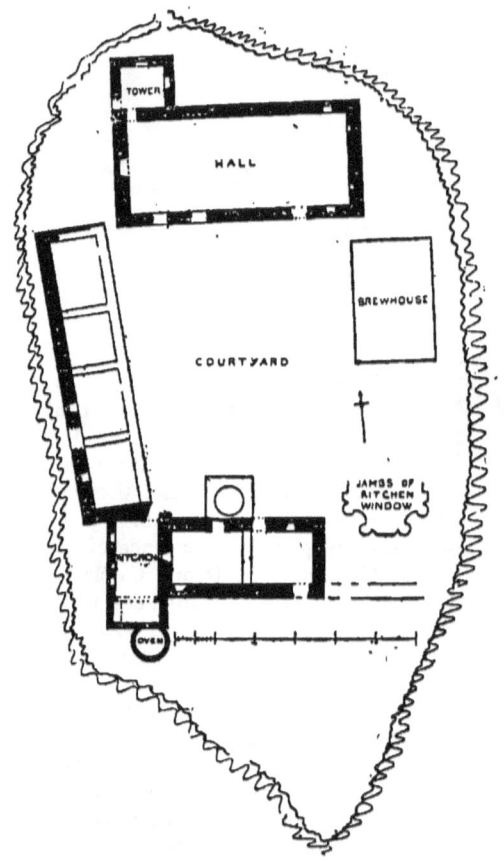

Plan of the Buildings on Inchtalla.
(By permission, from M'Gibbon and Ross's Castellated and Domestic Architecture of Scotland.)

Whether any portion of the building, which must have existed in his time, is to be found among the present ruins, is doubtful. The character and style of most of what remains point rather to a seventeenth century origin. Stones are to be found in the walls which must have come from the ecclesiastical buildings on the neighbouring island, and these appear to show that the erection could not have been earlier than the period of the Reformation. Some of these stones are to be found even in what is admittedly the oldest portion of the ruins—that at the south end of the island. In the tower-like building at the west end of the High House, for example, there has evidently been a stair leading to rooms above the kitchen; and the interior wall of this tower still retains some carved corbels, which have evidently been taken from the monastic buildings. The moulded side of one of the small windows in the kitchen wall is the mullion of a Gothic window, which also has obviously been abstracted from the Priory. It is possible, of course, that these Gothic fragments may have been inserted when repairs or additions were being made to the old house. If that be so, the High House, still standing as a ruin, may have been built at some more or less remote period prior to the Reformation. But the general arrangement of the buildings, the thickness of the walls, and the style of the work, no less than the circumstance that much of the materials seems to have been taken from the Priory, all indicate the seventeenth century as the period of erection of most of the buildings.

The plan is the common one of that period of a central court-yard surrounded by houses. But it must be added that this design is so loosely developed as to favour the idea that the buildings had not all been erected at the same time. The Hall, which makes the north side of the square, is evidently the most recent portion. It had apparently been built when the High House was either decaying or not considered sufficiently large or dignified for the family use; and may have been erected by the great Earl William (the seventh earl) when in the full flow of his prosperity. This suggestion—as well as the inference from architectural characteristics regarding the period of erection of the buildings—receives a certain amount of confirmation from a document in the State-Paper Office giving an account of "The Present State of the Nobility in Scotland: July 1st, 1592." In that paper the then earl, John, the sixth of the Graham line, and immediate predecessor of William, is noted as having his residence at *Kylbride*.[1]

The High House—at the south end of the island—was so called because it used to be loftier than the Hall at the north end. It has now lost something of its height, and is, in fact, greatly dilapidated. It is said to have formerly had heraldic devices over the doorway, which Mr. M'Gregor Stirling says had in his time been "partly abstracted." He adds—"From one of these devices, where the crest, representing (as is believed) an eagle *coupé*, is above a shield, the charge of which is not legible, it would appear that the oldest building was erected after the introduction of the first-mentioned emblem into armorial bearings."[2]

[1] State-Paper Office MS. printed in Tytler's History of Scotland, Proofs and Illustrations to vol. iv., No. xxiii.
[2] Notes on Inchmahome, p. 74.

Mr. Stirling thus speaks as if he had himself seen this heraldic stone. The statement must be left as it stands on his authority. There is now no vestige of heraldic device of any sort.

The lower apartment of this house measures thirty-six feet eight inches in length, with a breadth of fourteen feet eight inches. It has a vaulted roof. The space is divided into two rooms. The upper floor is also in two divisions. Access was had to these apartments by a stair—portions of which remain—inside a tower on the north side jutting into the court-yard. These were probably the family rooms when this house was inhabited. They are lighted by four openings in the south wall. The outside of this wall is peculiarly interesting. There are indications that it once had a kind of hanging gallery or wooden hoarding,[1] such as were sometimes used as a means of defence when the place was attacked, and perhaps also, in more peaceful times, as a place for enjoying the air and the prospect. About eight feet from the ground, and just under the openings in the wall already mentioned, are still to be seen the corbels on which the joists that supported the hoarding rested, as well as the "put-log" holes in which the ends of these joists were inserted; while the corbels for the wall-plate of the roof are also visible on the wall above

---

[1] A hoarding of this kind, called a *Bretess* (Fr. *Bretèche*) "was usually constructed over a gateway or portion of a wall liable to be attacked; it was of sufficient dimensions to hold several archers or cross-bowmen, and projected from the wall so as to allow openings to be made in its floor, through which stones or burning materials could be let fall on the heads of the besiegers. The sides of the bretess were provided with shutters or loops, for the discharge of arrows or bolts."—Audsley's Dictionary of Architecture, vol. iii. p. 257. The *bretèche* at Talla Castle must have been a mere architectural survival.

the windows. Still higher, a projecting stone band or table runs along the wall—intended to protect the roof of the hoarding at its junction with the wall from the rain-drip. Of the four openings, the two in the centre were probably windows. The other two were obviously doorways leading out to the platform of the hoarding. They were closed with doors opening outwards, as is shown by the checks in the rybats. Traces of a similar hoarding are discernible on the west side of the Hall.[1]

On the west end of the High House is the Kitchen—about twenty-five feet in length by ten feet in breadth. This includes a large arched fire-place at the south end, which measures nine feet nine inches by six feet six inches. Through a narrow opening in the wall, the kitchen and fire-place communicate with the oven built outside. Another opening leads into the ground floor of the High House. There are two very small windows—only about ten inches square—in the kitchen, looking to the west. Overhead a square tower seems to have risen to a considerable height. The remains of a circular stair in this tower have already been referred to.

Northwards from the kitchen, in a line parallel to the shore of the lake, runs a long building, about eighty feet in length, which was possibly appropriated to the household servants and other attendants on the earls. Only the wall on the side next the lake, and fragments on the north and south ends, are now standing. This wall has been peculiarly destitute of lighting. There are only two small

[1] See M'Gibbon & Ross's Castellated and Domestic Architecture of Scotland, vol. iv. p. 288.

windows in it—both in the southmost portion. Each of these seems to have lighted a separate room, and, judging from their positions, there may have been two other apartments in the length of the entire block.

On the north side of the court-yard stood, and still stands, the Hall, evidently the most recent of all the buildings on the island. It consists of an oblong house of about sixty feet in length by thirty feet in width, and two storeys high, with a square tower at the north-west angle. Over the doorway, which is towards the east end of the south wall, is a stone which appears to have had armorial bearings, but these are not now decipherable. The ground floor is one undivided room, with a great fire-place in the west end. It measures fifty-five feet in length, and is twenty-three feet four inches wide, and in the days of its inhabitation must have been a fine and imposing apartment. Fortunately, we are able to obtain a clear idea of the appearance of this room, and indeed, of the arrangement and furnishing of the whole House, in the time of the last earl. An inventory of the "haill Household Stuffe and Plenishing," taken on the 22nd of May, 1694, and preserved among the Menteith papers at Gartmore, has been printed by Mr. M'Gregor Stirling.[1]

The Hall—as this lower floor of the house was specially named—was draped with green drugget hangings, dependent from gilt rods. It had also two window curtains, a pair of virginals, my Lord and my Lady's portraits with green hangings before them, a large table, a folding table, and a

[1] Notes on Inchmahome, appendix vi. p. 159.

house clock with case. No mention is made of chairs in the furniture of the Hall, but a separate inventory is given of the chairs belonging to the house, in addition to those that are mentioned in connection with the various bedrooms. They numbered eighteen new red leather chairs, of which two were armed, and fourteen old leather chairs. Besides these, there were eighteen fine carpet chairs—two of them armed—and ten old carpet chairs. For lighting the Hall and the other rooms, the house had fourteen brass candlesticks, old and new, and as necessary adjuncts to these, two pairs of brass snuffers with their pans, besides two pairs which were broken, and also two pairs of snuffers made of iron; and—no doubt for the great Hall and on great occasions—two silver candlesticks, with snuffers, plate and chains of the same metal.

On the floor above the Hall were two bedrooms, entrance to which appears to have been obtained from behind. These were called respectively the East and the West Chambers. The furnishings of the East Chamber were mostly in blue, and those of the West in green. Moreover, the furniture of the former seems to indicate that it was meant for ladies' use, while that of the other seems rather to point to male occupancy. In the East Chamber—according to the inventory, hung with blue—was a standing bed with blue damask knot hangings lined with orange, having the pand of gimp silk, eight cane chairs—two of them being armchairs—a dozen of flowered satin cushions, two white window curtains, a looking-glass with olive wood frame, a fir table, two "standers," a blue damask table-cloth, and a coffer. In the West Chamber, hung with green drugget, were a large standing bed with green drugget hangings, lined with white and fringed on the inside, a glass with a black frame, two white crepe window curtains, with a large oak chest, a smaller chest, and a little table with a green table-cloth.

The square tower at the north-west had an entrance from the Hall. The ground floor of this tower was called "the laigh back-room." It had hangings of stamped blue cloth, two trunks covered with leather, two dressing boxes, one of olive, the other of sweet (fragrant) wood, and a large chest. This chest held a considerable quantity of holland and linen sheets, six large dornick table-cloths, eleven dozen new dornick serviettes, and four dozen towels.

A turnpike stair on the west side of the tower led to the upper rooms. That on the second storey was my Lord's Chamber. It contained a standing bed, with gold knops, hangings of stamped cloth, and pand of gimp silk with white linings and pand within. The whole room was hung with stamped cloth similar to that of the bed hangings. The rest of the furniture consisted of a chest of shotles (drawers), two cabinets—one of larger, another of smaller size—with shotles, a little table with a drawer, a looking-glass with a black "brissel" frame.[1]

Above my Lord's Chamber was the Wardrobe, which also served, as occasion required, for a bedroom. It held an old standing bed, two trunks, and four chests.

On the east side of the court-yard was the Brew-house, furnished with all the apparatus and utensils necessary for

---

[1] Brissel, *i.e.*, Brazil wood—the bright-red coloured wood which gave name to the country that produces it. This may have been dark through age, or stained.

o

brewing ale, and apparently cider, for the use of my Lord
and his household. For, besides a masking fat, wort
stands, and other apparatus for the manufacture of ale,
it had a "syder press and trough." To eke out the
somewhat limited accommodation of the mansion-house,
the upper part of the Brew-house was utilized for sleeping
room. This large chamber—which, from the warmth of
the Brew-house underneath, must have been very comfort-
able in the cold season, though the odour, when the
"browst" was on, must have been a trifle heavy—was
hung with green cloth, and had two beds. One of these
beds had hangings of "red scarlet" cloth, and the other
of green stuff, and they had each rods and pands "conforme."
Besides these there were a red scarlet resting-chair, a little
table with a red table-cloth, and, for use in emergencies
probably, a wooden folding bed. Built on to the ends of
the Brew-house were "to-falls," and these, too, were
appropriated as bed-chambers, and held between them three
beds—two of them hung with red cloth, and the third
with brown drugget.

With the buildings thus described crowded round the
central court, there was no vacant ground to spare for
other purposes, so that, as has been elsewhere stated, the
gardens had to find room on the neighbouring island of
Inchmahome, while the earls' pleasaunce was on the north
shore and their stables on the west shore of the lake.
But, though closely set, the buildings were airy enough,
with the open water all round. In fact, the strong winds
which often blow over the lake—especially from the west—
must have occasionally sent the spray well over them,

and this may have been the reason why the windows to the west are so few and small.

Some of the items in the inventory enable us to obtain glimpses of the mode of living in this island mansion at the time. Ale and cider would appear to have been the more common household drinks; while, for the heads of the family and guests, there were also brandy, sack, and wine—for the consumption of which liquors the earl had eighteen glasses. Meal girnels, flour kits, and baking tubs point to the supplies of daily bread. The large number of herring barrels shows that salt fish of that description was a considerable item in the daily menu; and the spits, branders, dripping-pans, frying-pans, ladles, and flesh-crooks tell their tale of more generous living. The vessels were mostly of pewter. When the seventh earl was disgraced by Charles I., and denied the payment of the pensions and other moneys to which he was entitled, he had to part with almost all his lands, and finally with his silver plate. This went to the laird of Keir in 1645 to satisfy a claim he had as security for the earl in certain of his transactions.[1] Neither Earl William nor his successor were ever in a pecuniary condition to replace this plate. The very short list of "silver work" that appears in the inventory must therefore have been the poor remains that had been left in 1645. The most important piece in this small collection is that mentioned first and specially as "ane large basone and lawer of silver." It would be interesting if we could believe that this was "the Mazer" gifted by the first Earl Malise to

[1] Red Book of Menteith, vol. i. p. 388.

his spouse, and transmitted from one generation to another as a family heirloom.[1] No doubt the silver vessels—such as they were—were reserved for special and great occasions in the castle.

Domestic crafts are represented by the "two little wheels, ane chack reel, four pair of tow cards, two pair of wool cards, and ane haire-clouth," as well as by the quantities of "new-made linning, harne, and dornick" among the stores. My Lord's personal wardrobe is set out in full detail—his coats of Spanish cloth, of velvet, and of scarlet and grey cloth; his vests of velvet and flowered silk; his Highland coats; his doublets, belts, and bandelier; his grey worsted and snuff-coloured, black and pearl-coloured stockings; and his two pairs of breeches of grey cloth, one pair of which was new. There were also saddles for my Lord and my Lady—the former embroidered, the latter of velvet; three pairs of pistols—one pair with iron stocks; an unusually large stock of night-caps; and, last of all, two house Bibles—"ane large and ane less."

The very small proportion of female properties in the inventory—besides the saddle, the only other thing mentioned is a skirt and a hood, "which was my Lady's" —is accounted for by the circumstance that the earl died a widower, his last wife—for he was twice married—Lady Katherine Bruce, having predeceased him in 1692. At her death, she left her own money, her gold watch, rings, bodily ornaments, and other trinkets to various relatives, so that little belonging to her was left in the house. Her

---
[1] See *infra*, chap. x.

Ladyship, moreover, was not much in love with her island home. Her rest was said to have been broken and her nervous system upset by the croaking of the frogs that persisted in holding their nightly concerts under the window of her chamber. Whether that were the case or not, it is certain that for some time she left her husband alone in the castle and went to reside in Edinburgh, and my Lord had much curious manœuvring to get her to return.[1]

The whole inventory does not give a very exalted idea of the wealth of this, the last Earl of Menteith, or of the grandeur of the castle in which he dwelt. It was taken on the 22nd of May, 1694; and, in September of that year, the Earl died. His household gear and other personal estate was left by him to his nephew, Sir John Graham of Gartmore, while what was left of the property of the old earldom—now reduced to narrow dimensions—went to the Marquis of Montrose. The house of Talla has not been inhabited since, but has been left for over two hundred years to neglect and decay. There is little wonder, therefore, that it should have become the utter ruin it now is. All over the island, around the roofless walls, and inside them too, has sprung up a dense natural wood, which, in its summer foliage, all but conceals the ruins from outside view.

[1] See *infra*, chap. xi.

CHAPTER VIII.

**The earlier Earldom of Menteith:
Menteith, Comyn, and Stewart Earls,
previous to 1425.**

"How forcy chieftains, in many bloody stours,
Most valiantly won landis and honours,
And for their virtue called noblemen."

"Old, unhappy, far-off things,
And battles long ago."

"The knights' bones are dust
And their good swords rust."

THE ancient Province of Menteith and Stratherne had doubtless its Mormaers, but no mention of any of them has been preserved. The old Celtic title of Mormaer passed into that of Earl (*Comes*) in the time of Alexander the First, that is, about the beginning of the twelfth century; and the first reference to an "Erl of Meneteth" appears in a statute of David I. (1124-1153), Alexander's brother and successor.[1] The name of this earl is not given. It may have been either Gilchrist —the first whose name has come down to us—or an unknown predecessor. From this statute, as well as from a later one of William the Lion (1165-1214), it is known that these old Earls of Menteith had jurisdiction in the districts of Cowal and Kintyre.[2]

[1] Acts of the Parliaments of Scotland, vol. i. p. 603.   [2] *Ibid*, vol. i. p. 372.

GILCHRIST.[1]

Earl Gilchrist is a mere shadow on the page of history. Nothing is known of him beyond the name—and that only from its occurrence as witness to certain royal charters. In 1164, he witnessed a charter granted by Malcolm IV. to the Abbey of Scone,[2] and again he was witness to a deed whereby William the Lion made a grant of the burgh of Glasgow to Jocelin, the Bishop of that place, somewhere between 1175 and 1178.[3] Sir William Fraser has put the date of Gilchrist as from about 1150 to about 1180.

MURETACH.

His successor—Earl Muretach or Murdach—is equally shadowy. He is known as having witnessed an agreement between the Prior and Canons of St. Andrews and the Culdees there in 1199 or 1200.[4] He was certainly dead by 1213, as in that year there was a quarrel about the succession. His tenure of the earldom may therefore be reckoned as extending from 1180 to 1212 or 1213.

MAURICE (SENIOR AND JUNIOR).

After Muretach, the earldom was held in succession by two brothers, both named Maurice. The elder could have been in possession, if at all, only for a short time, as his claim was immediately challenged by the younger brother.

---

[1] An Earl Murdach is said to have been mentioned in the Cartulary of Dunfermline as living in the reign of David I. That is not the case. The mistake may have arisen from confusion with Murdach, the successor of Gilchrist.
[2] Liber Ecclesie de Scon, p. 8.
[3] Registrum Episcopatus Glasguensis, vol. i. p. 36.
[4] Registrum Prioratus Sancti Andree, p. 318.

The fact that the brothers bore the same name would seem to indicate that they were sons of Muretach by different mothers, and that the illegitimacy of the elder was the ground on which the earldom was claimed by the younger. But the documents leave us in the dark as to this. What we do know is that Maurice junior laid claim to the earldom "*sicut jus et hereditatem suam*," and that his right was acknowledged by the King (William II.), to whom the matters in dispute had been referred, while the elder brother was compensated by certain lands he was to hold in bailiary of the King, and which were to revert to the earldom on the death of the holder.[1] The agreement is dated at Edinburgh, 6th December, 1213.[2]

Maurice was one of the seven earls who, along with William Malvoisin, Bishop of St. Andrews, on the morning after the death of King William (5th December, 1214), carried the young Prince Alexander to Scone, and had him crowned and enthroned there on the 10th of the same month.[3] That he was Sheriff of Stirling we learn from the Chartulary of Cambuskenneth.[4] He held the earldom for about seventeen years, dying probably in 1230. He left two daughters — the elder, Isabella, married to Walter

---

[1] These lands included the two towns (*villae*) of Muyline and Radenoche, and the lands of Tum (Thom), Cattlyne, Brathuly, and Cambuswelhe. There were other lands he was to receive for the marriage portion of his daughters. Presumably these did not revert, with the others, to the earldom.

[2] This agreement is quoted in the *Inspeximus* granted by Henry III. of England, 20th September, 1261, to Isabella, Countess of Menteith, and her husband, John Russel : printed in the Red Book, vol. ii. p. 314.

[3] Fordun Gesta Annalia xxix. Vol. i. of Skene's edition, p. 280. The seven earls were Fife, Stratherne, Athol, Angus, *Menteith*, Buchan, and Lothian (Dunbar). See also Balfour's Annals, i. 38.

[4] Chartulary of Cambuskenneth, ed. by Fraser, p. 176.

Comyn, Lord of Badenoch, and the younger, Mary, who was the wife of Walter Stewart, third son of the High Steward of Scotland. With these two ladies may be said to have begun the many remarkable vicissitudes to which the Earldom of Menteith has, in the course of time, been subjected.

WALTER COMYN.

The Lady Isabella, the elder of Maurice's daughters, was married to Walter Comyn probably in January, 1231, and her husband at once assumed the style and dignity of Earl of Menteith. He was the second son, by the first marriage, of William Comyn, who had, by his second marriage, become Earl of Buchan. Walter Comyn was much older than his wife, and had, previous to his marriage, risen to high distinction in the affairs of the kingdom. The frequent appearance of his name as a witness to royal charters shows that he was frequently in the train of King William the Lion and Alexander the Second.[1] He became Lord of Badenoch about 1229.

Under the designation of Earl of Menteith, he rapidly rose to a position of influence in the management of Scottish affairs. The English King, Henry III., was

---

[1] He witnessed several charters by King William between 1211 and 1214 (Chartulary of Arbroath, &c.) In 1220 he accompanied Alexander II. when he went to York to make arrangements with Henry III. for marrying his daughter Joanna, and the agreement in the case was signed by Comyn, 15th June of that year (Red Book, vol. i. p. 14). Sir William Fraser says that in a document of date 1225, he is styled *Clericus domini regis*, or Lord Clerk Register. However, in the two charters granted—one at Kincardin, 18th August, 1226, and the other at Edinburgh, 20th July, 1227—by Alexander II. to the burgesses of Stirling, he is named (as witness) simply Walter Comyn. (See Charters and other Documents relating to Stirling, pp. 9 and 11).

endeavouring, by every means in his power, to reduce the kingdom of Scotland to a condition of vassalage, and there was a considerable party among the Scottish nobility that favoured the English interest. The Earl of Menteith as —since the death of his father, the Earl of Buchan, in 1233—the head of the powerful Comyn family, and a man distinguished by his ability both in the council and in the field of battle, was regarded as the leader of the patriotic party. He made the Comyn family for years the dominating factor in Scottish politics. On the death of Alexander II. (on the 8th of July, 1249), he acted promptly and successfully in the national cause. When the assembly of the nobles met at Scone for the purpose of crowning the youthful Alexander III., Alan Durward, the Justiciary, and others in the English interests endeavoured to prevent or delay the ceremony. They represented that the day fixed for the purpose was an unlucky one, and that the King could not be crowned without being previously knighted. But Menteith strongly urged the danger of delay as King Henry was known to be intriguing with the Pope to procure an interdict against the coronation on the ground that Alexander was his vassal and could not be crowned without his permission. He therefore proposed that the Bishop of St. Andrews should both knight and crown the young King. His advice was taken; and David de Bernham, the Bishop of St. Andrews, girded the boy with the belt of knighthood and the sword of State, and formally crowned him King of Scotland.[1] Shortly after this Menteith was appointed

[1] Fordun (ed. Skene), vol. i. pp. 293-4 (13th July, 1249).

The Lake of Menteith. 221

one of the guardians of the King, and for some years he appears to have been in pretty constant attendance on the royal person, as is shown by the various royal deeds to which he was witness.

In 1255 the Durward faction, supported by the influence of the English King, gained a temporary supremacy, took possession of the young King and Queen, and removed the regents and councillors. A deed was drawn up at Roxburgh which virtually gave to King Henry the entire management of the Scottish King and Scottish affairs. To this the Earl of Menteith refused to affix his seal, and in this refusal he was backed by the Bishop of Glasgow and the Bishop-elect of St. Andrews.[1] The Earl's party was the popular one, and the feeling against the English continued to grow. Gamelin, Bishop-elect of St. Andrews, succeeded in obtaining from the Pope a sentence of excommunication against the royal counsellors. Taking advantage of these favourable circumstances, Menteith ventured on the bold stroke of seizing the King and Queen at Kinross—28th October, 1257—and conveying them to Stirling. The English[2] faction was scattered, and Durward again took refuge in England. The next important step was to enter into a treaty with the Welsh (dated 18th March, 1258), who were at that time engaged in a struggle with Henry. But not long afterwards a compromise was concluded, in the arrangement of which the Earl bore a principal part. And thus, after a long struggle, he

[1] Tytler's History of Scotland (ed. 1867), vol. i. p. 6 ; Chronicle of Melrose, p. 181 ; Scotichronicon a Goodall, lib. x. cap. ix. ; Wyntoun, bk. vii. chap. x.
[2] Tytler's History, i. p. 7.

succeeded in freeing his country—for a time, at least—from the interference of the English monarchs.

He did not long survive this national service. He died unexpectedly—although he was now an old man—in November, 1258. In England, the report was that his death was caused by a fall from his horse; while in Scotland, it was rumoured, and generally believed, that he was poisoned by his Countess, who had conceived an attachment for an Englishman named John Russell, whom she married almost immediately after the Earl's death.

Walter Comyn, Earl of Menteith, was undoubtedly the foremost Scotsman of his time—able, energetic, courageous, and faithful to his country's independence. He appears to have been a great builder as, in addition to the Priory of Inchmahome, which he founded in 1238, he built, in 1244, the great Castle of Hermitage in Liddesdale,[1] and that of Dalswinton, or Comyn's Castle, in Galloway. He left no son to take his place—his son Henry having predeceased him—and his daughter Isabella was disinherited —so far as the earldom was concerned—along with her mother. The place of his burial is unknown. It may have been in the Priory which he had founded, although no evidence to that effect has been preserved, and the conduct of his Countess makes even the supposition doubtful.

Isabella of Menteith, who had brought the earldom to Walter Comyn, was probably, as has been said before,

[1] So says Sir W. Fraser, but by others the builder of this the second Hermitage Castle is said to have been Nicholas de Soulis. See M'Gibbon & Ross's Castellated and Domestic Architecture of Scotland, i. p. 524.

much younger than her husband, although, as she had
been his wife for twenty-seven years, she could not have
been very young at the time of his death. The accusation
of poisoning him was not proved, but her hasty marriage
to Sir John Russell naturally gave rise to much suspicion
and indignation. It may have added to this indignation
that probably some of the Scottish nobles had hoped themselves to receive the hand of the well-dowered Countess of
Menteith. At any rate she and her second husband were
thrown into prison and deprived of the estates. When
ultimately set at liberty they left the kingdom and retired
to England. There she made several attempts to recover
the earldom of which she had been despoiled, by appealing
first (1262) to Henry III. of England, who could do
nothing more than inspect her writs[1] and certify them to
be authentic—her late husband had effectually prevented
the authority of Henry from running in Scotland—and
next to the Pope, Urban IV. The Pope's interference was
resented by the King, Alexander III., and notwithstanding
the fact that the country was laid under a papal interdict,
it came to nought. The Countess never regained her
dignities or estates, nor did she return to Scotland. She is
supposed to have died about 1273. Who the John Russell
whom she married was, has never been clearly ascertained.
He has been called[2] "ignoble," but incorrectly. In the
Pope's letter committing the affair of Countess Isabella to
certain Scottish Bishops for judgment,[3] he is styled " a

[1] It is from these *Inspeximus* that we have the account of the dispute between the two Earls Maurice and its settlement.
[2] By Boece and Buchanan.
[3] Theiner's Vetera Monumenta, No. 237, p. 93.

noble man, John Russell, of the diocese of Ely." Most of those who have written of him content themselves with calling him "an obscure Englishman"; and *obscure* in the sense of *unknown*, he certainly is. One writer had dubbed him "a futile Englishman." The epithet has a kind of vague vigour about it, but does not seem to mean anything in particular. In fact, whatever has been written regarding his origin is of the nature of more or less plausible conjecture; and almost all that can be conjectured on the subject will be found in Sir William Fraser's "Red Book of Menteith."[1]

WALTER STEWART.

On the death of Earl Walter Comyn and the confiscation of the Countess Isabella, the earldom passed to a member of the noble House of Stewart. Lady Mary, the younger daughter of Earl Maurice, had been married to Walter Stewart, third son of Walter the High Steward of Scotland, and to her and her husband the earldom was adjudged, notwithstanding the efforts of the Comyns to retain it in their family. First of all, Sir John Comyn, younger brother of the deceased Earl of Menteith, forced the Countess Isabella, when she was in prison after the death of her husband, to renounce in his favour. On the ground of this renunciation he set up a claim to the earldom, but it was rejected. The next claim was made on behalf of William Comyn, Lord of Kirkintilloch, the son of this Sir John. William had married Isabella, the only daughter of the late earl, and on the death of

[1] Red Book, vol. i. pp. 44 and 45.

her mother, the elder Isabella, in 1273, a claim was advanced to the earldom on her behalf and that of her husband. Proceedings in support of this claim were instituted at York, but to no effect, as King Alexander would not permit an action affecting dignities and estates in his kingdom to be prosecuted in England or anywhere else furth of Scotland. The Comyns, however, did not yet give up their pretensions, till in 1285 a final settlement was made by the King and Parliament assembled at Scone. The result, a division of the earldom between the parties, seems to have been acquiesced in by both. It is thus stated by Wyntoun :—

> The Kyng than of his counsale
> Made this delyverans thare fynale ;
> That erldume to be delt in twa
> Partis, and the tane of tha
> Wyth the chemys assygnyd he
> Til Walter Stwart : the lave to be
> Made als gud in all profyt ;
> Schyre Willame Comyn till have that quyt
> Till hald it in fre barony
> Besyd the erldume all quytly.[1]

That is to say, that while Sir William Comyn received half of the great estates belonging to the earldom, Walter Stewart retained the other half, with the *chemys*, *i.e.*, the chief messuage or castle, and the dignity of Earl of Menteith.

Sir William Comyn died, without issue, in 1291; and Edward I. of England, who was at that time paramount in Scotland, directed the marriage of the widow to Sir Edmund Hastings in 1293. The Comyn portion of the estates of the earldom therefore now passed to the posses-

[1] Wyntoun, ed. Macpherson, vol. i. p. 397.

sion of this English knight. Sir Edmund was one of those who signed the famous letter sent by the earls and barons of England to Pope Boniface in 1301. The legend on his seal affixed to that document is "*S. Edmundi Hasting Comitatu Menetei*," and his designation is "*Dominus de Enchimchelmok*," which evidently means Lord of Inchmacolmok or Inchmahome.[1]

Seal of Sir Edmund Hastings, Lord of Inchmahome.

It is a curious fact that not long after this the other portion of the earldom, then held by Alan, son and suc-

---

[1] We may perhaps gather from this designation that the lake and its islands were in that half of the earldom which had been given to his wife, the Lady Isabella Comyn and her first husband. If that were so, the Castle of Inchtalla could not have been the *chemys* at the time. Possibly it may have been at Doune—although the erection of the present Castle there is generally assigned to a later period.

cessor of Walter Stewart, was taken from him by Edward (in 1306) and granted to Sir John Hastings, the elder brother of Sir Edmund. At that time, therefore, the whole lands of the earldom were held by these two brothers. But Edward apparently did not grant the title of Earl of Menteith to either—possibly to avoid displeasing either the one or the other. The dates of the death of Lady Isabella Comyn and her husband are not known. He is known to have been alive in 1314, but no doubt he and his brother had been cleared out of Menteith before that. King Robert was at Inchmahome in 1310, and it is not likely that the Hastings family were there at the time. With Isabella, all connection of the Comyns with the earldom of Menteith ceased.

To return now to the earldom under Walter Stewart, known to his contemporaries as *Balloch*, or *Bulloch* (*i.e.*, The Freckled). He was a personage of distinction before he came to be Earl of Menteith. After that, his position gave him still greater prominence and influence, and he took an ample share in the affairs of the kingdom. Although the Stewarts belonged to the English faction as opposed to the patriotic party headed by the late Earl of Menteith and the Comyns, the new Earl during his long life did much good service to his country. In valour and wisdom, and, indeed, in genuine patriotism, he was a worthy successor of the distinguished man who preceded him in his title. In his earlier life (1248-9), his brother Alexander and he had gone a-crusading, at least as far as Egypt, where they greatly distinguished themselves, with Louis the Ninth (Saint Louis) of France. Hence the crusader attitude of his effigy in the choir of the Priory of Inchmahome. Whether he bestowed benefactions on that religious house is not known; there is no evidence to show it; but documents are extant which prove his liberality to other churches, especially those of Kilwinning and Paisley.

He bore a prominent part in the battle of Largs, 2nd October, 1263, where his brother Alexander, the High Steward, who was in chief command under the King, was slain. Besides his actual share in the fighting, the Earl of Menteith was at the time Sheriff of Ayr, and as a duty of this office, had the charge of all the arrangements for defending the coast and watching the movements of the enemy.[1] After the successful issue of that battle, he was one of the nobles sent by the King to reduce to subjection the chieftains of the Western Isles—a task which was successfully accomplished. It was after this, in 1273, that he had the contest with the Comyn family for the earldom, the result of which has been already given.

He was one of the witnesses to the marriage contract between the Princess Margaret of Scotland and King Eric of Norway, settled at Roxburgh on the 25th of July, 1281, and gave his oath to see the deed faithfully carried out. Along with his Countess, he was of the company that attended the Princess to Norway in order to take part in the nuptial celebrations and witness the coronation. The expedition left Scotland on the morning of the 12th of August, and reached Norway on the evening of the 14th,

---

[1] The nature of these arrangements may be learned from the claim of expenses made by the Earl in connection therewith, as set down in the Exchequer Rolls, vol. i. p. 5.

so that the old ballad appears to be perfectly accurate on this point—

> They hoisted their sails on a Monday morn,
> Wi' a' the haste they may;
> And they hae landed in Norroway
> Upon the Wodensday.[1]

When the ceremonies they had gone to witness were concluded, the Earl and the Countess Mary, with the most of the Scottish nobles, returned home in safety; but a second ship, conveying the Scottish ecclesiastics who had taken part in the ceremony, and others, never reached Scotland. She went down, with all on board, probably in the neighbourhood of one of the Orkney Islands.[2] It is this tragic event that is the subject of the ballad just quoted—one of the oldest and finest ballads in the Scottish minstrelsy.

The Earl was again present at the Council held at Scone on the 5th of February, 1283, and appended his seal to the declaration subscribed by the nobles that, in the event of the death of King Alexander without further issue, the Maiden of Norway would be accepted as sovereign of the realm.[3] Alexander died without further issue on the 16th of March, 1285, and his grand-daughter, then about three years of age, became his successor. Meantime, those Scottish nobles who, from affinity or otherwise, thought

---

[1] Ballad of Sir Patrick Spens. See Aytoun's Ballads of Scotland, vol. i. p. 5.
[2] Professor Aytoun, in his introduction to the ballad, says that "in the little island of Papa Stronsay, one of the Orcadian group, lying over against Norway, there is a large grave or tumulus, which has been known to the inhabitants, from time immemorial, as 'The Grave of Sir Patrick Spens.'"—Ballads of Scotland, i. 2.
[3] Acts of the Parliaments of Scotland, i. 424.

they might be able to put in a claim for the crown should anything happen to the young Queen, began to prepare for such a possible contingency by forming parties for their support. The Earl of Menteith adhered to the party of the Bruces, and, along with other relatives, entered into a bond of mutual defence at Turnberry Castle in 1286.[1]

After the death of the Maid of Norway in 1290, he continued to take part in the negotiations regarding the succession. He was one of Bruce's Commissioners. On the 13th of June, 1292, he took the oath of fealty to Edward I. of England; but, while he tacitly acquiesced in Edward's decision in favour of Baliol—he could scarcely do otherwise—he seems privately to have been still for Bruce. He did not live, however, to give the latter effective help in his efforts to reach the throne. He died in the latter part of 1294, or in 1295.

He survived his wife, who had brought him the earldom, by several years. The Countess Mary was certainly dead before 1290, the date of his charter to the monastery of Kilwinning, in which he makes certain grants "pro salute anime mee et domine Marie *quondam* sponse mee, comitisse de Menetheht."[2] And it is probable that she died before 1286, when he gave the Church of Kippen[3] to the Abbey of Cambuskenneth, in order to obtain a burial-place in the Abbey, as his daughter-in-law, Matilda, not his wife, is mentioned as concurring in that grant. He was not,

---

[1] Printed in the Red Book, vol. ii. p. 219.
[2] Red Book of Menteith, vol. ii. p. 220.
[3] The tradition is that the earlier Earls of Menteith had their burial-place in Kippen. The Stewarts, of course, were buried in their Abbey of Paisley.

however, buried in Cambuskenneth. He rests, with his Countess Mary, near the high altar of the Priory of Inchmahome. The fine monument, which there preserves their memory, is elsewhere described.¹

Earl Walter had two sons—Alexander his successor, and the notorious Sir John Menteith of Rusky, whose career forms the subject of a separate notice.²

Seal of Walter Stewart, Earl of Menteith.

ALEXANDER.

Alexander, the elder son and successor of Walter Stewart, seems, as well as his brother Sir John, to have dropped the surname of Stewart and recurred to that of Menteith. He lived in very troubled times, and his tenure of the earldom was short. He must have been of age in 1286, when he was a signatory of the agreement at Turnberry. Along with his father, he swore fealty to Edward at Norham in 1291. Immediately after his accession he threw himself into the midst of the exciting

---

¹ See *supra*, chap. iv. p. 123.   ² See chapter ix.

events of the time. In the battle of Dunbar (1296), where he fought on the Scottish side, he was taken prisoner, and sent to the Tower of London.[1] But his confinement extended over only two or three months. Bruce and the Earl of Dunbar—both of them parties to the agreement of Turnberry—were then in favour with Edward; and it was perhaps to their friendly influence that his speedy release and restoration to his estates were due. On the 28th of August, 1296, at Berwick, he again took the oath to Edward, signing a document in which he acknowledged that he had received from the said King of England his earldom and its pertinents, together with its other vassalages, to hold at his pleasure; and swearing on the Holy Gospels, for himself and his heirs, to serve the said King well and loyally against all mortals.[2] Two of his sons, Alan and Peter, were left as hostages in the hands of the English King. Alexander was in England in the summer of 1297; but it is certain that he returned to Scotland before the battle of Stirling Bridge.[3] If he were at that battle at all—and there is no evidence that he was—he can scarcely have been in the ranks of the Scottish patriots, because, just after it, on the 26th September, 1297, a letter was addressed to him by Edward, thanking him for his fidelity, and requesting him to co-operate with the new Governor, Brian Fitz-Alan.[4] Nothing more is certainly known of Earl Alexander. He must have been dead before 1806, because Alan is mentioned as Earl in that year. By his

---

[1] Historical Documents relating to Scotland, vol. ii. p. 19.
[2] Ragman Rolls, p. 120.
[3] Historical Documents relating to Scotland, ii. 175. [4] Rotuli Scotiæ, p. 50.

wife Matilda—whose name only is known from the deed granting the Church of Kippen to Cambuskenneth—he had four sons, Alan, his successor, Peter, Murdach—who succeeded Alan—and Alexander. Where he died and where he was buried are alike unknown, though the conjecture is permissible that his Countess and he may have been interred in the burial-place which they had provided in Cambuskenneth Abbey.

ALAN.

The career of Earl Alan was short and unfortunate. It has been already stated that he and his brother Peter became hostages for the fidelity of their father to King Edward. They went with that King to the wars in Flanders in 1297, fitted out for the campaign at the royal expense.[1] It is possible that Peter was slain in this campaign; at any rate he is not again heard of. Alan succeeded to the earldom probably in 1303 or 1304. Duncan, Earl of Fife, made an entail of his earldom in favour of Alan;[2] but the latter, with his usual bad luck, never obtained possession. When Robert Bruce resolved to vindicate by force of arms his right to the Scottish crown, Alan supported his cause. In the fight at Methven Wood (1306) he was captured and sent as a prisoner to England, assigned to the keeping of Sir John Hastings. King Edward stripped him of his earldom and estates, and —as has already been stated—bestowed the latter on Hastings. Alan never returned to Scotland. He is sup-

[1] Accounts of the Keeper of the King's Wardrobe, 1296-7: Historical Documents, vol. ii. p. 138, *et seqq.*
[2] Red Book of Menteith, vol. ii. p. 257.

posed to have died in captivity. With his death the earldom of Menteith might be said to have ceased to exist. But the fact is the Scots never recognised the usurpation of Hastings. Alan left a daughter Mary, and she was regarded as the heiress and made a ward of the Crown. When Bruce succeeded in freeing the country from the English domination, the brothers Hastings were of course turned out of Menteith, and the two divisions of the earldom were re-united. Sir John Menteith of Rusky became guardian of the consolidated earldom on behalf of the Countess Mary. By a family arrangement, however, the earldom was for a time transferred to Murdach, the third brother of the late Earl Alan, on the condition that it should revert to his niece on her marriage, or in the case of his own death without male issue.[1]

MURDACH.

Murdach first appears under the style of Earl of Menteith as witness to a deed of King Robert in 1318. He received numerous gifts in lands and money[2] from that King, from which it may be inferred that he was regarded as a faithful subject. He continued this faithful service to Robert's son and successor, David II. He was distinguished by his gallant conduct at the battle of Dupplin, 12th April, 1332, when the Scottish regent, Earl of Mar, was disastrously defeated by Edward Baliol. This

---

[1] That Murdach was meant to be only a temporary earl is shown by the fact that at the time he was enjoying the style and dignity of Earl, Sir John Menteith—in the subscription of the letter from the Scottish barons to the Pope in 1320—still styles himself *guardian* of the earldom.—Acts of Parliament of Scotland, vol. i. p. 474.

[2] Exchequer Rolls, vol. i. p. 178, *et passim* (year 1329).

was the last of his fights. He fell on the field of battle.[1] His wife was probably the Alice, Countess of Menteith, who appears for several years later as a pensioner on the bounty of Edward III. As the arrangement which had been made with her husband threw her out of the possession of the earldom, she perhaps went to England and came under allegiance to Edward in the hope that, if he recovered the country, she would regain possession of the estate; and no doubt Edward also expected that in that case the advances he made to her would be repaid.

COUNTESS MARY AND SIR JOHN GRAHAM.

The earldom now reverted to the Lady Mary, the only child of Earl Alan. She had been brought up by her grand-uncle, Sir John Menteith of Rusky, and seems to have formed an enduring regard for that family. She was now about twenty-six years of age, and for the safety of her possessions in the disturbed state of the country it was necessary that she should have a husband to guard and protect them. Accordingly, she married in 1333 a gallant knight called Sir John Graham. The precise family of Grahams to which he belonged is uncertain, but he is supposed to have been a younger son of Sir Patrick Graham of Kincardine who was killed at Dunbar in 1296. If that were so, he must have been a man of mature years in 1333. As he was related to his wife "in the fourth degree of consanguinity," a papal dispensation had to be procured in order to legitimate the marriage already con-

[1] Wyntoun's Cronykil (edited by Laing), vol. ii. p. 388; Fordun (ed. Skene), vol. i. p. 354; and other authorities (Walsingham, Lanercost, Liber Pluscardensis).

tracted. Accordingly, a dispensation for the celebration of a new marriage was issued by Pope John XXIV. at Avignon on 1st May, 1334.[1] Sir John, in right of his wife, assumed the title of Earl of Menteith. He was one of the most distinguished soldiers of the time. In 1346, he went with King David II. on that invasion of England which resulted so disastrously. Had Menteith's advice been taken, the battle of Neville's Cross might have had a different issue. He entreated the King to allow him to charge the English archers in flank. "Give me but one hundred horse," he said, "and I will disperse them all." If David had but remembered the success of a similar movement in the battle of Bannockburn, he should have granted the request. But he refused. Menteith then attacked the archers at the head of his own followers. But they were too few to effect his purpose. His horse was shot under him, and with difficulty he was able to rejoin the main body.[2] The battle resulted in the slaughter of a great number of the Scottish soldiers, the capture of the King himself and many of his nobles—the Earl of Menteith among them. He was sent to the Tower of

---

[1] Theiner's Vetera Monumenta, No. 515, p. 262; the marriage appears to have been already contracted.

[2] The incident is thus described by Wyntoun :—

> Than gud Schyre Jhone the Grame can say
> To the Kyng, "Gettis me, but ma,
> Ane hundyre on hors wyth me to ga,
> And all yhone archerys skayle sall I:
> Swa sall we focht mare sykkerly."
> Thus spak he, bot he mycht get nane.
> His horse in hy than has he tane,
> And hym allane amang thame rade,
> And rwdly rwme about him made.
> Qwhen he a quhille had prekyd thare,
> And sum off thame had gert sow sare,
> He to the battaylis rade agayne.
> Sa fell it, that his hors bes slayne.
>
> —Wyntoun's Cronykil (ed. Laing), II. p. 475.

London. Orders arrived from Edward III., who was then at Calais, that the Earls of Menteith and Fife should be tried for treason. Instructions were also sent for the finding of the Court. Of course, a trial of this kind could have but one ending. The two earls were convicted, and condemned to be drawn, hanged, beheaded, and quartered, their heads to be placed on London Bridge, and the fragments of their bodies to be sent to York, Newcastle, Berwick, and Carlisle, there to hang in chains as a terror to the enemies of the King. The Earl of Fife, however, as a blood relation of the King, was spared; but in the case of Menteith no item in the horrible details of the brutal sentence was omitted. So, in the beginning of March, 1347, died this gallant soldier.

His widowed Countess remained in her island home, fully occupied with the composition of the family feuds that were raging in the neighbourhood,[1] and with the matrimonial alliances of her daughter. This daughter, Lady Margaret, was the only child of her marriage with Sir John Graham, and was born in 1334. As the heiress of an ancient and powerful earldom, she was no doubt a very interesting personage to the Scottish nobles of the time. She was, in fact, early and often married. The Popes—Clement VI. and Innocent VI.—had a good deal of business to do for her—no fewer than five papal dispensations having been granted for her four marriages.

The first of these marriages took place in 1348, when Lady Margaret had reached the age of fourteen years. Her husband was Sir John Moray, Lord of Bothwell, son

[1] See chap. xii.

of the brave and patriotic Sir Andrew Moray, who had been regent of Scotland in the minority of David II. Sir John lived but three years after his marriage, and died without issue. The Lady Margaret's widowhood was of short duration. An ardent wooer appeared in the person of Thomas, Earl of Mar, who, within six months after the death of Moray, obtained from Pope Clement VI. a dispensation for his union with the widow.[1] The document went astray, but the impatient Mar married without it, and then applied for a dispensation to have the union properly legalised. This was granted by Pope Innocent VI. in 1354.[2] But Mar's ardour did not endure. Scarcely had the papal dispensation arrived when he divorced his young wife—" at the instigation of the devil " *(instigante diabolo)*, says Fordun.[3] The Earl was the last male of his line, and was anxious for an heir; as no heir appeared, he got rid of his wife and married another— to be disappointed again, it may be added, and go to his grave without issue. The divorced wife—still little more than twenty years of age—returned to her mother and the solitudes of Menteith. The Countess Mary was then endeavouring, by every means in her power, to settle the bloody feud between the Menteiths and the Drummonds. With this end in view, she persuaded her daughter to marry the chief of the rival family, John Drummond of Concraig. This third husband was a man of much more mature years than his wife; for his daughter Annabella was already married to John Stewart, afterwards King

[1] At Avignon, 15th August, 1352.—Theiner's Vetera Monumenta, No. 601, p. 300.
[2] At Avignon, 29th May, 1354.   [3] Fordun a Laing, vol. i. p. 317.

Robert III.[1] The marriage took place in 1359, but it was discovered to be irregular, and a dispensation had to be obtained. This was granted by Innocent VI., in 1360, on the condition that the transgressors should erect and endow an altar in the Cathedral of Dunblane. As in this dispensation[2] Margaret is styled Countess of Menteith, it is not unlikely that her mother, in order the more strongly to commend the marriage to Drummond, demitted the earldom in favour of her daughter.[3] Not very long after this dispensation was received, John Drummond died—he does not seem to have taken the title of Earl of Menteith —and next year (1361) we find the Countess Margaret married for the fourth time. She was now twenty-six or twenty-seven years of age, and her matrimonial vicissitudes were at an end.

ROBERT STEWART, EARL OF MENTEITH, EARL OF FIFE, DUKE OF ALBANY.

The fourth husband was Robert Stewart, the third son of the Earl of Stratherne who became afterwards Robert II. This apparently was a marriage of political convenience, arranged between the parents. Not only, however, were the parties themselves connected by blood, but their relation-

---

[1] Drummond was doubly related to royalty, for besides being the father of Queen Annabella, he was the brother of Margaret Logie, the second wife of David II.

[2] Theiner's Vetera Monumenta, 640. The dispensation is dated 18th April, 1360. The marriage had taken place previously.

[3] In a charter granting the lands of Aberfoyle to John Drummond, the Lady Margaret is designed "Margaret of Moray, Countess of Menteith." Charter confirmed by David II. at Scone, 12th November, 1361. Printed in Red Book, vol. ii. p. 246.

ship was much complicated by the previous marriages of
the Countess, so that application had again to be made to
the Pope. Once more the dispensation was granted,[1] and
the grantees were ordered to found a chapel to the honour
of God in the city or diocese of Dunblane, and endow it
with an annuity of twelve marks of silver. On his marriage
Sir Robert Stewart took the style of Lord of Menteith;
and at the accession of his father to the throne (1370), he
was created Earl of Menteith. The Countess Margaret
lived to see her husband add the earldom of Fife to that
of Menteith. She did not, however, survive to see him
reach the higher dignity of Duke of Albany. She is
supposed to have died about 1380.

The earldom of Menteith had now come back again to
the Stewart family. Robert Stewart was the most famous
man who had ever held the dignity; but he is better
known to history by the titles of Earl of Fife and Duke
of Albany than by that of Earl of Menteith. His life and
achievements, moreover, belong rather to the history of
Scotland in general than to his special connection with
the district of Menteith, and need not here be narrated in
detail. We do not hear of his residing at Inchtalla,
although there are letters and deeds of his which are
dated from the Castle of Doune, which seems to have
been the principal messuage of the earldom during his
time, as it perhaps was in the case of some of the earlier
earls. The Castle of Falkland, however, was most frequently his place of residence.

[1] Dated 9th December, 1361.—Theiner's Vetera Monumenta, No. 645, p. 317.

He was born in 1339 or 1340, and was therefore about five years younger than his wife. Of his life previous to his marriage in 1361, nothing is known. In the Exchequer Rolls of 1364, he is designed simply Robert Stewart of Menteith.[1] As Lord of Menteith, he appeared in Parliaments held in 1367, 1368, and 1369.[2] His father was crowned at Scone as King Robert the Second on the 26th of March, 1371. That he was then created Earl of Menteith is inferred from the fact that, among the nobles who next day performed homage to the King, he is found under that designation. Why he had not assumed the title on his marriage with the Countess—as others had done in similar circumstances—is not clear; although it has been suggested that it might have been because of the jealousy with which David regarded the High Steward and his family.

Very soon after assuming the title, he added to his dignities and possessions the ancient earldom of Fife. Isabella, the widowed and childless Countess of Fife, entered into an agreement with him to the effect that, if he aided her to recover the earldom which she had been compelled to part with to others, she would resign it into the hands of the King for a regrant to be made to the Earl. In the indenture, which is dated 30th March, 1371,[3] the Countess recognised the Earl as her lawful heir, both by reason of the entail made by her father in favour of Alan, Earl of Menteith, the grandfather of the Countess

---

[1] Exchequer Rolls, vol. ii. p. 166.
[2] Acts of Parliaments of Scotland, i. pp. 501-507.
[3] This indenture is printed in Sibbald's History of Fife.

Margaret, and also because of the entail made by herself and her late husband, Walter Stewart, brother of the Earl of Menteith, in favour of the latter. That this agreement was carried out is shown by the fact of his witnessing a charter at Scone, 6th March, 1372, as Earl of Fife and Menteith. On the 4th of December, 1371, he had witnessed a royal confirmation at Dundonald as Earl of Menteith simply, so that the additional dignity must have been acquired between these dates. Fife, as the older dignity, thenceforth takes precedence of Menteith; and by the first title alone, in fact, he is generally known.

He was made keeper of the Castle of Stirling in 1373, and during his forty-seven years' tenure of that office he considerably strengthened the Castle.[1] In the same year, by a Grand Council of Parliament held at Scone, it was ordained that, failing John, Earl of Carrick, eldest son of King Robert, the succession to the throne should devolve on the second surviving son, the Earl of Fife and Menteith.[2] During the succeeding years Earl Robert was much with his father, who had great confidence in his business ability and activity. He received in consequence many grants of lands in various parts of the country, and other favours. He was made High Chamberlain of Scotland in 1382, and held the office till 1408, when he gave it over to his second son, the Earl of Buchan. His wife, the Lady Margaret Graham, must have died about 1383, and thereafter he married Muriella, daughter of Sir William

---

[1] Among other additions to the Castle, we learn from the Exchequer Rolls (iv. p. 164) that he built a chapel there.
[2] Acts of Parliaments of Scotland, vol. i. p. 549.

The Lake of Menteith.

Keith, Marischal of Scotland.[1] Towards the end of 1388, the King, feeling the infirmity of age, and knowing that his eldest son and heir apparent was physically disabled, submitted to his Council[2] a proposal that the Earl of Fife should be made Guardian of the Kingdom. And this was agreed to. When John, Earl of Carrick, ascended the throne, in 1390, as Robert III., the Earl of Fife still retained this position until at any rate 1392; that was the year in which the payment of his salary as Guardian ceased.

At a meeting of Parliament at Scone on the 28th of April, 1398, the Earl of Fife and Menteith was created by the King Duke of Albany, and at the same time his nephew, Prince David, Earl of Carrick and Athole, was created Duke of Rothesay. This is the first appearance of the title of Duke in the Scottish peerage. The ceremonies which took place at the investiture were on an elaborate and splendid scale. They are said[3] to have occupied fifteen days. Next year the Duke of Rothesay was appointed Lieutenant of the Kingdom for three years, with a Council of Advice, at the head of which was the Duke of Albany. The conduct of Rothesay in that position was such that the King, at the close of the period of office, wrote to Albany to have him arrested. This was done, and Rothesay was confined in the Castle of Falkland, where he died of

---

[1] Among the Stirling Charters is one granted by Robert, Duke of Albany, Earl of Fife and Menteith, and Governor of the Kingdom of Scotland, to St. Michael's Chapel "for the salvation of the souls of Margaret and Muriel, his wives." It is dated 26th June, 1407, and witnessed by (among others) Robert, son of Murdach, and grandson of the Duke.

[2] Held at Edinburgh, 1st December, 1388.   [3] Liber Pluscardensis, p. 332.

dysentery on the 26th of March, 1402. Pity for the untimely fate of the young Prince roused suspicions in the minds of the people, and a rumour got about that he had been starved to death by the instructions of his uncle Albany. These rumours in course of time crystallised into the well-known story related with circumstantial details by Bower.[1] At the request probably of Albany and the Earl of Douglas, brother-in-law of Rothesay—who were both implicated in the suspicion of foul play—an investigation was made by Parliament in 1402, with the result that the two nobles were pronounced innocent of the charge, and the Prince was declared to have died from natural causes.[2] This is likely enough to have been really the case, but the popular mind was never quite disabused of its suspicions.

After the expiry of the Lieutenancy of the Duke of Rothesay, and apparently before his death, Albany was appointed Governor of the Realm under the King. When Robert the Third, wasted with grief for the fate of Prince David, and heart-broken by the captivity of his only surviving son, the Prince James—who had been made prisoner by the English King, Henry IV., during a time of truce—sank under his misfortunes, and died on the 4th of April, 1406, Albany was chosen by the Estates[3] Governor of the Kingdom. This office he held till his death in 1420.[4]

---

[1] Scotichronicon, ii. p. 431. [2] Acts of Parliaments of Scotland, vol. i. p. 582.
[3] In a meeting held at Perth in June.—Wyntoun, bk. ix. ch. 26.
[4] Albany had a salary of £1000 as Governor (Exchequer Rolls, iv. pp. 152, 189, *et passim*), and an annuity of 200 merks as Keeper of Stirling Castle (*Ibid*, pp. 39, *et alia*). The resources of the earldom of Fife and Menteith have been estimated at £1200, and the whole income of the Regent at £2500—exclusive of certain allowances. See Introduction to the fourth volume of the Exchequer Rolls series by George Burnett, Lyon King at Arms.

Official Seal of Robert Duke of Albany.

This is not the place to narrate the events of that period. It is enough to say that, on the whole, he ruled well and wisely, and that the country enjoyed a measure of peace and made consequent progress during his government. All the time the Scottish Prince—and for a great portion of the time the Duke's own son, Murdach, also—

was a prisoner in England. It has been asserted that Albany made little effort for the release of his nephew, willing rather to leave him a prisoner so as to gratify his own ambition of ruling. But official documents show that throughout the whole long period of the captivity negotiations for the release of the Prince seldom ceased, although the English Kings, while plausible enough in their communications with the Scottish Governor, resolutely stuck to their prize. There are not wanting indications, however, that the Prince himself was not convinced of the sincerity of his uncle's desires for his release, and this may have been one of the causes of his otherwise inexplicable severity to the family of Albany when he did return to his kingdom.

Bower states that Albany died on the 30th of September, 1419, but the correct date must be put a year later. The Exchequer accounts show that he was alive in July, 1420,[1] and he granted a charter at Falkland on the 4th August of the same year.[2] He was thus over eighty years of age at his death. He was buried in Dunfermline Abbey. His widow, the Duchess Muriella, survived till 1449—the Exchequer Rolls show that a pension of £66 13s 4d annually was paid to her from 1428 to 1449.[3] He had a family of four sons and six daughters. Murdach, the eldest of his family and the only son of Countess Margaret, succeeded his father. John, the eldest son of Muriella, was that gallant Earl of Buchan, the Constable of France, who was slain at Verneuil, 18th August, 1424. The third

---

[1] Exchequer Rolls, iv. p. 310.   [2] Reg. Mag. Sig. lib. iii., No. 81.
[3] Exchequer Rolls, vol. iv.; accounts for those years.

son, Andrew, died in 1413. Robert, the fourth son, is known to have been alive in 1431.

It was recently the fashion among Scottish historians to decry the character of the Duke of Albany. He has been spoken of as cowardly, crafty, cruel, cold-blooded, unscrupulous, and selfishly ambitious. The earlier historians, Bower and Wyntoun,[1] on the other hand, refer to him in terms of the highest praise. As these historians, although contemporary in their lives with Albany, wrote after his death, they could have been under no temptation to colour their estimates in his favour. Rather, considering the conduct of James I. and his obvious ill-feeling towards his uncle's family, they might have been expected to say as little in his praise as they possibly could. Their testimony, in the circumstances, must be held therefore as strongly in his favour.

MURDACH STEWART, DUKE OF ALBANY, EARL OF FIFE AND OF MENTEITH.

Robert Stewart was succeeded in his dignities by his eldest son, Murdach, who thus became the second Duke of Albany, as well as Earl of Fife and of Menteith. Murdach was the son of Lady Margaret, and was born probably in 1362. In 1389 he was appointed, by Robert III., Justiciar of Scotland north of the Forth.[2] In one of the documents issued in his justiciarship, he is designed Lord of Apthane,[3]

---

[1] Scotichronicon, lib. xv. c. 37. Wyntoun (Cronykil, lib. ix. c. 26) calls him "a mirror of honour and of honesty."

[2] Acts of the Parliaments of Scotland, vol. i. p. 557.

[3] He received the *Abthania* of Dull—or rather £136 as an equivalent for its revenues—from his father.—Exchequer Rolls, vol. iv., Introd.

but, in most of them, his style is Lord Kinclevin, and that was generally his title during his father's lifetime.[1] In pursuance of a treaty made between his father and Duncan, Earl of Lennox, at Inchmurrin in Lochlomond (17th February, 1392), he married Isabella, the eldest daughter and heir of Lennox.[2]

He was taken prisoner by the English in the battle of Homildon, 14th September, 1402, and underwent a long captivity in England. Notwithstanding repeated embassies and negotiations for his release, he did not receive his freedom till the year 1416, when he was exchanged for the young Earl of Northumberland, who had been long held prisoner in Scotland.[3]

After his return he was appointed lieutenant to his father the Governor, and when the latter died in 1420, he succeeded him in his high office. It is more than likely that he was appointed to the office by Parliament, but there is no extant documentary evidence to that effect.[4] He was fifty-eight years of age when he assumed the Governorship in succession to his father, and, if we are to credit the statement of the contemporary historian Bower, he did not hold the reins with the same firm hand as his predecessor.[5] He was troubled also, it appears, by the disobedience and turbulence of his sons. But his tenure

---

[1] A charter of Robert Duke of Albany, granting an annual rent to the chaplain of St. Michael's Chapel in the Castle of Stirling (dated at Perth, 26th June, 1407), is witnessed by "Robert Steward, eldest son of our dearest son and heir, *Murdach Steward, Knight.*" But this was during Murdach's captivity in England. See Stirling Charters, p. 29.

[2] Fraser's The Lennox, vol. ii. p. 43.   [3] Rotuli Scotiæ, p. 214.

[4] He succeeded his father also as Keeper of Stirling Castle, and drew the allowance for that office—200 merks.—Exchequer Rolls, iv. 338, &c.

[5] Scotichronicon (Goodall), ii. 467.

of the government was not destined to be long. Negotiations were resumed for the release of King James, and, after many delays, resulted at last in the return of the King in the beginning of the year 1424.

One of the first acts of the King, on arriving at Edinburgh in April of that year, was to arrest Sir Walter Stewart, the eldest surviving son of Duke Murdach, and to send him prisoner to the Bass.[1] Two other barons were arrested at the same time. For what reason these arrests were made is not by any one stated.

At the coronation of the King and Queen at Scone, on the 21st of May, 1424, the King was placed in the royal chair by Duke Murdach, in virtue of the ancient privilege of the Earls of Fife; and at the same time his son, Alexander Stewart, received the honour of knighthood from the King.[2] This did not look as if James was bent on the destruction of the House of Albany. But the storm soon burst. Later in the year the Earl of Lennox, Albany's father-in-law, was seized and committed to prison. And in the month of March next year, while a meeting of the Estates was being held at Perth, the King ordered the arrest of Duke Murdach himself,[3] his secretary, and his son Alexander, the recently made knight. Only one of Albany's family, his second surviving son James, eluded the King, and after several exciting adventures, found refuge in England, and finally in Ireland.[4] The Duke's castles of

[1] Walter Stewart was arrested on the 13th of May, 1424.—Scotichronicon, lib. xvi. c. 9; Exchequer Rolls, iv. 386.
[2] Fordun a Goodall, vol. ii. p. 482. [3] On the 14th March, 1425.
[4] A safe conduct to Ireland was granted to James Stewart by Henry VI., 10th May, 1429.—Rotuli Scotiæ, ii. p. 265.

Falkland and Doune were seized. In the latter was found the Duchess Isabella, who was sent, with the other prisoners, to St. Andrews Castle. Afterwards she was transferred to Tantallon Castle, while her husband was sent to Caerlaverock, where he was confined in a portion of the castle known thereafter as Murdach's Tower.

The local traditions differ as to the scene of Duke Murdach's capture. One places it at a spot still called by the name of Murdach's Ford, on the old road between Doune and Dunblane, where a small stream is crossed by the road, not far from the farm of Anchors Cross, and about a mile from the town of Dunblane; while a second legend affirms that he was taken from his castle on Dundochill, a small island in Loch Ard.[1] Both traditions are probably in error. He and the others appear to have been seized while attending the Parliament at Perth.

After these arrests the Parliament was adjourned, to meet again at Stirling on the 18th of May. The first of the captives to be brought to trial was Walter Stewart, who was convicted and executed on the 24th of the month. Next day witnessed the trial, conviction, and execution of the Duke of Albany, his son, Sir Alexander Stewart, and his father-in-law, the Earl of Lennox. Five persons of subordinate rank, who had been engaged with James Stewart in his attack on Dumbarton Castle, were, at the

---

[1] The foundations of a strong building, locally called Murdach's Castle, can still be traced on this island, and the people of the district say that it was built by this Duke of Albany as a residence. It seems too small, however, for that purpose; but it may have been a hunting seat or tower of refuge for some of the earlier Earls of Menteith. There were earlier Murdachs among them.

same time, put to death with horrible tortures.[1] The execution of the Albanies took place on what is known as the Heading Hill, the northernmost spur of the ridge that runs out from the Castle rock of Stirling. From here, as Sir Walter Scott has said, the Duke might see the towers of the Castle of Doune, in which he had been wont to live in princely state.[2] The bodies of the unfortunate victims of the royal severity were interred in the Church of the Dominican Friars, on the south side of the great altar.

The nature of the charges made against the Albanies has not been preserved. Walter Stewart is stated in the Scotichronicon[3] to have been indicted for robbery (*de roborea*), but in what instance or instances is not stated. It is obvious that James had resolved on the extermination of the family, but why must remain an unsolved problem. Certain expressions in recently published letters of his lead us to think that he did not believe the late Duke of Albany had done all he might have done to obtain his restoration,

---

[1] According to the Scotichronicon (vol. ii. p. 483), they were torn to pieces by horses, and the mutilated fragments of their bodies suspended on gibbets.

[2] According to Sir Walter Scott, the name of Gowlan Hills—as he calls the knolls to the north of the Castle—originated in the lamentation (*Scottice, gowling*) made by the populace and onlookers at the time of this execution. This popular etymology, however, must be taken with caution. The Scottish people have never at any time been demonstrative in the expression of their griefs; and at that period scenes of cruelty were not so uncommon as to have been likely to move them to tears and lamentation. If Gowlan was the original in use before any local records that have been preserved, it perhaps represents the Gaelic "guallan" (*i.e.*, shoulder), a word which aptly enough designates the topographical relation of the hills to the Castle rock. But the name of the hills in the Burgh Records is invariably written *Gowane* (or *Govane*)—the form still in common use—never *Gowlan*. Against this can only be set the monkish *montes dolorum*, and the occurrence of *Gowlan* once, at least, in the Kirk Session Records of the seventeenth century.

[3] Cupar MS. quoted in Fordun (Goodall), vol. ii. p. 483, *note*.

and he may have cherished a suspicion that the family had purposed to supplant him on the throne. Or the popular opinion of the time, as expressed in a contemporary account of the murder of James I., quoted by Pinkerton,[1] may not be far from the truth—" the people ymagynd that the Kyng did rather that vigorious execucion upon the Lordes of his kyne, for the covetise of thare possessions and goodes, thane for any other rightfull cause, althofe he fonde colourabill wais to serve his entent yn the contrarye."

Murdach and his sons were men of tall stature[2] and splendid presence, and the Earl of Lennox was a venerable man of eighty years of age. Moreover, the Duke had been an easy-going ruler, and was popular with all classes, while his son Walter was a general favourite. Among the people, therefore, their fate was greatly lamented; and, if the King imagined that, by this instance of inflexible severity, he would strike terror into the hearts of the haughty and turbulent nobles, his hopes were disappointed. He succeeded only in inspiring some of them with a spirit of hatred and revenge, which issued some years later in his own assassination (1436).

The possessions of the Duke of Albany were forfeited, and the earldoms of Fife and Menteith now came into the hands of the King. Of the sons of the Duke, Robert, the eldest, had died without issue before 1421, Walter and Alexander perished with their father in 1425, and James, surnamed *More*, was outlawed, and died in Ireland in 1451. His daughter, Isabella, married Sir Walter Buchanan of Buchanan.

[1] Pinkerton's History, vol. i., appendix, p. 453.
[2] Homines giganteæ staturæ.—Fordun (Goodall) ii. p. 483.

CHAPTER IX.

Sir John Menteith and the Capture of Sir William Wallace.

"The fause Menteith."

"Rycht suth it is, a martyr was Wallace."

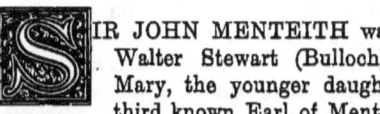IR JOHN MENTEITH was the second son of Walter Stewart (Bulloch), who had married Mary, the younger daughter of Maurice, the third known Earl of Menteith, and in right of his wife, had succeeded to the earldom.[1] Sir John, therefore, though he is always known as Menteith, or de Menteith, was by birth a Stewart of the family from which came the Kings of Scotland. The date of his birth may be placed some time between 1260 and 1265. He had, at any rate, arrived at manhood in 1286, when he was a party to a bond entered into by the Earl of Dunbar and his sons, Walter Stewart, Earl of Menteith, and his sons (Alexander and *John*), Robert Bruce, Lord of Annandale, and his sons, and other noblemen, to adhere to the party of Richard de Burgh, Earl of Ulster, and Sir Thomas de Clare. This bond, which was entered into a few months after the

---

[1] See *supra*, p. 224.

death of Alexander III., was in effect an agreement to support the claim of Bruce to the throne.[1]

When Baliol attempted to throw off the yoke of Edward, Sir John of Menteith was one of his supporters. He and his elder brother Alexander—who had by this time become Earl of Menteith—were in the Scottish army that was routed at Dunbar on the 28th of April, 1296, and were both made prisoners on that occasion.[2] He remained in captivity in England—first at Nottingham, afterwards at Winchilsea—for over a year, but he secured his liberation and the restoration of his lands in Scotland by agreeing to serve King Edward in his French wars. The expedition, on which he bound himself to serve, sailed for France on the 22nd August, 1297, and returned in March, 1298. The probability is that after having fulfilled the conditions of his liberation by serving on this expedition, he returned as soon as possible to Scotland; but there is no authentic evidence by which his movements at this time can be traced.

On reaching his native land, he did not long remain faithful to the interests of the English King. The statement that he accompanied Wallace and Sir John Graham on a punitive expedition against the men of Galloway in the month of August, 1298, rests on the authority of the *Relationes Arnaldi Blair*.[3] But we have the more certain

---

[1] It is dated at Turnberry, Carrick, 20th September, 1286.—Hist. Doc. Scot., vol. i. p. 22.

[2] Calendar of Documents relating to Scotland, vol. ii. No. 742.

[3] These Relationes consist of extracts from the Scotichronicon. The particular passage referred to here is not found in the edition of Fordun and Bower's work published *cura* Goodall, but it is supposed to have been part of one of the two missing chapters in book xi., the writer of which book was Bower, not Fordun. See also Balfour's Annals, vol. i. p. 84, where the same statement regarding Menteith is made.

authority of the public documents that he was at this time and later a member of the patriotic party opposed to the supremacy of Edward. In a communication to Edward, of date October, 1301, he is designated "The adversary of the King."[1] And the King's adversary he continued for some time longer to be.

The next glimpse we have of him in the historic scene may be regarded as characteristic both of his own disposition and of his attitude towards the troubles of his country. In September, 1303, he made his appearance at Berwick, along with Sir Alexander Meyners, to negotiate a truce with the English. But when he saw the state of destitution to which the Irish troops serving in the English army were reduced, he refused to proceed with the negotiations, thinking, no doubt, that starvation would soon drive them from the country. He was evidently willing to be on the patriotic side so long as it appeared to have any chance of success. These chances of success, however, seemed to disappear when the army of the Regent Comyn was defeated by Edward on the banks of the Forth at Stirling in December, 1303. The result of this defeat was the submission of the whole of the Scottish nobles and barons to the English King, save only two. Wallace and Sir

---

[1] Calendar of Doc., vol. ii. p. 437, No. 1255. This seems to give some confirmation to the statement of Blind Harry that Menteith, some time after the battle of Stirling, joined the party of Wallace. Harry's authority—especially in regard to dates—is not to be implicitly trusted, unless confirmed from other evidences; but his words—if we may venture to quote a writer whom Lord Hailes said everybody refers to but no one ventures to quote—are as follows :—

"Schir Jhon Menteith was than off Aran lord,
Till Wallace come, and maid a playne record :
With witnes thar be his ayth he him band,
Lants to kep to Wallace and to Scotland."

—Schir William Wallace, by Henry the Minstrel, Scottish Text Society Edition, book vii., 1200.

Simon Fraser alone held out; but the latter was compelled at length to give way, and Wallace was left alone, irreconcilable, and marked for death by his implacable enemy.

Menteith was, of course, one of the barons who gave in their submission to Edward, and he seems to have been speedily taken into favour by that monarch. Within three months of his submission he was formally entrusted with the custody of the Castle, town, and Sheriffdom of Dumbarton. The grant, which is dated at St. Andrews, 20th March, 1304,[1] was probably a renewal, under the authority of the English King, of offices formerly held by him in the Scottish interest.

And now we come to the event in the life of Sir John Menteith which has lived in the memory of his countrymen while all his other doings have been forgotten, and which—whether it was after all an evil but necessary consequence of the office he held rather than the result of a covetous and treacherous character—has branded him as the representative traitor in the estimation of the Scottish people, and left his name to be execrated by them from that time to the present.

So determined was King Edward on the capture of Wallace that he not only set a price upon the head of the patriot, but issued the most stringent orders to the captains of his forces and the Governors of the Castles and towns to be constantly on the watch to seize him. He even made this capture a condition of the restitution of their estates to the barons who had given in their submission to his will; so that not only Menteith but

[1] Hist. Doc. Scot., vol. ii. p. 474.

many others were interested in the capture of the hero.[1] Besides all this, he offered bribes to certain persons to undertake the enterprise. Ralph de Haliburton, one of the prisoners taken from Stirling Castle on the fall of that fortress, was sent to Scotland, under the charge of Sir John Mowbray, with instructions to search for Wallace and effect his capture. It is not clear what share, if any, these two had in the event. Neither is it quite certain who it was that actually discovered the hiding-place of Wallace and betrayed him to Menteith. Blind Harry attributes the treachery to a young man, a relative of Sir John, and engaged by the latter for the purpose.[2] Langtoft[3] says that a servant, to whom he gives the name of " Jack Short," was the traitor, and that, acting on his information, Menteith came and seized Wallace when in bed. The popular imagination, as represented by the minstrel, has added numerous romantic incidents, that all tend to deepen the stain of the treachery. These need not be mentioned here. They are in want of confirmation. So also is the statement made by other Scottish writers that Wallace finally surrendered to Sir John only on a promise that he was to be secretly set at liberty, and that it was necessary to submit to being made a prisoner temporarily that his life might be saved from the overwhelming English force by which he was surrounded. It is not necessary to believe all these things. But, after all, the fact remains, proved by historical evidence, that it was Menteith who was

[1] Palgrave's Historical Documents relating to Scotland, p. 276.
[2] " His syster son."—Schir William Wallace, &c., xi. 950.
[3] Langtoft Chron., p. 329.

responsible for the capture of the hero, and also that treachery of some sort—whether directly arranged by him or not—was employed in the capture. The most trustworthy historians, both English and Scottish, who wrote most shortly after the event, leave no doubt of this.[1] It is no less certain that he was rewarded by the English King for his share in this business. In a memorandum of the English Council, quoted in Palgrave's Historical Documents,[2] mention is made of 40 marks "to be given to the valet who spied out William Waleys," of 60 marks to be divided among others who were present, and "a hundred livres for John of Menteth." And he had other rewards. He was chosen a Scottish Commissioner by Edward, and was accordingly one of the ten Scottish representatives who met in the Union Parliament at Westminster in September, 1305. He was made one of the Council of the Royal Guardian of Scotland (Sir John de Bretagne),[3] and he was continued in the office of Sheriff and keeper of the Castle of Dumbarton. In 1306, Edward still further marked his high satisfaction with his conduct by giving him the ward of the Castle and Sheriffdom for life; and in June of the same year he conferred on him the earldom of Lennox.[4]

Next year, after the death of Edward I., we find his son and successor, Edward II., communicating with

[1] Chronicle of Lanercost; Wyntoun's Cronykil; Fordun and Bower's Scotichronicon; The Arundel MS.; The Scala Chronica, &c. The words of Fordun are quite distinct: "In the year 1305 William Wallace was craftily and treacherously (*fraudulenter et proditionaliter*) taken by John of Menteith, who handed him over to the King of England."—Historians of Scotland: Fordun, ed. Skene, vol. ii. p. 332.

[2] Palgrave's Hist. Doc., p. 295. [3] *Ibid*, p. 305. [4] *Ibid*, p. 293.

Menteith as Earl of Lennox, and "one of his faithful in Scotland."[1] This faith, however, he did not long retain. The fortunes of Robert Bruce were rising, and Sir John went over to his side. His name is found among those attached to the answer sent by the Scottish nobles, who acknowledged Bruce as their King, to the message in which the King of France recognised his sovereignty. This letter was drawn up at St. Andrews, 16th March, 1308.[2] Thereafter he seems to have been as much in the confidence of Bruce as he had formerly been in that of the English Kings. He had now, however, to drop his claim to the earldom of Lennox, for Malcolm, the real Earl, was one of King Robert's most intimate friends. Possibly his tenure of the earldom had been but a shadow; at any rate, he does not appear to have made any difficulty in surrendering it. He seems even to have been on friendly terms with Earl Malcolm. In the year 1309 he was one of the Commissioners appointed on behalf of King Robert to treat for a peace with the Earl of Ulster, the English Commissioner.

From this time to his death there are but few notices of Menteith in the records. The story of his attempted treachery to Robert Bruce in the Castle of Dumbarton, narrated by Bower,[3] and more circumstantially by Buchanan, is probably mere legend. He was pardoned by the King, says Buchanan, on condition that he should take his place in the front of the battle at Bannockburn, and

[1] Rymer's Fœdera, ii. 22.
[2] Acts of the Parliaments of Scotland, vol. i. p. 289.
[3] Scotichronicon, lib. xii. cap. 16 and 17. These two chapters are omitted from some of the MSS.; but are to be found in those of Cupar, Perth, and Dunblane.

R

there await the issue. "There," says the historian, "the man, otherwise treacherous, served the King faithfully, and behaved with so much bravery, that by his exertions that day he not only procured pardon for his former deeds, but even an ample reward for his conduct."[1] It will be observed that in this story Buchanan makes it a condition of Sir John's pardon that he should take his place in the Scottish ranks at Bannockburn. The inference therefore is that the date of the treachery of Dumbarton was immediately or, at the most, shortly before that battle. But it has been shown that Menteith was in favour with Bruce some years previous to the fight at Bannockburn. An entry in the Chartulary of Dunfermline shows that he was with King Robert in the neighbourhood of Stirling in November of 1313, seven months before the battle.[2] That Menteith fought at Bannockburn is likely enough, although there is no certain evidence to that effect. That he was much engaged thereafter in public affairs and much in the confidence of his sovereign, is manifest from the little we do know of his later life. He is said—on somewhat doubtful authority—to have accompanied Edward Bruce on his expedition to Ireland in 1315. If that were so, he did not remain till the end of that unfortunate adventure, for in 1316 he was sent, along with Sir Thomas Randolph, on a special mission to Ireland.[3] He was one

---

[1] Aikman's Translation of Buchanan's History, vol. i. p. 428.

[2] Sir John Menteith was witness to a charter of King Robert, dated at Cambuskenneth, 14th November, 1313, by which the King granted to the Church of Dunfermline the Church of Kinross and Chapel of Orwell.— Registrum de Dunfermleyne.

[3] Rhymer's Fœdera, ii. 302.

of the Scottish barons who subscribed the famous Memorial to the Pope, dated at Aberbrothock, 6th April, 1320, in which they vindicated the right of their country to independence, and declared their resolution to maintain it.[1] He signs this letter in the style of Guardian of the earldom of Menteith. Although Murdach was at this time earl, he was holding the title only temporarily with the consent of the Lady Mary, daughter of the late Earl Alan, who was under the guardianship of her father's uncle, Sir John Menteith. The latest public act of his of which we have any notice was in 1323, when, in company with Randolph, Earl of Moray, the Bishop of St. Andrews, and Sir Robert Lauder, he went to Newcastle and negotiated a truce for thirteen years with the English King.[2] He probably did not long survive this last national service. He certainly died before King Robert.[3]

Sir John Menteith, besides possessing the lands of Rusky, seems also to have inherited as his portion of his father's earldom, the lands of Arran and Knapdale. He had two sons and two daughters. The eldest son, Sir John, is styled Lord of Arran and Knapdale, and so is his son—also a Sir John. With the third John, the direct line of descent ended. Rusky was inherited by the second son, Sir Walter. The direct Rusky line of descent terminated in the fourth generation in two heiresses—Agnes Menteith, who married, 1460 or 1461, John Haldane of

[1] Fordun a Goodall, vol. ii. p. 277; and Anderson's Diplomata Scotiæ, where a *facsimile* of the document is given, plate li.; Acts of the Parliament of Scotland, vol. i. p. 291.
[2] Rymer's Fœdera, ii. 521; Acts of Parliaments of Scotland, i. 479.
[3] Robertson's Index to Missing Charters, p. 18.

Gleneagles, and Elizabeth, who married, much about the same time, John Napier of Merchiston. Between these the estates of Rusky were divided. Collateral branches of the family are descended from John, the second son of Sir Walter Menteith of Rusky.

Sir John Menteith was obviously an able man of affairs, and, not less clearly, a valiant soldier. If his steady patriotism is not so evident, it can at the least be said that in this respect he was only a fair representative of the Scottish nobility of that period, whose allegiance seems to have varied with what they considered their personal interests. Unfortunately, however, for his reputation with posterity, it was into his hands that the national hero was betrayed; and, when we consider the passionate devotion of the Scottish people to the memory of Wallace, there is scarcely room for wonder that the name of Menteith should have come down in the traditions of the country as that of the greatest traitor in the national history *(immanis proditor)*. He had certainly once fought on the same side with Wallace in the national wars, and there is therefore no inherent improbability in the statement made by Scottish writers that he was acquainted and even friendly with the hero. It is not, however, necessary to believe that they were on the terms of close intimacy implied in the repeated statement of Blind Harry that Wallace had been Menteith's "gossip,"[1] *i.e.*, the god-

---

[1] "Schyr Jhon Menteth Wallace his *gossop* was."
—Henry the Minstrel, xi. 795.

"Twys befor he had his *gossop* been."
—*Ibid*, viii. 1598.

"For cowatice, Menteth, apon fals wys
Betrayeit Wallace, at was his *gossop* twys."
—*Ibid*, xi. 847-8.

father of one or more of his children: even although Blind Harry is, in this instance, supported by the authority of John Major—a historian who is careful to guard himself against being supposed to give unlimited credit to Henry's writings. Major affirms that the greatest intimacy was supposed to exist between Wallace and Menteith,[1] and distinctly says that Wallace had been godfather to Menteith's two children. The statement therefore may be taken, not as a gratuitous invention of the blind minstrel, but as the common belief. There is no nearly contemporary evidence, however, in proof. It may have been merely one of those figments by which the popular imagination endeavoured to deepen the baseness of the treachery.[2]

The popular feeling of later times against Menteith fails to take into account the character, morally and politically, of the period in which and the men among whom he lived. He does not appear to have been worse than the other Scottish nobles of the time. They took oaths and broke them with the same facility. Their country was little to them; their own interests were everything. They were all equally bound by Edward, as a condition of their personal safety and security of their estates, to hunt down the outlawed patriot, and it need not be doubted that the most of them would have been glad enough to commend themselves to the favour of Edward by the capture. Neither must it be forgotten that, for the time, Menteith was an

---

[1] Ipsi Vallaceo putatus amicissimus.—Major, De Gestis Scotorum, lib. iv. ch. 15.
[2] The fact that Menteith *had* two sons may be held as accounting for, although it does not justify the belief, or prove the statement.

English officer, in the pay of the English King—however little that may say for his patriotism. But to him—and not to any of the others who were engaged in the search— it fell to apprehend Wallace, and that under circumstances in which treachery (whether directly concocted by him or not) was undoubtedly involved, and his memory has had to bear the odium. That his conduct was not reckoned unpardonable, or even disgraceful, by his fellows at the time is evident—however curious it may seem to us now—from the way in which he was received into favour by King Robert the Bruce. Under that King he did good service to his country, as the notes regarding his later career, which have been given above, will show. Blind Harry has been accused of originating the feeling of abhorence with which Menteith has so long been regarded by his countrymen. But that is not so. He had been denounced by Scottish, and even English, writers before the time of the Minstrel. In fact, the latter is the only early Scottish writer who exhibits any feeling of tenderness for Menteith. He represents him as not entirely lost to honour. In the interview with Sir Aymer de Vallance, he makes Sir John say that it would be a "foul outrage" to sell the patriot, and he represents him as consenting to effect his capture only on the assurance that the life of Wallace would be spared and his person kept in safety.[1]

The popular estimate of the character of Menteith, and the detestation of the treachery which led to the capture of Wallace, was formed long before Blind Harry's time. For example, the persistent tradition of the district is that

[1] See book xi. 809, *et seqq.*

when the Drummonds attacked the Menteiths at the Tar of Rusky,[1] and slew three of their chiefs, they were urged by the desire to avenge the perfidy of Sir John on his descendants, and eager to exterminate the whole hated race. That may not have been the real reason of the attack, but the tradition is a very old one—older possibly than Blind Harry, who was not born till more than a century after the fight of Rusky.

There is a curious legend, referred to by Sir Walter Scott, regarding the signal that was made for setting on Wallace as he sat or lay in the cottage at Robroyston in fancied security, and all unwitting of treachery. It affirms that when arrangements had been completed for surrounding the cottage with the soldiers of Menteith, the domestic traitor—Jack Short, Menteith's nephew, or whoever he was—was to watch the time when the hero was quite off his guard and had laid aside his arms, and then to give a silent signal to his confederates by turning upside down a loaf which had been laid on the table. There must, by this account, have been more than one traitor within the hut, or the operation must have been watched from the outside, through the door or the window.

The story is not a very likely one in itself, and is not found in any reputable author—not even in Blind Harry. In fact, the Minstrel's account represents the traitor, Menteith's nephew, as waiting till Wallace and his faithful friend, Kerle, were fast asleep, and then going out to inform his uncle of the fact. The circumstance, however,

---

[1] For this fight and its consequences see *infra*, chap. xii.

that the traitor is represented as a "cuk" (cook), may have given some countenance to the tradition, or even originated it. Purely legendary as it is, the story long continued to live, and nowhere more vigorously than in the country of the Menteiths, where it was employed by jealous neighbours as a means of annoying those of the name.

Sir Walter says that "in after times it was reckoned ill-breeding to turn a loaf in that manner, if there was a person named Menteith in company; since it was as much as to remind him that his namesake had betrayed Sir William Wallace, the champion of Scotland."[1] To "whummle the bannock"—as the performance was called in the vernacular—before a Menteith was regarded as offering him a deadly insult. Till not so very long ago, it used to be resorted to when the intention was, either in joke or seriously, to irritate a person of that name—sometimes with unpleasant results to the practical joker. A local writer of about forty years since[2] asserts that even in his own time he had known a fiery Menteith take signal vengeance on one who had dared to "whummle the bannock" before him.

The tradition is now dead in the country of the Menteiths. The stranger may "whummle the bannock"—even in the presence of a Menteith, should he happen to meet one, for the name is now rare in their old country—without any fear of consequences. The action will not likely be regarded as having any significance whatever.

[1] Scott's Tales of a Grandfather, second series, chap. vii., *sub finem*.
[2] Dun's Summer at the Lake of Menteith, p. 26.

It must be added, however, that the feeling of hatred against Sir John Menteith has not yet been eradicated from the heart of the Scottish people. It will probably continue to exist as long as the memory of Wallace is cherished by his countrymen.

Sir John's Castle of Rusky has already been noticed. Tradition avers that he died there, and was buried in the Priory of Inchmahome; but no stone marks the place of his interment. There is no evidence in support of the statement, unless we regard the fact that his father was buried there as rendering it not unlikely.

CHAPTER X.

The First Six Earls of Menteith of the Name of Graham: 1427-1597.

"The gallant Grahams."

"A race renowned of old,
Whose war-cry oft has waked the battle-swell,
Since first distinguished in the onset bold,
Wild sounding when the Roman rampart fell."

AFTER the death of Murdach, Duke of Albany, the earldom of Menteith was in possession of the Crown till 1427, when it was granted by James I. to Malise Graham, in compensation for the earldom of Strathern, of which he had some time previously been deprived by the King on the ground that it was a male fief. The new earldom of Menteith did not, however, comprise the whole of the ancient possessions. James I. reserved to the Crown the eastern part of the old earldom, with its messuage of Doune Castle, and thus formed what was called the Stewartry of Menteith. The charter of erection of the new earldom—dated at Edinburgh, 6th September, 1427—enumerates the lands included in it. These may be said generally to extend from the lake of Menteith westwards.[1] As the Castle of Doune, along with the eastern lands, thus became the property of the Crown, Inchtalla became the residence of the earls, and the Lake of Menteith and its Islands were more closely connected with these Graham earls than with their predecessors. There they resided for more than two centuries and a half, great men in their own country-side, and gallant fighters all of them, although not—with one or two notable exceptions—conspicuous in the history of the country.

MALISE, FIRST EARL.

Seal of Malise Graham, First Earl of Menteith.

Malise Graham was related to the royal family on both sides of his descent. His father, Sir Patrick Graham, son

[1] The lands of Craynis Easter and Craynis Wester, Craguthy Easter and Wester, lands of Glasswerde, Drumlaen, Ladarde, Blareboyane, Gartnerthynach, Blareruscanys, Foreste of Baith the Sidis of Lochcon, lands of Blaretuchane and of Marduffy, of Culyngarth, Frisefleware, Rose with the Cragmuk, Inchere, Gartinhagel, Bobfresle, Bovento, Downans and Baleth, Tereochane, Drumboy, Crancafy, Achray, Glassel and Cravaneculy, Savnach, Brigend, Lonanys and Garquhat, Drumanust, Schanghil, Ernetly and Monybrachys, Gartmulne and Ernomul, Ernecomy, Achmore, the Porte and the Insche with their pertinents. No mention is made of any castle or dwelling, so that the buildings on Inchtalla were probably not in use—if they existed—at this time. (Charter printed in Red Book of Menteith, vol. ii. p. 293).

Sir Patrick Graham of Kincardine, by Egidia, niece of
Robert II., married the Princess Euphemia, daughter of
David, Earl Palatine of Strathern, eldest son of Robert's
second marriage. Malise was therefore a great-grandson
of King Robert the Second. He was but a youth when
he was denuded of the earldom of Strathern by the King,
and he could scarcely have reached his majority when he
received the grant of the new earldom of Menteith. There
is ground for believing that even after recieving the
earldom he did not for some years, at any rate, enjoy
the revenues. Within two months—in November, 1427—
he was sent to England as one of the hostages in security
for the payment of the King's ransom. And the Exchequer
Rolls show that the rents of the earldom were in the hands
of the King up till 1434[1] at least. In England Malise
remained for a quarter of a century, and married there.
He obtained his release, 17th June, 1453, only on the
condition that his eldest son, Alexander, should take his
place as hostage. Alexander accordingly went to England,
and never came back from his exile.

Earl Malise, after his return, was a fairly regular attender
at meetings of Parliament, but was never very prominent
in their business.[2] He seems to have been a favourite with
James III., who, on the 8th of February, 1466, granted
him a charter erecting the town of Port into a burgh of
barony, "for the singular favour which we bear towards

[1] Exchequer Rolls, vol. iv. pp. 530, 560, 589, &c. These accounts give the names of the various *camerarii* of Menteith, from Patrick Don in 1431 onwards.

[2] He was present in the Parliament of 1455 when the Douglasses were declared traitors by John II., and he appended his seal to the instrument of forfeiture.—Acts of Parliament, ii. 75, &c.

our beloved cousin Malise, Earl of Menteith, and for making provision for ourselves and our lieges, in the highland of Menteith, in the time of the huntings and at other times."[1] There were royal forests and hunting lodges both at Glenfinlas and at Duchray,[2] and it was while making their way to the latter forest especially that the royal hunting parties would require accommodation at Port of Menteith. He remained faithful to James III. in the rebellion which led to the death of that King and the establishment of his son, James IV., on the throne. Old as he was, he raised his men and went to the assistance of his King, and, in the battle of Sauchie, held the command of the men of Stirlingshire and the West, who formed the rear division of the royal army.[3] He did not long survive the King—dying probably in 1490, after holding the earldom for more than sixty years.

He was twice married. About the identity of both wives there is considerable dubiety. The first wife was married in England, and was therefore most likely an English lady. By some writers she has been called Anne Vere, daughter of the Earl of Oxford, or Jana Rochford. Mr. Graham Easton names her "Lady Jana de Vere, daughter of Aubrey, tenth Earl of Oxford."[4] In the Protocol Books

---

[1] Charter printed in Red Book, ii. p. 297.

[2] In the Exchequer Rolls are notes of sums paid for building a hall and chambers at Glenfinlas in 1459 (vi. p. 579), and for repairing the hunting lodge at Duchray in 1469 (vii. p. 614) The fermes of the lands of Duchray were assigned to the King in 1461 (vii. p. 62). Donald Neyssoune was the royal forester of Menteith in 1467 (vii. p. 485).

[3] Balfour's Annals, i. 213; Tytler's History of Scotland, vol. ii. p. 239; and other Scottish Histories.

[4] See Graham, Earl of Menteith, by Walter M. Graham Easton, in the Genealogical Magazine for June, 1897.

of Stirling, she is certainly called, and by Earl Malise himself, Lady Jonet—which may or may not be (as Mr. Graham Easton suggests) a Scotch corruption of the English Jana. Besides this determination of the lady's name, the transactions recorded in the Protocols are otherwise so interesting, that the passage may be quoted in full:—
"23rd October, 1476. Malize, earl of Menteth, sound in mind and body, out of natural affection, and considering the manifold services and most tender good deeds done to him in youth and age by his dearest spouse, Lady Jonet, Countess of Menteith, in the realms of England and Scotland, gave and bestowed to her for her life-time a silver-gilt horn gilded on the surface with gold, a dish called *le Masar*, a silver cup, a missal book, with other things suitable for celebrating mass; nine silver spoons and a silver salt-fat, gilt on the top, having a beryl stone *(lapidem birraneum)* set in the middle, acquired by his own conquest and industry, from him and his heirs to the said Lady Jonet, and that by placing a gold ring on her finger.

"Done in the chamber of the said earl, in the isle of Inchtolloch, the second hour after noon.

"The same day, the said earl bestowed all and sundry the foresaid jewels on John Graham, his son natural, for his good deeds and services, also giving him sasine of a carucate of land called *le Akyr* in the burgh in barony of Port and Shire of Perth."[1]

Although the Earl here speaks of his old age, he married again after the death of Lady Jonet. At the time of his death, the name of his Countess was Marion or Mariota—

[1] Extracts from Stirling Burgh Records, 1519-1666, appendix, p. 260.

supposed to have been a Campbell of Glenorchy. She was no doubt much younger than her husband. She married again shortly after his death. In 1491 she was the wife of John of Drummond.[1]

By his two wives the Earl had five sons and one daughter. The eldest son, Alexander, who had taken his father's place as a hostage in England, died there previous to 1471, without issue.

The second son of Earl Malise is said by Sir William Fraser to have been John, whom he designates—without authority—Master of Menteith or Lord Kilpont.[2] He is followed by Mr. W. M. Graham Easton, who, however, simply designs John as "of Kilbride."[3] Both genealogists appear to be wrong. Sir William Fraser puts the death of John as before 1478, because in an instrument of sasine in that year, Patrick Graham is described as son and heir of Earl Malise; while Mr. Graham Easton dates the death as before 19th April, 1471, so as to suit the circumstance —apparently unknown to Fraser—that, in a Stirling Protocol of that date, Patrick is styled "son and heir of Malise, Earl of Menteith."[4] The fact, however, is that in the Exchequer Rolls, "John le Graham, son of Malise, Earl of Menteith," is found receiving a certain annual "fee," in virtue of letters under the King's privy seal, from 1467 to 1473.[5] The inference seems clear that since Patrick is designated "son and heir," within the limits of these years,

[1] Acta Auditorum, p. 154.   [2] Red Book, vol. i. p. 296.
[3] Genealogical Magazine for June, 1897, p. 71.
[4] Stirling Protocol Book, 1469-84 (Abstract, p. 5).
[5] Exchequer Rolls, vol. vii., pp. 486, 574, 624; and viii., 70, 172.

he must have been senior to John.[1] Patrick Graham predeceased his father, but left two sons, Alexander and Henry, the former of whom succeeded his grandfather in the earldom.

John, whom we must therefore call the third son of Earl Malise, is designed "of Kilbride," of which property he received a charter under the great seal in 1469. He has come down in tradition as "John of the Bright Sword." It must be added that in the tradition he is usually called the *second* son of the Earl of Menteith. This may well enough be explained by the circumstance that Alexander, the Earl's eldest son, from his long captivity and death in England, could hardly have been well-remembered in Menteith; and also that the proud title John bore is always connected with him as of Kilbride, and possibly when he received that estate—certainly very shortly after —Alexander was dead, and John was the *second surviving* son of the Earl. The traditional epithet indicates that he must have been a warrior of renown, but none of the special exploits which gave him the title have come down to us. There is a further tradition that he was the ancestor and founder of the Grahams of Netherby and other families of Border Grahams.[2] This tradition has not been verified.

---

[1] The question of the seniority of Patrick and John has been fully and ably discussed in an article on "John Graham of Kilbride," signed B., in the Scottish Antiquary, vol. xi., No. 43, p. 108. To this article the reader is referred.

[2] "John Graeme, second son of Malise, Earl of Menteith, commonly surnamed *John with the Bright Sword*, upon some displeasure arisen against him at Court, retired with many of his clan and kindred into the English Borders, in the reign of King Henry the Fourth"—Henry IV. was dead before John Graham was born—"where they seated themselves, and many of their posterity have continued there ever since."—Introduction to the History of Cumberland, quoted by Sir Walter Scott in Notes to the Lay of the Last Minstrel. There appear, however, to have been Graemes on the Borders before the time of "Bright Sword."

The Lake of Menteith. 275

It awaits further genealogical investigation. The date of John le Graham's death is uncertain. He seems to have been alive in 1478, and it is not unlikely that he survived several years beyond that time.[1]

Lady Euphame Graham, the daughter of Earl Malise, married Sir William Stewart of Dalswinton.

By the Countess Mariota the Earl had two sons, John and Walter, who had charters of lands from their father; but they do not concern the present narrative.

ALEXANDER, SECOND EARL.

Seal of Alexander, Earl of Menteith.

Alexander Graham, grandson of Earl Malise, was infeft in the earldom in 1493. The "malis" had been "in the kingis handis the space of thre yheris."[2] The cause of delay in infeftment is not stated, but it must have arisen

---

[1] Stirling Protocol of 7th March, 1477; Instrument of Sasine, 8th October, 1478.—Red Book, vol. i. p. 302. John of Kilbride appears to be the John of the protocol of 1476, quoted above. Although described there as "son natural," it does not seem to be a necessary inference that he was illegitimate. It would have been an extraordinary—almost indecent—proceeding on the part of the Earl, to conjoin an illegitimate son with his Countess in the disposal of his jewels.

[2] Precept of sasine from William, Lord Ruthven, Sheriff of Perth; printed in the Red Book, vol. ii. p. 302.

S

either from the part the last Earl took with James III., or because Alexander was under age. On the 6th of May, 1493, Michael Dun, bailie of the Sheriff of Perth, came "to the shore of the lake of Inchmahomok, near the Coldon, on the ground of the lands of Porth," and there, by giving earth and stone, in the usual manner, invested Alexander Graham in the possession of the earldom of Menteith. The particular spot where the investiture took place is described as "at the shore of the lake of Inchmahomok, between the said lake and the Coldone," and the time as the twelfth hour at noon or thereabout.

Earl Alexander was a member of the King's Council which sat at Stirling, 25th August, 1495;[1] and the records of the Scottish Parliament show that he attended a meeting of that body on the 10th of July, 1525.[2] A bond which he and other noblemen and gentlemen of Perthshire entered into at Perth, 27th May, 1501, with King James IV., wherein they engaged to do their utmost to suppress crime within their bounds, and bring the criminals to justice, gives indication of the disturbed state of the country and the prevalence of lawlessness at the time, as well as the methods by which that energetic King was endeavouring to restore order. The nobles, however, were still forming parties among themselves, and providing for their own interests in the old way of "bands" for mutual defence and support. Such a bond was entered into at Edinburgh, 20th November, 1503, between Alexander, Earl of Menteith, and James, Earl of Arran, Lord Hamilton,

[1] Acta Dominorum Concilii, p. 385.
[2] Acts of the Parliaments of Scotland, ii. 292.

the instrument bearing to be written in "the court of the monastery of St. Colmoc, in the island called Inchmaquhomok."[1]

It was in Alexander's time that the first perpetual Commendator made his appearance at Inchmahome. The Earl himself was present at the ceremony of institution, 15th March, 1529.[2]

The large family of the late Earl Malise had rendered it necessary to grant charters of lands in the earldom to his younger sons for their support. It was the policy of Alexander to redeem these lands; and we find a transaction of this sort recorded in the Stirling Protocol Books, under dates 15th and 16th July, 1533. This was the sasine of William, the eldest son of Alexander, and his spouse, Margaret Mowbray, in the lands of Miltoun and Kirktoun of Aberfoyle, and sundry others mentioned, which had been lawfully redeemed from Walter Graham, the youngest son of the deceased Earl.[3]

Earl Alexander had married Margaret, daughter of Walter Buchanan of Buchanan. Of his two sons, William, the elder, succeeded him. The younger is said to have been the ancestor of the Grahams of Gartur. In the sasine above referred to, he is simply called Walter Graham, the Earl's son. The Earl died in 1536 or 1537.[4]

---

[1] Red Book of Menteith, vol. ii. pp. 303 and 306.
[2] Extracts from Records of Stirling, vol. i. p. 266.
[3] *Ibid*, vol. i. p. 268.
[4] The Macgregor raiders were troublesome in the time of Earl Alexander. On 15th November, 1533, the "robbers of the clan Gregor" were put to the horn for stealing forty cows from him and his son William, Master of Menteith.—Pitcairn's Criminal Trials, i. 164*.

WILLIAM GRAHAM, THIRD EARL.

Seal of William Graham, Third Earl of Menteith.

The infeftment of William Graham, third Earl of his line, took place on the lands of Ernchome, on the shore of the lake of Inchmahome, on the 16th of May, 1537.

While still Master of Menteith and Lord Kilpont, he had married, in 1521, Margaret, daughter of John Moubray of Barnbougle. His family by this lady consisted of five sons and two daughters. One of these daughters, Margaret Graham, became the second wife of Archibald, fourth Earl of Argyle. The marriage was solemnized at the Church of Inchmahome on the 21st of April, 1541—the celebrant being John Youngman, Canon of the Monastery.[1] The other, Christian by name, was married to Sir William Livingstone of Kilsyth.[2] Of the sons, John, the eldest,

---

[1] Stirling Protocol Books under date.

[2] Both Sir William Fraser and Mr Graham Easton make Christian Graham, wife of Sir William Livingstone, a daughter of John, the fourth Earl. But it does not seem possible that Earl John could have had a daughter of marriageable age in 1553 (his eldest son and successor was not of age for at least fifteen years later), previous to which time both writers agree in saying Lady Christian was married. All doubt on the point is removed by a clause in the will of Robert Graham of

succeeded his father in the earldom. The others held various lands within the earldom, which need not here be enumerated. But it may be mentioned that it was through one of these sons, Robert, that Gartmore came into possession of the family.[1] This property belonged to one Alexander Makauly of Erngobil, who, on the 23rd of May, 1547, granted Robert Graham a charter of the two merk land of Gartmore—charter granted at Inchmahome, and witnessed by James Bad, Canon of the Monastery; and on the 3rd May, 1554, a charter of sale of the twelve merk land of Gartmore was granted by Walter Macaulay to the same Robert Graham.[2]

Beyond various business transactions in lands, little is known of the life of Earl William. But his death, which took place in circumstances in which comedy and tragedy are intermingled, has kept his memory alive in the traditionary lore of the district. It is almost needless to say that the story, as narrated by local tradition, assumes different forms, and that these forms vary both as to the names of the combatants and the cause of the quarrel in which the Earl fell. One story makes the victim, not the

---

Gartmore (second son of William, the third Earl), in which he bequeaths "six ky and a bull or forty merks in hir choise" to *his sister Cristane, Lady Kilsyth*. Moreover, the inventory of Robert's daughter, Margaret Graham, was given up by Lady Kilsyth, *her father's sister*.

[1] Sir William Fraser makes Robert the third son. Mr Graham Easton says he was the second. Their names were John, Andrew, Robert, Gilbert, and Walter. Mr Graham Easton makes Andrew the youngest of the family.

[2] On the death of Gilbert Graham of Gartmore, the last laird of his line, without issue, in 1634, his sister Agnes succeeded. She had been previously married to John Alexander, a younger son of the first Earl of Stirling, her petition for service as her brother's heir bearing that it was made with the consent of her husband. Gartmore was sold in in 1644 to William Graham of Polder, who was made a baronet in 1665.

Earl himself, but one of his sons.[1] According to this account, the Murrays of Athole had come down on a foray into the realms of Menteith, and were intercepted and driven up the Pass of Glenny by the Grahams, led by a younger son of the Earl, when, at the summit of the Pass, an Athole man, from his concealment behind a tree, mortally wounded the young Graham as he was rushing past in the pursuit. Another version sends the men of Athole to the Isle on a friendly visit. The Earl happened to be out at the time, but his dinner was cooked and waiting his return. The Murrays, probably thinking it a good joke, gathered up the roasted fowls destined for his dinner, and took their departure. Soon the Earl arrived, and, learning what had occurred, set off in eager and angry pursuit up the slopes of Mondhui. The leader of the Murrays turned in a friendly way, no doubt intending to explain the joke, and, as he saw the Earl fitting an arrow to his bow, he shouted out as he handled his own: "Over me and over you." "No," cried the incensed Earl, "in me and in you." And *in* him it was, for the Murray's arrow pierced his heart. His men, however, drove the enemy over the hill, and returned with their dying master to the Isle.

In commemoration and in proof of this story, it is pointed out that the Grahams of Glenny and Mondhui were long known to the countryside as "Hen Grahams." And in this connection a veracious local legend tells the following gruesome tale. Once on a time a Graham and

---

[1] It is certain, however, from authentic documents, that all the Earl's sons survived their father.

a Macgregor had a quarrel on the hillside above the lake. Angry words were bandied, and the Macgregor's vocabulary of abuse being exhausted, he bethought him of the opprobrious epithet, and was just about to give it utterance, when the Graham, divining his intention, whipped out his sword, and smote off his opponent's head so swiftly that he cut off the words along with it, and "Hen Graham" escaped from the lips of the severed head as it rolled down the hill.

When we turn from these local legends to more trustworthy accounts, we find that it was not the Murrays of Athole, but the Stewarts of Appin, led by the famous Donald nan Ord (Donald of the Hammers) who were responsible for the Earl's death. In an account of the family of Invernahyle, in a MS. communicated by Sir Walter Scott to Jamieson's edition of Captain Burt's Letters, the story is told in the following terms:—

"One time, as returning from Stirlingshire, on passing through Menteith, his (*i.e.*, the Hammerer's) party called at a house where a wedding dinner was preparing for a party, at which the Earl of Menteith was to be present; but, not caring for this, they stepped in and ate up the whole that was intended for the wedding party. Upon the Earl's arriving with the marriage people, he was so enraged at the affront put upon his clan, that he instantly pursued Donald, and soon came up with him. One of the Earl's men called out ironically,

'Stewartich chui nan t' Apan,
A cheiradhich glass air a chal.'

The Lake of Menteith.

One of Donald's men, with great coolness, drawing an arrow out of his quiver, replied—

'Ma tha 'nt Apan againn mar dhucha,
'S du dhuinn gun tarruin sin farsid';[1]

i.e., 'If Appin is our country, we would draw thee *(thy neck)* wert thou there'; and with this took his aim at the Menteith man, and shot him through the heart. A bloody engagement then ensued, in which the Earl and nearly the whole of his followers were killed, and Donald the Hammerer escaped with only a single attendant, through the night coming on."[2]

In "The Stewarts of Appin"[3] the story is told in substantially the same way, but—as might be expected—

---

[1] These Gaelic couplets appear to be incorrectly given, and badly spelt. The first may be translatable thus:—

"You Stewart black from Appin,
You tinker sallow upon kail."

The "tinker," of course, was meant as a hit at the upbringing of Donald in the smithy. The second couplet may be translated:—

"If the Appin be ours as a country,
'Tis black for us (or, *possibly*, it is necessary for us) to draw a shaft."

In Sir Walter's own version of the affray, as given in the account of Donald the Hammerer (Tales of a Grandfather, vol. i. p. 424, edit. 1892) the taunt of the Graham appears thus in English:—

"They're brave gallants these Appin men,
To twist the neck of cock and hen."

And Donald replied:—

"And if we be of Appin's line,
We'll twist a goose's neck in thine."

And he states that Donald escaped with a single follower.

[2] Letters from a Gentleman in the North of Scotland, &c., edited by R. Jamieson, vol i. Introduction, p. xxiii. Sir Walter Scott adds, in a note:—"As the quarrel began on account of the poultry devoured by the Highlanders, which they plundered from the earl's offices, situated on the side of the Port"—Sir Walter must mean the *lake*—"of Menteith, to accommodate his castle in the adjacent island, the name of *Gramoch an gerig*, or *Grames of the hens*, was fixed on the family of the Grames of Menteith."

[3] The Stewarts of Appin, by John H. J. Stewart and Lieutenant-Colonel Duncan Stewart (Edinburgh, 1880), p. 168.

with a colour rather more in favour of the Stewarts. They are represented, not as on a marauding expedition to the lowlands, but as returning from the battlefield of Pinkiecleuch. It is not denied that they ate the wedding dinner, but they were travel-worn and hungry; and when the Grahams overtook them on the hill, they insulted them in a way the Stewart blood could not stand.[1] Finally, it is asserted that, in the conflict which followed, while the Earl of Menteith and most of his men were slain, "the Appin men marched off in triumph, the pipers playing the Stewarts' march."

The earliest version of the tale—unless Sir Walter's Invernahyle MS. be of older date—is that given very shortly by Duncan Stewart, which must have been written before 1730, as that is the date of the author's death. He says simply:—"This Donald of Innernahail commanded a party of men at the battle of Pinkie; and in his return was attacked by the Earl of Menteith, in resentment of *a little malverse* some of Stewart's men had been guilty of in their march, when the Earl and some few of his friends and followers were killed."[2]

---

[1] One of the Grahams taunted them thus:—
"Yellow-haired Stewarts of smartest deeds,
Who could grab at the kail in your sorest needs."
To which a Stewart replied:—
"If smartness in deeds is ours by descent,
Then I draw—and to pierce you this arrow is sent."
The Homeric way in which the representatives of the Grahams and the Stewarts in this clan fight taunt each other in epigrammatic verses need not be taken as invalidating the substantial truth of the story. No doubt, the earliest forms of it were arranged by the bards of the clans, and certainly the allusions to the "kail" and the "hens" were very unlikely to have been invented without a basis of fact. We know that Donald of the Hammers himself was a noted *improvisator*, and was in the habit of launching stinging epigrams at his opponents in the field and the council.

[2] A Short Historical and Genealogical Account of the Royal Family of Scotland and of the Surname of Stewart, by Duncan Stewart, M.A. (Edin., 1739), p. 196.

Duncan Stewart and the authors of "The Appin Stewarts" are both wrong regarding the date of the incident.¹ Whatever the Stewarts were doing in Menteith at the time, they could not be returning from the battle of Pinkie. That battle was fought in September, 1547, when John Graham, the son of William, was Earl of Menteith. The death of Earl William must be dated in 1543, or, at the latest, early in 1544.

JOHN GRAHAM, FOURTH EARL.

John Graham succeeded his father in 1544, although he was not infeft in the earldom till the 26th of May, 1547. He at once began to take an active part in the affairs of that troubled time. He was present at the Convention held at Stirling on the 3rd of June, 1544, which suspended the Earl of Arran and transferred the regency to the Queen-mother. He signed the agreement then drawn up as "John Erle of Mentieth."² Between that date and his infeftment he attended several meetings of Privy Council.³ It was in his time that the island of Inchmahome afforded a refuge to the young Queen Mary.⁴ But the statement made by Sir William Fraser,⁵ and repeated by Mr. Graham Easton,⁶ that he accompanied the young Queen Mary to France as one of her guardians, seems to be erroneous.

---

¹ For the scene of the occurrence see *supra*, p. 27.
² Document in the State-Paper Office, first published by Tytler.—History of Scotland, vol. ii., notes and illustrations, Y.
³ Register of the Privy Council of Scotland, vol. i. pp. 22, 60.
⁴ See page 171.   ⁵ Red Book of Menteith, vol. i. p. 318.
⁶ Genealogical Magazine for June, 1897, p. 78.

The Lake of Menteith.

Lords Erskine and Livingston were the guardians of the Queen. Besides, the date given by both writers—August, 1550—is manifestly wrong. The young Queen left Dumbarton for France in the end of July, 1548.[1] In September, 1550, however,[2] the Queen-mother, Mary of Lorraine, left Scotland on a visit to France, and the Earl of Menteith may have been one of her large retinue.[3] If so, he probably returned to Scotland with her in the following year, as he was present with her at a meeting of Privy Council at Stirling on 20th March, 1552. He was certainly one of her active partisans for several years, sitting in various Parliaments; and, apparently in reward for his activity and fidelity, he received (16th August, 1554) a commission as Justiciar of the earldom and stewartry of Menteith.

In 1559 his political attitude was changed. He joined the Lords of the Congregation at Perth, and was in their army when that town was surrendered to them in June, 1559.[4] Thenceforth he steadily adhered to the Protestant party. He was one of their leaders at the siege of Leith. He sat in the Parliament of 1560 which established the Reformation.[5] He was one of the twenty-four members nominated by the same Parliament, out of whom the Council of Twelve was to be chosen.[6] And although he was not one of the elect Twelve, yet he was certainly

[1] Diurnal of Occurrents, p. 47; and numerous other authorities.
[2] Lesley's Historie of Scotland (Scottish Text Society), vol. ii. p. 335.
[3] The writer has not been able to find any evidence to this effect. Sir William Fraser gives no authority for his statement.
[4] Calderwood's History of the Kirk of Scotland, i. p. 476.
[5] Acts of the Parliaments of Scotland, ii. p. 525.
[6] Tytler's History of Scotland (ed. 1864), vol. iii. p. 132.

present at one at least of the meetings of the Privy Council.[1] He subscribed the first Book of Discipline.[2] Calderwood notes his presence in the General Assembly in June, 1564;[3] but he must have died very soon thereafter.

He left a widow, Marion Seton, daughter of Lord Seton, who was subsequently married to John, tenth Earl of Sutherland, and along with her husband was poisoned in July, 1567, at Helmsdale, by Isabel Sinclair, wife of Gilbert Gordon of Gartay.[4] By the Countess Marion he had two sons—William, his successor, and George, said to be the ancestor of the Grahams of Rednoch—and one daughter, Lady Mary, married to John Buchanan of Buchanan.

WILLIAM GRAHAM, FIFTH EARL.

William Graham was not of age at his father's death, and the earldom was in the hands of the Crown for upwards of seven years. His infeftment did not take place till the 20th of November, 1571.[5] But Earl William, like his father, was a precocious politician, and was busy with affairs of State before he attained his majority. He was one of the Commissioners of Parliament who received the demission of Queen Mary,[6] and he attended the Coronation of James VI. at Stirling, 29th July, 1567.[7] He took part

---

[1] Acts of the Privy Council of Scotland, i. p. 192.
[2] Calderwood's History, &c., ii. p. 50.   [3] *Ibid*, p. 282.
[4] Gordon's Genealogical History of the Earldom of Sutherland, i. p. 146.
[5] Red Book, vol. i. p. 325.
[6] Signed at Lochleven, 24th July, 1567.
[7] In the Parish Church, Knox preaching the sermon.—Register of Privy Council of Scotland, i. 537, 541.

The Lake of Menteith. 287

in the battle of Langside (13th May, 1568)[1] with the Regent Moray, and attended many meetings of Privy Council and Parliament held thereafter.[2] He married, in 1571, Margaret Douglas, daughter of Sir James Douglas of Drumlanrig and widow of Edward, Lord Crichton of Sanquhar. After the death of Regent Moray, he continued to enjoy the favour of the Regents Mar and Morton, and was a member of the Council of the latter. And when King James had assumed the royal authority, he was appointed one of the Councillors Extraordinary.[3]

During this Earl's time one of those local feuds, which were unhappily so common in Scotland, broke out between the Grahams of Menteith and their neighbours the Leckies, on the south side of the Forth. What the original cause may have been is not known. It is said in the records of the affair[4] to have been "licht and slendir." But the quarrel increased in intensity till several persons on both sides of it had lost their lives, and the Privy Council had to intervene. An attempted arrangement resulted only in a further outbreak of violence; and finally, the Earl of Menteith and Walter Lecky of Lecky were summoned to appear before the Council. This was on the 23rd of May, 1577. In February, 1578, Hugh, Earl of Eglinton, and George Buchanan of Buchanan became sureties for the Earl, under a penalty of £5000, that he would appear before the Council on the 1st of April following and bind himself,

---

[1] Calderwood, vol. ii. p. 415.   [2] *Ibid*, iii. p. 119.
[3] Acts of the Parliaments of Scotland, vol. iii. pp. 4, 47, 48, 56, 84, 115, 119, &c. Register of Privy Council, vol. iv. pp. 24, 27, 97, 320.
[4] Register of Privy Council of Scotland, ii. pp. 612, 672, 729.

his servants and dependants, to keep the peace and observe good order in the country. But the Earl was now John, a mere child, and the unruly Grahams and Leckies did not at once bury the hatchet. For at least five years longer the quarrel went on, and again made its appearance in court in the beginning of 1593, when it is to be hoped it was finally settled.[1]

Earl William died in 1577, leaving two young sons, John and George, and a daughter, Lady Helen.

JOHN GRAHAM, SIXTH EARL.

John Graham could scarcely have been more than five years of age at his father's death, and he was in minority for the greater portion of his tenure of the earldom. He was placed, as a ward of the Crown, under the guardianship of his uncle, George Graham of Rednoch, who was consequently known to legal and family documents as the Tutor of Menteith. In October, 1587, in virtue of a dispensation obtained from the King (James VI.), he was infeft in the earldom, although not yet fifteen years of age. In the same month, with consent of his curators, he entered into a marriage contract with Mary Campbell, sister of Duncan Campbell of Glenorchy, who brought him a dowry of eight thousand merks. In a MS. in the State-Paper Office, noting "the Present State of the Nobility in Scotland,"

---

[1] Pitcairn's Criminal Trials, i. 282 :—23 January, 1592-3, John, Earl of Menteith, finds John Blair of that ilk, John Graham of Knockdolean, and Robert Graham of Thornick cautioners in 10,000 merks that "he sall in nawayis invade or persew Walter Lekky of that ilk, his kin, &c., in the deadlie feid standing betwix" them. And Walter Lekky finds John Murray of Polmaise his surety in 3000 merks.

and dated 1st July, 1592,[1] the condition of this Earl is described as follows:—Earl of Menteith: surname, Graham: religion, young: of nineteen years: his mother, daughter to the old Laird of Drumlanrig: married to Glenorchy's daughter: house, Kylbride.[2] He was not distinguished in the history of the times, and little is known of his private life, beyond accounts of lawsuits with his mother and quarrels with his relations.

He died in December, 1598, leaving one son, William, and a daughter, Christian, who married Sir John Blackadder, of Tulliallan, a Nova Scotian Baronet.

[1] Printed in Tytler's History of Scotland, proofs and illustrations to vol. iv., No. xxiii.

[2] The fact that Earl John's *house* was Kilbryde Castle may indicate that by this time the old castle of Inchtalla had fallen into decay, and may be held as countenancing the supposition advanced in the chapter (vii. p. 205) on the existing ruins, that these represent buildings of seventeenth century origin, which were probably either erected wholly of new, or very largely rebuilt, by William the seventh Earl, son and successor of Earl John.

CHAPTER XI.

The Last Two Graham Earls of Menteith, 1598-1694.

"Wha climbs too high, perforce, his feet mon fail."

"Base Fortune, now I see that in thy wheel
There is a point, to which when men aspire
They tumble headlong down. That point I touched."

WILLIAM GRAHAM, SEVENTH EARL OF MENTEITH, EARL OF STRATHERN, FIRST EARL OF AIRTH.

ILLIAM, the seventh of the Graham Earls of Menteith, was, both from the length of his tenure of the earldom and the nature of his public services, the most distinguished of his line. His long life was not without its vicissitudes. After his entry on public life, he rose rapidly to the highest place in the councils of his country and the esteem of his sovereign, and still more suddenly he fell from his high estate. Deprived of his only son by the dagger of an assassin, stripped of titles and harassed by creditors, he spent his old age in poverty and distress.

He was born probably in 1588,[1] and was thus the third

---

[1] Sir Harris Nicolas—History of the Earldoms of Strathern and Menteith, p. 29—says he was born in 1589, but Sir William Fraser gives reasons to show that the date must be placed earlier.

The Lake of Menteith. 291

minor who, in succession, had inherited the earldom. The wardship was given to his mother, along with James and George Elphinstone, and after passing through the hands of George Balfour, came to Sir Colin Campbell of Lundie, his mother's second husband.[1] He was infeft in the earldom in August, 1610. In 1612, he married Lady Agnes Gray,

Seal of William Graham, Seventh Earl of Menteith.

daughter of Patrick, Lord Gray. The marriage settlements gave rise to some litigation with his mother, but this was amicably arranged, and the mother—whose second husband was by this time dead—renounced all claims on the estate in consideration of an annuity of seven hundred merks.

[1] Ward given to his mother and the Elphinstones in 1598; in 1600 disponed to George Balfour, who in turn transferred it to Lundie.

T

The young Earl had decided talents for business; and these he exhibited at the outset of his career in two ways. First of all he undertook the task of arranging and making inventories of the contents of his charter chest in the island of Talla. This business he did not quite complete, as certain *memoranda* appended to the inventories show. "Twa hundreth evidentes not inventored" were in "ane meikle greit quhyt buist within the chartour-kist." The original charter of the earldom with "twa uther greit evidentis" were in "ane little coffer bandet with brass, and the key of the same hanging at it," and a "little kist" contained all the discharges, while there was "the number of ane hundreth and fyftie evidentes lying louss in the charter-kist of the lordschippe of Kilpont, quhilk is not inventored."[1] In the next place, he set himself to redeem the lands which had been alienated from the earldom and were now in the possession of others, and in this he was very successful. An instance of his care for the moral and spiritual welfare of the district was his purchase of the patronage of the Church of Aberfoyle from the Bishop of Dunblane, and the presentation of a minister (John Cragingelt, A.M., 1621). There was a nominal parson of Aberfoyle at the time, but he was a pluralist and non-resident,[2] so that—in the words of the Bishop's Resignation — "that desolate congregation of Aberfule presentlie hes great necessitie of ane pastor, quhair never

[1] Inventory in the charter-chest of the Duke of Montrose: printed in the Red Book, vol. i. p. 333.
[2] Mr. William Stirling, who had been presented to the parsonage of Aberfoyle, 27th August, 1571, had also the vicarage of Kilmadock and a manse in Dunblane, and to these, in 1574, was added the cure of the Parish of Port.—Fasti Eccl. Scot., vol. ii. p. 718.

in no man's memorie leving thair wes ony resident minister to preatche the word of God, nor minister his holie sacramentis, quhairthrow the maist pairt of the paroschinneris thairof remanes in great blindness and ignorance."[1] In return for the right of patronage, the Earl added £100 (Scots) yearly to the stipend, besides giving the teinds of Boquhapple and Drumlean, and securing the manse and glebe to the use of the minister.

His first transaction with King James appears to have been in connection with the affair of the "earth-dogges" elsewhere referred to,[2] and from that King he received his first public appointment, when, on the 15th of February, 1621, he was made Justiciar "within his hail boundis of the erledome of Menteithe, for the speace of ane yeir allanerlie," for the suppression of the crimes of theft and "pykrie," which had become too common in the district. In that year also he attended his first Parliament.[3] But it was under Charles I. that he rose to high distinction in the political affairs of the kingdom. On the 27th of December, 1626, he was appointed by the King a member of the Privy Council of Scotland and a Commissioner of Exchequer. On 21st February, 1628, he was installed President of the Privy Council in succession to the Earl of Montrose deceased; and in 1631 he was made President for life. Also in 1628 (11th of July) he had received the additional appointment of Justice-General for Scotland. This dignity, which had formerly been hereditary in the Earl of Argyll, was con-

[1] Red Book, vol. ii. p. 320.
[2] See *supra*, p. 99.   [3] Acts of the Parliaments of Scotland, vol. iv. p. 593.

ferred on the Earl of Menteith for one year; but the commission was renewed in the following year, and he continued to hold the office till 1633. In 1630, he was further honoured by being made a member of the Privy Council of England.

Earl William was now about the summit of his power, trusted by the King, and undoubtedly the most influential man in His Majesty's kingdom of Scotland. But he was laying the foundations of future difficulties for himself. The expenses of frequent journeys to London on the public business, and the general expenditure which his great position necessarily involved, together—if we are to believe the Earl himself—with the extravagances and unbusiness-like stupidities of his Countess, were getting him steadily into debt, which afterwards was the cause of the greatest misery to him, and eventually obliged him to alienate great portions of the property of the earldom. He was the recipient, certainly, of numerous promises and pensions from the King, but the promises—like most of those of Charles—were not often fulfilled, and the pensions were seldom, if ever, paid. The list of these visionary gifts is a curious one. In 1628 he was granted a pension of £500 a year for life, to be paid out of the Exchequer of Scotland. In the following year, the King issued a warrant for a gift of £5000 sterling to the Earl, and also instructed the Earl of Mar, Lord Treasurer of Scotland, to pay him £500, because he had "furnished roabes for the Judges of our Circuite Courts, and sent out his deputies in that our service upon his own charge." Again, in 1630, on the Earl's resignation of his claim to the lands of the earldom of Strathern, the King granted a precept to the Lord High Treasurer, the Earl of Morton, for payment to him of £3000 sterling. In the beginning of 1631, the Lord High Treasurer was ordered to pay him the sum of £8000, and again, in the end of the year, £15,000. This seems to imply that the previously promised sums had not been paid, and were now included in this gross sum of £15,000. But none of this reached him. When the Earl's misfortunes had overtaken him, he wrote to the King reminding him that the expenses he had incurred in his service had never been repaid, and beseeching him either to satisfy his creditors or suffer him to leave Scotland. The King proposed to give him for the satisfaction of urgent creditors 132,000 merks, and until that sum was paid £500 yearly; also, to buy his house near Holyrood for 18,000 merks, and to give 30,000 merks for the Countess's pension of £500. None of these sums were paid. In 1641 again the King acknowledged a debt of £5000 to the Earl, and instructed the Lords of the Treasury to give him a lease of the free rents of the lordships of Fife and Menteith, calculated to amount to £700 a year, until the debt should be paid. The Treasury, however, did not obey the royal command, and on the 18th of March, 1643, the King again issued a warrant to the Treasury for a payment of £7000 out of the revenues of the customs. This, too, was disregarded; and no further effort was made by Charles I. to pay his debts to the Earl of Airth.[1] It is scarcely to be wondered at. His subjects were getting more and

---

[1] The documents instructing these facts are all either printed or referred to in the Red Book of Menteith.

more beyond his control, and his very life was now in danger.

Throughout the whole of this wretched pecuniary business one can see that the King was not without a sense of the good service that had been rendered him by the Earl of Menteith, and was not untouched by feeling for the calamities that had overtaken him. It is also obvious that the Earl had numerous and not too scrupulous enemies among the nobles and the official class in Scotland. One wonders, however, at the King's impotence in the control of the government of his northern kingdom. His usual obstinacy seems to have deserted him. It was not an instance of the duplicity for which he has often been blamed. The Scottish Treasury calmly disregarded all his precepts and warrants, all his orders and instructions.

Charles II., while at Portend, on the shore of the Lake of Menteith, in the year 1651, acknowledged the royal indebtedness to the Earl. He wrote that he had seen the warrant of his " umquill father of ever blessed memorie " for the principal sum of £7000 sterling and £700 yearly till that principal was paid, and added, we " doe heirby promise on the word off ane prince to sie it faithfullie payed when ever we find occasione." Occasion was so long in arising that the word of a prince was forgotten. The Earl survived till the Restoration, but died not long after, without an opportunity of jogging the royal memory. His grandson and successor tried it, but his faith in the word of princes, if he had any, was also doomed to disappointment. In the petition which he presented to the

King in 1661 he put the amount of the debt due to his grandsire at upwards of £50,000.

Let us return to the Earl at the height of his prosperity, and note the causes of his downfall. An Act had been passed by James VI., in 1617, allowing those who might desire to make claims to heritable estates a period of thirteen years in which to investigate and make up their claims. Taking advantage of this Act, Menteith laid claim to the earldom of Strathern, from which his ancestor Malise had been ejected by James I. The lands which had been annexed to the Crown he renounced in favour of the King, as he did his right to the earldom, "provyding thir presentis nor noe clause thairof prejudge me and my foirsaidis of our right and dignitie of bluide perteining to us as aires of lyne to the said umqhile David, Erle of Stratherne." In consequence of this renunciation, and to mark his satisfaction therewith, the King was pleased to issue a patent, dated 31st July, 1631, ratifying and approving to Earl William of Menteith and his heirs-male the title of Earl of Strathern. While Strathern renounced all claim to those lands of the earldom which had been annexed to the Crown, he prosecuted his claims to the others—with sufficient success to make enemies of those who thus either were deprived or feared they might be deprived of their possessions. Besides the properties acquired through these claims, he also made about this time considerable additions to his estates by purchase. The barony of Drummond or Drymen was acquired from the Earl of Perth in 1631. In 1632 he bought the lands, with the tower and fortalice, of Airth from the Earl of Linlithgow, and a royal charter re-erected these lands into a new barony of Airth.

Now it was that his troubles began. His enemies—of whom the ablest, if not the highest in rank and position, was Sir John Scot of Scotstarvet—saw in his assumption of the title of Earl of Strathern a means of his overthrow. They had a statement drawn up and presented to the King in which they insinuated that, if the Earl was recognised as the legitimate heir of succession to Prince David, there might be danger to the present royal family: they affirmed that to restore the earldom of Strathern to the successors of Malise Graham was an insult to the memory of James I., and would justify the murder of that monarch by Sir Robert Graham, the Tutor of Malise; that the revenues of the Crown would be prejudiced and many honest gentlemen ruined in their estates by the separation of the earldom from the Crown; and that James VI. had refused to grant the title even, much more the earldom, to any subject, on the ground, as he said, that he had no more for the blood and slaughter of King James the First.[1] To add to the force of these and other insinuations, the King was also informed that the Earl had made it a boast that "he had the reddest blood in Scotland." By these accusations it is evident that the suspicions of the King were aroused, but he was as yet unwilling to give up his friend. He is reported to have said that "it was a sore matter that he could not love a man but they pulled him out of his arms." However, he recalled the title of Strathern,

[1] Sir John Scot's True Relation (Sir Harris Nicolas's History of the Earldoms of Strathern and Menteith, app. p. xxviii.)

The Lake of Menteith.

and reduced all the documents in connection with the grant. To make some compensation he granted a patent for the creation of a new earldom, that of Airth, which was therefore (21st January, 1633) conferred on Menteith.[1]

But his enemies were not satisfied. They desired his complete ruin, and to that end accused him of treasonable language which they affirmed had been used by him. On the 1st of May, 1633, a Commission was appointed by the King to examine these charges and, in particular, as to a statement alleged to have been made by Airth that "he should have been King of Scotland, and that he had as good as or a better right to the crown than the King himself." The Earl, in an interesting letter to the King,[2] absolutely denied having used this language—"words which I protest to God I never spoke." The same letter also gives indication that the vultures were already gathering for their prey, for he informs His Majesty that he was the "subject of obloquy of the whole kingdom, and his creditors had already served inhibitions against him as if he were a bankrupt." The King arrived at Holyrood on the 15th of June, 1633; and the Commission for trying the case met on the 10th of July following. Airth, while steadfastly denying that he had ever uttered any such words, submitted himself absolutely to the King's pleasure. The Commission found the charge proven. Then the Earl, at the

---

[1] The earldom of Menteith was annexed to the new creation of Airth, with the precedence due to the Earls of Menteith by virtue of the charter of 1427.

[2] In the charter-chest of the Duke of Montrose: printed in the Red Book of Menteith, i. 369.

suggestion of Traquair, signed the following submission to the King :—

Sir,—Having examined myself from my infancie, I cannot, upon my soule, remember that ever I spok those words as ar conteined in Sir James Skeene his paper, zit finding by the depositiones of persones of qualitie to zour Majestie that sum such words may have escaped me as in law may bring my lyf and fortune in zour Majestie's reverence, I will not stand outt, bot as guiltie, in all humilitie submitt my self at your Majestie's feett.

AIRTHE.[1]

At Halliruid Hous, the 15 Julij, 1633.

The King's decision was declared on the 8th of November. The Earl had to give up his posts as President of the Privy Council and Justice-General, together with his pension of £500, and everything else that had been granted to him by the King; and he was ordered to be confined to his own house and the bounds thereof.

He retired to Airth, and his creditors immediately began to swoop down on him. He wrote to the King informing him that he had had to sell one barony and mortgage another, and that those friends to whom he had given his lands in security had obtained a decree before the Lords of Session, and were now taking possession, so that he would be denuded of them at Whitsunday. He had the right of reversion at the following Martinmas, but, if the debts were not paid then, all was gone, and he was a landless noble. He entreated His Majesty to satisfy these

---

[1] Original at Traquair: printed in Red Book of Menteith, i. 376.

cautioners; or, if not, to give him leave to retire from the kingdom to some place "where he might live and die obscurely and not see the fall of his house."[1] The King promised, and issued warrants, which seem, as usual, to have been neglected. It is, perhaps, to this first disappointment that another pathetic letter[2] to the King refers, in which he again begs permission to go out of the country, "that I sie not," he says, "such miserie, not having bene bred that way." After all, means were found to pacify some of the Earl's creditors, and stave off final ruin.

After his treatment by the King, it is rather wonderful that the Earl of Airth continued faithful to his cause. Yet he not only did so, but so exerted himself as to some extent to regain the royal favour. In 1636, the King sent him a letter of thanks for his services in capturing a Highland freebooter called John Dhu Roy Macgregor—a brother of Gilderoy—in securing whom a near kinsman of the Earl had been slain.[3] In 1637, his confinement to the bounds of his own earldom came to a close, by the King's command, and in a letter dated 17th March, 1638, a London correspondent, who signs himself Jo. Wishart, congratulates him on his restoration to the royal favour, which he compares to a "resurrectione frome the grave."[4] This year—1638—was that in which the opposition to the King's measure in Scotland rose to its height, culminating in the signing of the National Covenant. The Earl steadily

---
[1] Letter written from Airth, dated 3rd April, 1634.
[2] Preserved among the Menteith Papers at Gartmore, and printed in full in Notes on Inchmahome, p. 151.
[3] Letter printed in Red Book, li. 58.
[4] From the Gartmore Papers: printed in Notes on Inchmahome, p. 141.

discountenanced this movement—so far as his influence extended—and he and his son, Lord Kilpont, were severally thanked for their conduct at the time, and informed that His Majesty would acknowledge their affection to his service in a real manner when occasion should offer.[1]

As symptomatic of his growing favour with the King, he was, in 1639, again appointed a member of the Privy Council, and was requested to attend His Majesty's Commissioner—the King seemed to think the latter required to be watched—as one of the Council, at the meeting of the Assembly and the Parliament to be held that year. Of the proceedings at these meetings he sent a confidential account to the King, and was afterwards instructed to repair in person to Hampton Court for conference and to learn His Majesty's further pleasure. When the Covenanting war broke out, the Earl of Airth and his son were, of course, for the King. They were made Lieutenants of Stirlingshire for raising men for the royal army; and they executed their commission with much vigour. Lord Kilpont served with distinction under Montrose, but his career was cut short by his assassination, in Montrose's camp at Collace, by his kinsman and retainer, James Stewart of Ardvoirlich.

Meanwhile, the Earl's pecuniary embarrassments continued. The lands of Airth had been apprised from him in 1638. Mondhui was wadset in 1641 to Walter Graham of Glenny on a letter of reversion which was afterwards (in 1652) renounced. Kilbride was disposed of in 1643; and his silver-plate went to satisfy the claims of the Laird of

[1] Printed in Red Book, ii. 59.

Keir in 1645. He was now pretty well plucked. During the supremacy of the Commonwealth he could not look for assistance. In fact, the poor remains of his possessions seem to have suffered further dilapidation at that time. His house of Airth was made a garrison by Cromwell's troops.[1] General Monck, from Cardross, 17th May, 1654, ordered him to cut down the woods of Milton and Glassart in Aberfoyle parish, as being " great shelters to the rebells and mossers." In August of the same year, the parish was burned and wasted by the English army, cultivation was utterly ruined for the time, and the houses destroyed. The house of Drymen, also, with its furniture, was burned.[2]

He lived to see the restoration of Charles II. to the throne, but not much more. He was alive and staying at Inchtalla—where he seems to have spent the most of his later life—on the 1st of January, 1661, for that is the date of a letter addressed to him by his son-in-law, Sir John Campbell of Glenorchy, who had come to pay his father-in-law a New Year visit, and to consult him about his affairs, but could not get access to the island on account of the ice. Next month his grandson is mentioned as second Earl of Airth and Menteith.[3]

The Countess survived him. Their domestic life had its disagreements, some of which are most amusingly told—not

---

[1] Act of the Parliaments of Scotland, vol. vi. p. 687.

[2] Petition presented to Parliament in 1663 by William, second Earl of Airth.—Acts of Parliaments of Scotland, vol. vii., app. p. 100.

[3] This is the statement of Sir William Fraser (Red Book, vol. i. p. 390); but a letter is extant, written to him by his grandson, then still Lord Kilpont, on the 13th April, 1661.

the less amusingly, perhaps, because the Earl is in downright earnest about it all—in a manuscript written by his own hand.[1] He speaks of her Ladyship as "my divelish wyf," "this wofull wyfe of myne," "that wicked woman," and, with bitter irony, "this wyse woman of myne," "my prudent wyfe," "my goode wyfe," and tells a sad tale of her lamentable ongoings, which were bringing debt and ruin upon him. She had, without her husband's knowledge, bought from her "false uncle," the Earl of Carrick, his pension of 9000 merks yearly from the Exchequer, for which she agreed to pay him the sum of 7000 merks a year, Lords Forrester and Tulliallan becoming securities for the payment. The payment fell into arrears, and the Earl of Carrick "put hard at the Lord Forrester, intended a process against him, and took infeftment of his lands of Corstorphine." To relieve Forrester the Earl had to pay, "in layed doune money," 42,000 merks. "This," he cries out, "wes one of my divelish wyf hir wys actes, fortie two thousand mks., 42,000 merks!" Next, when again the Earl was in London, his "prudent wyfe" married her second daughter, Margaret, to Lord Garlies, eldest son of the Earl of Galloway, giving in tocher 27,000 merks, for which sum again she gave some of her husband's friends as cautioners; and before the "said doghter went home to her awin, she was four thousand merks more;" but in his indictment of his wife, the Earl—as they do in the law courts—restricts the total sum to "threttie thousand merks." All this money, he says, was as much lost to

[1] Printed in the Notes on Inchmahome, app. iv. p. 145-150, from papers at Gartmore.

him as if it had been cast into the sea. The Earl of
Galloway was nearly related to him, their estates were far
apart, the children of the married couple had died, and
for the sum given as tocher he might have married three
of his daughters to barons in his neighbourhood, any one
of whom would have been more useful to him than the
Earl of Galloway. In the third place, she wanted him
to buy a house in Edinburgh, instead of paying rent for
the little house he dwelt in there "besyde the Churchyaird,
pertaining to one Ridderfoord." He refused, notwithstanding her protestation that it would serve as a house for
the lands of Kinpont. After that, however, in some
transactions with the Earl of Linlithgow, he bought from
that nobleman a house at the back of Holyrood Abbey,
paying for it 8500 merks, "and it wes no ill pennieworth,
for it wes worth the money." But no sooner had he
gone again to London than his wife set all manner of
tradesmen to re-edify the house, so that he calculates
that it cost him in all 25,000 merks, but he "will only
sett doune heir 20,000 merks." And after all, when he
had to leave Edinburgh, he disponed the house to his
son James, and within two years it took fire and was
totally burned. This calamity could scarcely be laid to
the blame of the Countess, but he cries in his vexation,
"so becam of everie thing that the unhappie woman, my
wyfe, hade hir hand intoo." The speculations of the
Countess had now cost her husband, according to his
reckoning, 92,000 merks. "Bot," he says, "this is nothing
to that which will follow heireefter." This was a business
venture in coal and salt. The Earl had a coal heuch and

six salt-pans at Airth, which were let on a nine years' lease to William Livingstone, "ane very honest man," at a yearly rent of 2500 merks in money and a supply of coals—estimated at 500 merks—to the house of Airth. The Countess had been persuaded by "sum unhappie bodies" that she could make 6000 merks a year out of the works if they were in her own hands. Her lord, however, refused to break the lease, which had still some years to run, as Livingstone was a good tenant and paid regularly. "So shee parted in ane greate snuffe, and shee tooke ane uther way to worke." She harassed Livingstone, and withdrew the tenants and workmen from his service, so that he came to the Earl and, "with tears in his eyes," offered to surrender the lease on any terms his Lordship might think just. Out of pity he gave him 4500 merks. The Countess then went to work with great energy, sunk great and deep "sumps," erected a water mill and a horse mill, and built two new salt-pans, all at great cost, and all without her husband's authority. We are given to understand that this, like the other business speculations of the energetic lady, came to sad grief; but the amount of deficit which her husband had to make good is not mentioned, as the Earl's narrative of his wife's delinquencies has been interrupted, and breaks off abruptly.

The Earl of Airth had a large family—six sons and four daughters. The eldest son, John, Lord Kilpont, was killed at Collace, 6th September, 1644. The second son, Sir James, became Governor of Drogheda, and had a daughter, Helen, who was much in evidence in connection with the negotiations for settling the earldom in the time of its last holder. Robert, Patrick, and Charles are known only by name. Archibald was a country gentleman, and a douce elder in Port of Menteith Parish Church. Of the daughters, Mary was married to Sir John Campbell of Glenorchy, Margaret was the young lady disposed of by her managing mother to Lord Garlies, Anne became the wife of Sir Mungo Murray of Blebo, and Jean is only a name.

William, the eldest child and only son of Lord Kilpont, succeeded his grandfather in the earldom.

WILLIAM GRAHAM, EIGHTH EARL OF MENTEITH, SECOND EARL OF AIRTH.

This Earl, who held the title for thirty-three years, gives one the impression of eccentricity; although it must be admitted he had a rather hard time of it. All his life he had to struggle with comparative poverty and general ill-health. His domestic relations were not happy: he divorced his first wife, and had difficulties with the second. He had no children by either; and was greatly worried by questions of the succession. A large portion of his time was spent in dunning the King and endeavouring to obtain payment of the arrears of pensions and other debts due to his grandfather; and it is to be hoped he found some pleasure in this pursuit, for profit of it he had none. The only pleasurable bit of excitement that came into his life was when he hunted the Covenanters in his neighbourhood. He professed that he enjoyed this—rejoicing with special delight over the capture of one Arthur Dugall, an obstinate Covenanter of Kippen, " who was the verie first man that did harbor and reseat the horrid murderis of the lat Archbishop of St. Androws."[1] He lamented that he had narrowly missed Hackstoun and Balfour, who happened to be at the same conventicle at which Dugall was taken. He wished, with all his soul, that he had "one sure bout" of them, so that he might more fully prove his affection to His Majesty's service. "I doubt not," he wrote, "to put them in a verie great fear, all betwixt Dumbarton and Stirling, and sall put them from thes disorderly mittings, for on all occassions I'll hazard my life for the royall interest." For his encouragement in this laudable frame of mind, the valiant Earl received the acknowledgments of the Privy Council, and a message from the King, that he would show him the royal favour "upon a fitt occasion." It is scarcely necessary to say that the fit occasion never came. In 1681, his friend and relative, Claverhouse, also wrote him from London, complimenting him on having "taken his trade off his hand," and having become "the terror of the godly." "I begin to think it tyme for me," he added, "to set a work again, for I am emulous of your reputation." In all of which phraseology one can detect something like a sneer, or, at least, a smile, at the valetudinarian Earl and his man-hunts in the wilds of Kippen.

A good deal of the Earl's correspondence has been preserved, and it is both interesting and amusing. He strews his page—especially when he is labouring under excitement—with irrelevant *whiches* in the most lavish way.

---

[1] The correspondence of the Earl on this and other subjects is in the charter-chest of the Duke of Montrose, and has been printed in the Red Book of Menteith, from which the quotations here given are taken.

Here is an instance in a letter to his uncle, Sir James Graham—"Let him know if he wold be welcum, *wich* for my sak at least ye will admit of a visit from himself *wich* will be soon as you ar pleased to return a favorable ansyre to me in his behalf; *wich* my Lord Marquis of Montrose has wreatten a letter to you on his behalf." Sairey Gamp could not have bettered that.

Much of this correspondence deals with what was his most pressing business all his life through—the attempt to raise money for his immediate needs, and to satisfy his ever-pressing creditors. Writing to the Earl of Wemyss, from The Isle, on the 18th November, 1667, he declares that he is "warpt in a laberinth of almost a never ending truble," and not the least trouble is that he cannot make his Lordship payment of his claim against him. "What I sal doe this year," he goes on to say, "the Lord knows, for I know not. Both myself, land, woods, ky and horses, I lay all befor your Lordship, doe as it seemeth good in your eyes, for on everie syde I am perplext by to pressing credditors, and in consenc this terme of Martimis they wil get no monyes tho' they should tak my life."

A letter written from "the Ile," 27th June, 1681, to James, third Marquis of Montrose, furnishes an instance —not without its ridiculous side—of his continued impecuniosity. He had resolved to "ride the Parliament" at Edinburgh next month, and was determined to make as brave a show as his rank required. He was to have four footmen in livery—footmen were probably cheap in Menteith at that time—but he had no suitable robes for himself. Those that had belonged to his grandfather had been destroyed in the English time, and he had never been able to procure new ones. He therefore earnestly besought the Marquis to obtain for him from some earl the loan of his earl's robes, foot-mantle, velvet coats, and other things necessary for his appearance in proper Parliamentary outfit. He promised to use them only for one day, and to keep them carefully so that none of them should be spoiled. With a touch of vanity he added, "the last tyme when I reid the Parliament, I cearied the secepter," and, as if it would be taken as a guarantee of his honesty, he reminded the Marquis that on that occasion he "head the lene of the deces'd Earle of Lowdian's robes." He further asked "the lene of a peacable horse," as it seems he was troubled with gouty affections both in his hands and feet. He did attend the meeting of Parliament, so it is to be assumed that he succeeded in getting "the lene" of an earl's robes and a sufficiently peaceable horse.

Another interesting section of the Earl's correspondence concerns the succession to the earldom. He had no children. The nearest heir was his uncle, Sir James Graham, who resided in Ireland, and was now an old man.[1] This Sir James had one unmarried daughter, named Helen; and it is around this young lady that all the correspondence circles. The well-known John Graham of Claverhouse offered himself to the Earl to be adopted as

[1] Sir James Graham, second son of William, the seventh Earl, married Margaret Erskine, daughter of the Earl of Buchan, and had by her one daughter, Marion, who was married to Walter Graham of Gartur. By his second wife, Isabella, daughter of the Bishop of Armagh, he had a daughter named Helen or Eleanor.

his son and to be married to Helen Graham. The letter in which he makes this offer is extremely interesting, clever, and plausible. He tells how Julius Cæsar had no occasion to regret his want of issue, because in his adopted son (Augustus) he secured a faithful friend and a wise successor, neither of which he could have promised himself by having children of his own, " for nobody knows whether they begit wyse men or fooles, besids that the tays of gratitud and friendship ar stronger in generous mynds than those of natur." "I may say," he adds, "without vanity, that I will doe your family no dishonor, seing there is nobody you could mak choyse of has toyld so much for honor as I have don, thogh it has been my misfortun to atteen but a small shear." His proposal was that the Earl should settle the succession on Helen Graham and her heirs, that she should then be married to himself, and in this way, as he pointed out, the earldom would be preserved in the family of Graham. He had seen the young lady, and professed the greatest devotion. He protested that it was not for the expected honour she was to receive that he desired to gain her hand: he would take her "in her smoak."

The Earl was willing to agree to this arrangement, but Sir James and his wife—we are not informed of the feelings of the young lady—were not. An arrangement was then made with the Marquis of Montrose, by which the earldom of Airth and Menteith was to be provided to the Marquis on condition of his marrying Helen Graham and securing the Earl in a life annuity of £150. This proposal was well received by Sir James and his lady and by the fair Helen herself; and all seemed to be in good train for success when the Marquis, proving faithless, went off and married another.

Meantime the charter conveying the lands and honour of the earldom of Menteith to the Marquis of Montrose had received the signature of the King. Sir James Graham made representations to his Majesty, with the result that the portions concerning the peerages and the lands of Airth were cancelled, and the gift was restricted to the lands of the earldom of Menteith only. Thus it happens that the estates of the ancient earldom—or rather, the small portion of them then left—are now in the possession of the Duke of Montrose, while the titles are in the air, waiting for the advent of a claimant who shall prove himself an undoubted representative of the family. The Earl was, after all this, urged by Claverhouse to recall the disposition to Montrose, and to make him his heir, and again recommend him to Sir James Graham, who, he hinted, would not now be averse to accept him as a son-in-law. Miss Graham, however, was given in marriage to Captain Rawdon, heir apparent of the Earl of Conway.

The disposition of the estate was never recalled, although the Earl, after a letter received from his uncle in 1683—in which it is plainly stated that there had been a combination between Montrose and Claverhouse to overreach the poor old man—resolved to visit the Court next year and submit the whole affair to the King. But, the Marquis of Montrose having died in April, 1684, he was dissuaded by John, Master of Stair, from going to Court at the time. Stair's letter to the Earl is somewhat contemptuous in tone—as if he were dealing with a crank with whom it was difficult to have patience. It lets us know the curious fact that Menteith, who was now fifty years of age—possibly in the hope of yet having a natural successor to his titles—had married a second wife, and that before the divorce from the first had been completed. The letter does not spare the Earl :—" I shall never believ yow have bein so ill advysed as to have entred into another mariage till this was dissolved, if it be possible. I must say it's hard to determin whither yow hav bein more industrious to preserv or destroy yourself : only I am convinct they do not thriv that medle with yow."

In all the marriage and succession correspondence, Claverhouse proves himself a very clever writer. He shows much ingenuity in his ways of putting things, and his style is not only clear and vigorous, but even graceful. It contrasts with the obscure and fumbling manner of the Earl. The latter generally confines himself to not very clear statements of business; but in one letter addressed to the Marquis of Montrose after the latter had got married —not to Helen Graham—he attempts a poetical compliment, thus :—" Be pleased to present my verrye humble servise to my speciall good Ladey, to whom I heave sent some chirries "—no doubt from the fruit gardens at Inchmahome : it was the 27th of June, old style—" *to kiss hir fair handis, who blushes that they are not worthe to present themselves to so vertious and excelant a Ladey.*" But he does not often break out in that way. And, after all, he does not come out of the affair worst. He was honest, and his intentions were good; but he wanted adroitness and possibly suppleness. The Marquis of Montrose appears but little in the correspondence. Sir James Graham's letters show him a clear-headed man of business.

The Earl's first wife was Anna Hewes—to judge by the name, an Englishwoman—but really nothing is known regarding her. The decree of divorce is dated 19th July, 1694, but it would appear that even before it was issued he had, greatly daring, married again.[1] The second wife was Katherine Bruce, daughter of Thomas Bruce of Blairhall. In the Earl's circumstances it was praiseworthy, and even necessary, to practise economy; and he set about it in his usual fussy way. He drew up a paper in which he minutely specified the quantities of provisions and materials and sums of money that were to be allowed annually to my Lady for the maintenance of the house. This document shows that there must have been a fairly numerous household on the island at the time, and is of interest as indicating the sort of fare on which they lived. He allows four score bolls of good oatmeal—"quhilk is to be layed in the old girnell in the Isle, and my Ladie to keep the keye of it," and three score bolls of bear to be made into malt, "in my Lord's oune kill at the stables." Cheese must have been a favourite article of diet, as forty stones of it are allowed, "whairof ten stone Glaschyle cheese." The Glassachoil

---

[1] The Earl charged his wife with infidelity—one of the co-respondents, it may be noted, was the novelist Fielding—and the lady replied with a similar charge against her husband, a plea of connivance, and an allegation of bigamy on account of his marriage with Catherine Bruce while legal proceedings were still pending. The whole wretched history of the case and the curious manipulation of legal forms by which the bigamy charge—of which the Earl really was guilty—was evaded and finally departed from, may be found in the law reports. (Fountainhall's Decisions, pp. 248-308).

cheese was perhaps a superior brand, reserved for the family circle. Butter was not in such common use—only ten stones of good salt butter being required. For fish, two thousand herrings were allowed, and all the fishes "that can be had in the loches and waters there." Her ladyship might also supplement the allowance of meat with "all the veneson and wyld foule that can be gotten." The allowance of eggs was a hundred dozen, " or else six pounds Scots theirfor." That works out at ten for a penny sterling—eggs were cheap in those days. Four stots, ten quarters old, were to supply the fresh meat, and eight fat kyne and oxen for "mairts"; besides "all the reek hens, poultrie, and capones in the bounds of Menteith and Drummond." The milk for the house was to be supplied by five new-calved cows to be kept on Portend, and one good cow in the Easter Isle (Inchmahome) both summer and winter. My Lady was to have three hundred merks (£16 13s. 4d. sterling) for her clothes and purse, and four hundred merks "for whyte bread, flour, sheugar, spycerie and aquavite, brandi, reasins, plume demis and soap"—a modest sum, surely, for such a miscellaneous catalogue of luxuries. All this, and much more—set down at length in the agreement—was formally subscribed by my Lord and my Lady, before witnesses, at the Isle of Menteith, on the 1st of January, 1685.

It is not surprising that the Countess soon got tired of this over management, and went off to Edinburgh. The story was that she could not stand the croaking of the frogs outside her chamber window, but the probability is that it was the croaker within who was the chief cause

of her flight. At Edinburgh she remained, evincing no
disposition to return, until the Earl got alarmed, and commissioned his man of business there to tempt her back
with promises and agreements. In this he was successful.
A marriage contract—there had been none before—was
drawn up, and signed by the parties on 16th and 18th
March, 1687. This contract contains a clause very characteristic of the Earl. After providing the estates to the
eldest son—should there be a son—of the marriage, it
gives 20,000 merks to the daughters—if there should be
daughters—indicating at the same time that these 20,000
merks existed as yet mainly or only in the imagination,
and depended for their materialisation on the "freugall
and verteows leiving" of the Earl and his Countess. The
lady undertakes to reside in the Isle with her husband,
and when his lordship is absent, to stay at home at their
ordinary place of residence. By these arrangements, the
domestic harmony was restored, although the Earl, notwithstanding all manner of frugal and virtuous living,
remained all his life hard up, and found it anything but
easy to maintain his household.[1]

[1] The impecuniosity of the Earl is indicated in the traditionary story of
"Malise Graham and the Roe-skin Purse." As told by M'Gregor Stirling it
runs thus :—" The last Earl of Monteath being obliged, for the reason already
mentioned (*i.e.*, debt) to retire to the asylum for debtors, the Abbey of Holyrood,
applied to one of his vassals, and his kinsman and namesake, Malise Graham,
of Glassart, on the southern shore of Loch Catherine, for such a supply of money,
or such security, as might relieve him. Faithful to the call of his liege lord,
Malise instantly quitted his home, dressed like a plain Highlander of those days,
travelling alone, and on foot. Arriving at the Earl's lodging, he knocked for
admittance, when a well-dressed person opening the door, and commiserating his
apparent poverty, tendered him a small piece of money. Malise was in the act
of thankfully receiving it, when his master, advancing, perceived him, and chid
him for doing a thing which, done by his pecuniary friend, might tend to shake

The Lady Katherine died early in the year 1692. Two years later—in September, 1694—the Earl himself passed from his troubles. His estate had already been disposed of to the Marquis of Montrose. His personal property—it was not much, or valuable[1]—he left to his nephew, Sir John Graham of Gartmore, on condition that he paid certain debts and legacies, provided for the decent burial of the Earl, and erected a monument for him and his Countess. To what extent his wishes were obeyed is stated elsewhere.[2]

APPENDIX.

THE MURDER OF LORD KILPONT AT COLLACE.

JOHN, LORD KILPONT, was born in or about 1613. When his father held the title of Earl of Strathern, he married Lady Mary Keith, eldest daughter of the Earl Marischal, receiving with her a dowry of £30,000 Scots, while the lady was infeft in the baronies of Kilbride and Kilpont,

---

his credit more than ever. The Highlander, making his appropriate obeisance, but with the utmost *nonchalance*, took from his bosom a purse, and handing it to his lordship, addressed him in the following words, originally in Gaelic, but now translated :—' Here, my lord, see and clear your way with that. As for the gentleman who had the generosity to hand me the halfpenny, I would have no objection to accept of every halfpenny he had.' The story declares that his lordship's necessity was completely relieved, and that he instantly returned with his faithful vassal to his castle in the Loch of Monteath."—Notes on Inchmahome, p. 12.

[1] See the inventory and details of his personal possessions, chap. vii. pp. 209-215.

[2] See chap. iv. pp. 116-118.

and received an annuity of 1000 merks out of the barony of Drummond. The contract is dated 11th April, 1632, and the marriage took place in the course of that year. Lord Kilpont acted as his father's assistant in the justiciarship of Menteith, and in that capacity was instrumental in bringing to justice the noted robber, John Dhu Macgregor. For this service he was thanked by the King in 1636. He also received a letter of thanks in 1639 for his steady adherence to the King's interest as against the Covenanters.

In 1644 the Committee of Estates authorized him to assemble the men of Menteith, Lennox, and Keir, in order to guard the passages to Perth against the Irish levies who were on their march from the west. With this force, amounting to about 400 men, he was posted at the hill of Buchanty, in Glenalmond, when he was met by Montrose at the head of the Irish and Highland troops, and so far from resisting, he went over to him with the whole body of troops under his command.

The battle of Tibbermuir was fought on the 1st of September. After a rest of a few days in Perth, Montrose crossed the Tay on the 5th of September, and pitched his camp at Collace. That night he gave an entertainment to his officers to celebrate the victory at Tibbermuir. After the banquet a quarrel of some sort arose between Kilpont and his intimate friend, James Stewart of Ardvoirlich, who had shared his tent and his bed, which ended in Stewart stabbing his friend with his dagger and escaping from the camp. The murderer fled to the Covenanting army, where he was received by Argyll, and promoted ultimately to the rank of Major. The body of Lord Kilpont was conveyed to Menteith and interred in the Chapter House of the Priory of Inchmahome.[1] Lady Kilpont was so affected by the death of her husband that she lost her reason. A bitter feud which lasted long between the Grahams of Menteith and their friends and the Stewarts of Lochearnside was another consequence. Kilpont's son was a boy of about ten years of age at the time of his father's death, but he never forgot the circumstances. At the very earliest opportunity he had, that is, immediately after the Restoration in 1660, he tried to open the question of his father's murder by a petition to the King. After his accession to the earldom, he addressed the King again on the subject. Neither of these petitions had any effect. But the Earl continued to cherish his feeling of resentment, and as late as 1681, in a letter to the Marquis of Montrose, he refers to one Robert Stewart, who had purchased Stragartney, as "the treterous son of that cruell murderer of my faither, who was his Lord and Master."[2]

The motive of Ardvoirlich in this slaughter of his friend is obscure, and the accounts are somewhat conflicting. The sources of information in regard to it are three. First, there is the story as told by Wishart, the Chaplain of Montrose. This was the version that was before Sir Walter Scott when he wrote the *Legend of Montrose*, and it of course reports the incident from the Royalist point of view. Next there is the account handed down in the Ardvoirlich family, and sent by one of the members of that family to Sir Walter, who published it in a postscript to his story.

[1] See chap. iv. p. 111.
[2] Letter in the Red Book of Menteith, ii., p. 192.

That, as might be expected, puts the action of Stewart in a distinctly more favourable light. And, in the third place, there is the statement of the circumstances in the Act of Parliament which ratified the pardon for the deed previously granted by the Privy Council, which—if it may not be held as an absolutely impartial statement—may at least be taken as putting the case in a light that was not regarded as unfavourable to Ardvoirlich.

Wishart accuses Ardvoirlich, whom he calls "a base slave," of a plot to murder Montrose. He endeavoured to draw Kilpont into the plot, and when the latter expressed his detestation of the villainy, he stabbed him with many wounds before he had time to put himself on his guard; then killing a sentinel, he escaped in the darkness. He adds—" Some say the traitor was hired by the Covenanters to do this; others, only that he was promised a reward if he did it "—the distinction seems rather a fine one. "However it was, this is most certain, that he is very high in their favour unto this very day; and that Argyle immediately advanced him, though he was no soldier, to great commands in his army." And he concludes with a touching account of Montrose's tribute to his dead friend— " Montrose was very much troubled with the loss of that nobleman, his dear friend, and one that had deserved very well both from the King and himself; a man famous for arts, and arms, and honesty; being a good philosopher, a good divine, a good lawyer, a good soldier, a good subject, and a good man. Embracing the breathless body again and again, with sighs and tears he delivers it to his sorrowful friends and servants, to be carried to his parents to receive its funeral obsequies, as became the splendour of that honourable family."[1]

The family account is to the effect that Stewart was not a subordinate of Kilpont, but in an independent command; and through his intimacy with Kilpont he had induced the latter to join the royalist cause. The Irish levies, when coming from the west under the command of Colkitto, had plundered the lands of Ardvoirlich, and of this Stewart complained to Montrose, but obtained no redress. He then challenged Colkitto, and Montrose, on the information and advice of Kilpont, it is said, put both under arrest and then patched up a sort of reconciliation. But Stewart was far from being satisfied; and after the banquet, when the friends had returned to their tent, he broke out into fierce reproaches against both Kilpont and Montrose. Kilpont replied also in high words. From words they went to blows, and Stewart, who was a man of great strength, slew Kilpont on the spot. He fled after the deed and, for his own safety, was obliged to throw himself into the hands of the Covenanters.[2] This account frees Ardvoirlich from the accusation of treachery to Montrose, though it represents him as a man of violent temper.

The Act of Parliament narrates that John, Lord Kilpont, being employed in the public service against James Graham, then Earl of Montrose, the Irish rebels and their associates, did treacherously and treasonably join himself and induce

[1] Wishart's Commentaries on the Wars of Montrose, quoted by Sheriff Napier in his Memoirs of Montrose, ii. 446.
[2] Legend of Montrose, Postscript to Introduction (edit. 1829).

400 others under his command to join the said rebels; that Stewart and some of his friends, repenting of their error, resolved to forsake their wicked company, and imparted this resolution to Kilpont, who endeavoured, "out of his malignant dispositione," to prevent them, and fell a struggling with the said James, who, for his own relief, was forced to kill him, along with two Irish rebels who resisted his escape; and that then, with his son and friends, he came straight to the Marquis of Argyle and offered their services to the country.[1]

The particulars in this narrative would in all probability be supplied by James Stewart himself, and they seem, in every point, to contradict the family tradition. No mention is made of the plot to murder Montrose ascribed to him by Wishart, but in other respects the account of that writer is confirmed. He tried, according to this statement approved by himself, to make Kilpont false to the cause of the Royalists, and killed him when he did not succeed. It is quite possible that the statement may be not altogether ingenuous, as he might suppose that his zeal for the Covenant would be likely to condone the offence of killing one of its enemies. But if not accepted as it is, the plot to assassinate Montrose must still stand on a footing of at least equal authority with the grievance against Colkitto as the cause of the quarrel which ended so fatally.

[1] Acts of the Parliament of Scotland, vol. vi. pt. i. p. 359 (1st March, 1645).

CHAPTER XII.

Some Miscellaneous Matters of Greater or Less Interest.

"Old, unhappy, far-off things,
And battles long ago."

"O gentle reader, you will find
A tale in everything."

FEUD BETWEEN THE MENTEITHS AND DRUMMONDS IN THE FOURTEENTH CENTURY.

"In their baronial feuds and single fields,
What deeds of prowess unrecorded died!"

ABOUT the middle of the fourteenth century a deadly feud arose between the Menteiths and the Drummonds. The origin of this feud is obscure. A local tradition has come down to the effect that it arose from the hatred the patriotic Drummonds bore to the family of the man who had treacherously captured Wallace and handed him over to the English King, and that it was their fixed determination to wipe out for ever the whole kin and name of Menteith. That is a quite incredible story—

although one can well enough conceive how it might commend itself to the popular mind, and even be connived at by the Drummonds as giving a fairly plausible excuse for their acts of violence. The quarrel, no doubt, originated in a more vulgar, but unfortunately usual cause in Scotland—the mutual jealousies of two neighbouring families anxious for supremacy. The immediate occasion of the outbreak was the slaughter of Brice Drummond of Boquhapple, a cousin of John of Drummond, in 1330. The contention then rose to its height till at last a fierce clan battle was fought at the Tor—or Tar—of Rusky, about a mile north-east of the Lake of Menteith. In this fight three sons of Sir Walter Menteith[1] of Rusky, named Walter, Malcolm, and William, were slain. The Campbells of Argyle were also involved in this quarrel in alliance with the Menteiths. The battle of the Tar, so far from ending the quarrel, only increased the enmity of the clans, and reprisals and bloodshed devastated the countryside. At last the King (David II.) found it necessary to interpose his royal authority in the interests of humanity and peace.

An agreement was accordingly made on Sunday, 17th May, 1360, "upon the banks of the river Forth, near Stirling, in presence of Sir Robert of Erskyne and Sir Hugh of Eglinton, justiciars of Scotland, and of Sir Patrick Grahame, and many other noblemen and upright gentle-

---

[1] Sir Walter Menteith was the second son of Sir John, the captor of Wallace. He succeeded his father in Rusky, while his elder brother John was Lord of Arran and Knapdale.

men."[1] In compensation for the slaughter of the three Menteiths and other injuries done to them and their adherents, John of Drummond agreed to give up the lands of Rosneath in the earldom of Lennox to Sir Alexander Menteith of Rusky, the eldest son of Sir Walter, and his heirs. These lands, it may be said, had not been long in Drummond's possession. They had been given to him by the Countess Mary of Menteith, when she was arranging a marriage between him and her daughter Margaret, greatly with a view to staying the existing feuds between the families. This gift and the marriage were both prior to the agreement here recorded. The lands of Rosneath, therefore, now came back to a branch of the family of their former possessors. Drummond also bound himself and his friends to leave the Menteiths unmolested for the future.

On the other hand, the Menteiths pledged themselves to faithfully observe the agreement, to live henceforth at peace with Drummond, and to aid him against the Campbells of Argyle, should these rise up against him. And both parties, " embracing each other sincerely with affection, bound themselves to others with the constancy of a solid mind, as if dissension had never prevailed between them."

Then the principal parties to the treaty—John of Drummond, Maurice Drummond, and Walter of Moray, on the one part, and John and Alexander of Menteith, and

---

[1] The original of this agreement is preserved in Drummond Castle. A copy (with translation by Mr. George Horne) was printed by M'Gregor Stirling in his Notes on Inchmahome: Appendix iii., pp. 121 *et seqq.*

Walter of Buchanan, on the other part—gave their oaths by touching the holy Evangels. To make security still more secure, the High Steward of Scotland, as the principal relation of both parties, and other related nobles, solemnly ratified the treaty, and promised that, if it were infringed (which God forbid!), they would proceed against the party guilty of such infringement.

A final clause was added to the effect that if the Menteiths should compass the death of John of Drummond, or any of his adherents, or should not oppose any one who did so, the lands of Rosneath should return to Drummond. The latter part of this clause has probably reference to Gillespie Campbell and his son Colin, who had previously aided the Menteiths against Drummond, and whom the former professed themselves unable to bind. Their hostility to Drummond was, however, bought off by the Countess Mary, who persuaded them to acquiesce in the agreement by a gift of her lands of Kilmun and other considerable grants of land in her barony of Cowal.

By these means the peace was assured, and friendship and good neighbourhood was maintained between the families. The lands of Rosneath never returned to the Drummonds. They remained with the Menteiths till, in 1455, they were annexed to the Crown.[1] Since 1489 they have been the property of the family of Argyle.

[1] The Menteith possession of Arran had also by this time terminated. John of Menteith, Lord of Arran, died in or before 1387. And in that year, Janet Keith or Erskine, who had become the representative of the family, resigned Arran to the Crown in exchange for an annuity of £100 from the burgh fermes and fishings of Aberdeen.—Exchequer Rolls vol. vi. p. xcvi.

The Lake of Menteith.

THE BEGGAR EARL.

"A blessing on his head,
And, long as he can wander, let him breathe
The freshness of the valleys, let his blood
Struggle with frosty air and bitter snows;
And let the chartered winds that sweep the heath
Beat his grey locks against his withered face."

"And in a mendicant behold a Thane."

The person who bore the name of the "beggar Earl" was not so called in any metaphorical sort of way, or because of his comparative poverty, but in sad and literal fact. He was actually and really a beggar for many years, wandering about the country living on the alms of the charitable.

When the eighth Earl of Menteith died in 1694, he left nothing behind him but an empty title. The Marquis of Montrose had his estates—what had been left of them; and Sir John Graham of Gartmore had his personal property—burdened with the payment of his debts, which not improbably were in excess of the value of the legacy. In these circumstances it is little wonder that candidates for the dignity of the earldom were slow in making their appearance. For fifty years no one was found to put in a public claim to the title.

But on the 12th of October, 1744, when the Scottish peers were assembled at Holyrood to make one of their elections of Representatives to the House of Lords, as the roll was being called, they were surprised to see a young man rise and answer to the name of Earl of Menteith—a call which had elicited no response for the last half-century. On the name being called, says the official record, "compeared William Graham, who answered thereto, and being asked to describe himself because that title had been for some time in abeyance and disuse of any person taking it up, he answered that he was a student of medicine in Edinburgh, and was executor confirmed to the last Earl, as would appear from an extract of the testament lying in his process before the Lords of Council and Session."[1] He therefore claimed to take the oath and declaration qualifying him to take part in the election.

There is no doubt about his pedigree; although whether it entitled him to the dignity of Earl of Menteith is another question. He was the direct descendant of Lady Elizabeth Graham, one of the three daughters of that Lord Kilpont who fell at Collace, and sister of the last Earl William. This Lady Elizabeth had married, in December, 1633, William (afterwards Sir William) Graham of Gartmore; and to them were born a son, Sir John, and a daughter, Mary. Mary Graham married James Hodge of Gladsmuir, advocate, and had a daughter, also named Mary. When Sir John Graham of Gartmore died in 1708 without issue, Mary Hodge was served next and lawful heir to her uncle, and was confirmed executrix dative to him in 1713. She married, in 1708, her cousin, William Graham, who was a younger son of Walter Graham of Gallangad. Of this marriage the claimant of the earldom was the second son. His elder brother, James, had died in the beginning of the year 1740. Although there is ground to believe that James

[1] Minutes of Evidence before Committee for Privileges in Petition of Robert Barclay-Allardice, p. 88.

regarded himself as the representative of the Earls of Menteith, he is not known to have taken any steps to assert his claim. That claim was now taken up by his brother and heir; and hence the appearance which so startled the Scottish peers at Holyrood in 1744.[1]

William Graham resembled the last known Earl in two respects. He appears to have been somewhat eccentric, and he was always in want of money. On the death of his elder brother—who died without issue—he had been confirmed executor to Sir John Graham of Gartmore, his grand-uncle; but, on the 24th of May, 1740, he renounced his interest in Gartmore to Nicol Graham, for the sum of one thousand merks wherewith to purchase "chirurgical instruments and utencils and phisicall and chirurgical books," and to maintain himself withal during his study for his profession.[2]

The step he now took was a most unfortunate one for himself. It seems to have utterly unsettled him, and rendered him unfit for work of any kind and disinclined to earn his own livelihood. Instead of becoming —as he might have become—a fairly respectable medical practitioner, he sank into the half-crazed mendicant he eventually became, claiming always his shadowy rank in the midst of beggary.

For a period of seventeen years he continued to present himself at the occasional meetings for the election of peers.

---

[1] These facts regarding the descent of the beggar Earl are taken from the Minutes of Evidence in the peerage case formerly referred to, and may be found in the print thereof, pp. 33-130.

[2] Printed Evidence, p. 83.

He attended and voted at the meetings held in October, 1744; August, 1747; March, 1749; July, 1752; November, 1752; and 5th May, 1761.[1]

Then the House of Lords took notice of his case, and summoned him to appear before a meeting of the Committee for Privileges on the 1st of March, 1762, to show by what authority and on what grounds he took upon himself the title. That meeting he did not attend. Probably he had no means to take him to London, and no one to assist, and certainly his own conviction of his rank could not have been made stronger by any favourable decision of the House of Lords. The result of his failure to attend was an order issued by the Lords on the following day, prohibiting him from using the title until his claim should be properly examined and duly allowed.[2]

He did not desist, however, from calling himself by the name he fancied he had a right to; but he went to no more meetings of peers thenceforth. Indeed, it is said that whenever such a meeting approached, he fled in disgust from the neighbourhood of Edinburgh, and betook himself to the country. His claim never, during his lifetime, was examined or allowed. He made no further effort; but he clung to the empty title, with feeble obstinacy, to the very last. Without a profession and without means, nothing was left for him but the beggar's wallet, and for several years he wandered about the country, subsisting on the contributions of old friends and neighbours. For he preferred to work the district around his native place

[1] Printed Evidence, pp. 88-90.   [2] *Ibid*, pp. 90, 91.

of Gallangad, where many must have known him and had a kindly feeling for the poor and demented old man. A witness at the peerage trial, who remembered having frequently, in his boyhood, seen him on his rounds, describes him as "a little man—a little clean man, that went about through the country. He never saw him act wrong or anyone act wrong to him. He was just a man asking charity. He went into farm houses and asked victuals, what they would give him, and into gentlemen's houses."[1]

It was in this district that he came to his melancholy end. When on one of his journeys in the summer of 1783, in the parish of Bonhill, he would appear to have become faint and left the road to lie down in a field. There, on the morning of the 30th of June, his body was found lying some twenty or thirty yards from the roadside by some workmen who were passing on their way to Bonhill. Thus died a beggar's death by the roadside one who—whether he was entitled to be Earl of Menteith or not—had, at any rate, the blood of the royal family of Scotland in his veins.

The body was carried to the parish church, and buried by the parish authorities. The "beggar Earl" was, however, saved the last indignity of a pauper's funeral, for the family of his sister, who had married an exciseman of the name of Bogle, paid the expenses incurred in his burial, amounting in all to £3 5s. 6d. The account rendered, apparently by the session clerk, who had managed the arrangements for the interment, was found in the reposi-

[1] Printed Evidence, p. 143.

tories of Mrs. Bogle, the wife of the "Earl's" nephew, and is sufficiently curious to deserve reproduction.[1]

Acct. of the Expence of William Graham Earle of Monteath's founrill, Jully th. 1st, 1783.

	£	s	d
To a coffin and mounting by John M'Allaster,	0	18	0
To creaps and dressing by Thos. M'Bean,	0	14	0
To two women dressing th. corps when brought to th. church,	0	2	6

Accot. to John Alexander.

	£	s	d
To brandie,	0	8	0
To whiskie,	0	4	8
To bread,	0	2	6
To whiskie when th. corpse was found,	0	3	4
To th. bellman, brandie and beer,	0	0	6
To diner for a man and woman, and horse hay,	0	1	6
To a shirt,	0	5	0
To th. mor. cloath,	0	4	0
To bell and grave digging,	0	1	6
	£3	5	6

Bonhill, August th. 20th,
   then received th. above in full,
      per me, JOHN ALEXANDER.

John Bogle, the exciseman who had married William Graham's sister Mary, was anxious to set up a claim to the dormant earldom for his family; but his only son, John, a miniature painter in London, was lukewarm. After the death of the latter, his sister, Mary Bogle, made some pretensions to the succession. But the claim of the Bogles was never adjudicated upon, and with the death of Miss Mary Bogle, the line of Lady Elizabeth Graham became extinct.

[1] Printed Evidence, p. 145.

SUBSEQUENT CLAIMANTS OF THE EARLDOM.

The descendants of the other sister of the eighth Earl—Lady Mary Graham—afterwards put in claims to the earldom. Robert Barclay-Allardice, of Ury and Allardice, descended from Lady Mary, who it was averred was the elder sister of Lady Elizabeth, preferred his claim to the title of Earl of Airth in 1834, and again to the earldoms of Strathern and Menteith, as well as that of Airth, in 1840. Voluminous evidence was taken in this suit, and it is from the minutes of that evidence that the particulars given above are derived.

In May, 1838, Sir William Scott of Ancrum petitioned for the dignities of Airth and Menteith as the heir of line of Walter Graham of Gallangad, and lineal representative of Sir John Graham of Kilbride, son of Malise, first Earl of Menteith. The petition was referred to the House of Lords, but no measures were taken to follow it up, and Sir William was understood to have abandoned his claim.

In 1839, still another claimant appeared for the earldom of Airth. This was Mrs. Mary Eleanor Bishop, wife of Nicholas Donnithorne Bishop, of Cross Deep Lodge, Twickenham, in the County of Middlesex. She presented a petition to the House of Lords on the 22nd of July, 1839, in which she stated that while she had no desire to assert her own right to the dignity, she was anxious to protect the interest of her grandson, James Bogle Denton Graham Matthews, the infant son of her daughter and only child. The petition was referred to the Lords' Committees for

Privileges. The claim was founded on the Bogle descent of the petitioner, but on investigation it turned out to be a bogus one. It was asserted that Mrs. Bogle, the "beggar Earl's" sister, left a son Andrew Bogle, who was father of James Andrew Bogle, father of Mrs. Bishop. It was proved, however, that Mrs. Mary Bogle had no son called Andrew, and that all her descendants were extinct.[1]

In 1870, the Barclay-Allardice claim was renewed by the daughter and heiress of the previous claimant. Opposition was offered by William Cunningham Bontine of Gartmore, who maintained that the title of Earl of Menteith was transmissible only to heirs-male, and claimed it, therefore, in right of male descent from Malise Graham, the first Earl. Neither of these claims has yet had final adjudication.

As has been mentioned already, Mr. Graham Easton has tried to make out that the right to the dignities belongs to the family of Grahams of Leitchtown, but no formal claim to them has been made on their behalf, and Mr. Easton's opinions are strongly controverted by other expert genealogists, who seem rather to favour the claims of Gartmore. The Barclay-Allardice claim assumed that the dignities were descendible through females, while the others proceed on the understanding—which, having regard to the charter of Earl Malise, seems really to be the case—that they were limited to heirs-male.

[1] Sir Harris Nicolas's History of the Earldoms of Strathern, Monteith, and Airth, 1842, p. 178.

THE LAST EARL AND THE GRAHAMS OF DUCHRAY—
FRACAS AT THE BRIDGE OF ABERFOYLE.

The account of the incident now to be narrated is taken from the records of the Privy Council. It illustrates the difficulty of serving legal writs on the Highland borders at that period. Among the neighbours with whom William, the eighth Earl, had debts and disagreements, was John Graham, laird of Duchray. The Earl had procured "letters of caption" against Duchray and his son, Thomas Graham, but for some time he found it impossible to put these into execution. No sheriff-officer was willing to enter Duchray Castle with his writs. At length, what seemed to be a favourable opportunity presented itself.

The younger Graham was to have a child baptised at the Kirk of Aberfoyle on the 13th of February, 1671, and it seemed to the Earl that, not only the father of the child, but old Duchray and the whole family would be likely enough to be present at the interesting ceremony. He resolved, therefore, to seize the opportunity for serving his letters of caption. Having collected a number of his friends and servants, and taking with them the messenger-at-arms, Alexander Muschet, he intercepted the christening party at the Bridge of Aberfoyle. Duchray seems to have had warning of the intentions of the Earl, for, in addition to the ministers and elders of Aberfoyle and the indispensable baby, he had with him a strong party of his friends and tenants, all well armed. Muschet and his attendants advanced to execute the writ, the Earl with his armed followers remaining at some little distance behind. But

when the messenger informed Duchray that he must
consider himself his prisoner, the latter defied him to lay
hand upon him, and, taking from his pocket a paper which
he alleged was a protection from the King, he shouted,
"What wad ye dar? This is all your master!" The
baby was set down on the ground, and the Duchray men,
with swords, guns, and pistols, fell fiercely on Muschet and
his satellites, and, threatening loudly that they would slay
half of them and drown the rest in the Forth, drove them
back upon the Earl and his friends. The latter at first gave
way, but quickly rallied, and a stubborn fight ensued. The
Earl himself narrowly escaped the bullets of the assailants,
and several of his servants were wounded, one of them—
by name Robert M'Farlane—having two of his fingers shot
away. At last his party was fairly driven from the field,
and turned in full flight to Inchtalla. After this little
interruption of the ceremonies of the day, it is to be hoped
that the Duchray Grahams completed the celebration of the
christening in a peaceful and Christian frame of spirit.

Duchray's "protection," as it turned out, was no protection at all against his apprehension for a debt, but a
document bearing reference to quite another matter—his
removal from certain lands. Nevertheless, it may have
served his purpose at the time by giving a certain air of
legal authority to his resistance of the officer. His own
followers were not likely to require any such pretext; they
were probably indifferent enough to any legal authority
whatever. But it may have imposed upon the minister and
elders, who, it is to be hoped, were spectators merely, and
not participants in the combat.

The Earl, foiled in this attempt at force, had again recourse to the law, and this time with greater success. Duchray was imprisoned in the Tolbooth of Edinburgh, and only released on giving sufficient caution that he would keep the peace towards the Earl of Airth and his tenants.

Two Local Legends: I.—The Butler and the Witches.

This legendary tale was taken down by the Rev. W. M'Gregor Stirling from the narration of the Rev. Dr. Macfarlane of Drymen. One of the Earls of Menteith—which one, the tale does not condescend to say—was entertaining a company of his friends in the halls of Inchtalla, when it was found that the supply of liquor was running out. Late though it was, he summoned his butler and ordered him to set off at once for Stirling, procure the necessary supply, and be back as early as possible next day. The butler immediately took his cask, and, unmooring the boat, proceeded to row himself to the shore. As he neared it he observed two "honest women" among the reeds at the margin. Watching them, he saw each cut a bulrush for herself, then crying the one to the other, "Hae wi' you, Marion Bowie!" and "Hae wi' ye, Elspa Hardie!" they mounted their bulrushes, and immediately rose sailing into the air.[1] The butler, seized with a sudden impulse,

[1] According to the testimony of the witches themselves in the Criminal Trials, "Horse and hattock!" was the usual exclamation when they mounted their bulrushes or broomsticks and rode off on their nocturnal journeys through the air; but there is no reason why "Hae wi' ye" should not have been equally effective.

also cut a bulrush, and shouting "Hae wi' ye!" found himself flying at lightning speed through the realms of space. Together they descended in the palace of the King of France, where, being invisible, they enjoyed themselves in their several ways. The butler, in some mysterious manner, never let go his cask; and finding himself in the royal cellar, he replenished it with the choicest wine. But that was not all. In case the truth of the marvellous story of adventure he had to tell might be doubted, he resolved to carry off a memento of his visit, and so laid hands on the King's own drinking cup of silver. Then, with the cup and barrel, getting astride of his bulrush again, another "Hae wi' ye!" brought him back to the servants' hall at Inchtalla, where he was found by the Earl in the morning sound asleep beside his barrel. The Earl, thinking that he had drunk too much and neglected his message, awoke him and began to reproach him with his dereliction of duty, when the butler, begging his lordship's pardon, informed him that he had got the wine, and much better wine than could be found in the burgh of Stirling. Then he told the whole story of his adventure, and in confirmation, not only pointed to the full cask, but handed over the valuable silver cup he had brought with him. The Earl believed, or affected to believe, the story, and that day entertained his guests with a wine the quality of which astonished them all. The silver cup, with the *fleur de lis* and the royal arms of France, also graced the board.

The legend does not put anything like a date to this wonderful story; but witches had a high time of it in Scotland for a long period, and they were specially rampant in the time of the wise and learned James the Sixth. Had the adventure happened in the reign of that monarch, and reached his Majesty's ears, it would have been no joke for the butler and the two "honest women." And where were the minister and Kirk Session of Port ? Or was it that the Earl was so grateful to them for having been the means of getting him out of the difficulty with his guests, that he saved them from the rebukes and punishments of the civil and ecclesiastical authorities ?

While the story is purely imaginary, it is quite possible that there may have been two reputed witches at one time in the district answering to the names of Marion Bowie and Elspeth Hardie, from whose reputation it originated. But these names are not to be found in any of the numerous accounts of trials for witchcraft. If the names, like the story, are pure invention, it must be said that they are well imagined. Elspa Hardie and Marion Bowie have the distinct flavour of witchery about them.

II.—RIVAL LONG-BOWS.

This story, at any rate, deals with two real persons— William, the eccentric last Earl of Menteith, and James Finlayson, a well-known writer or law-agent of Stirling in the latter portion of the seventeenth and beginning of the eighteenth centuries. The two seem to have been on friendly terms. They had some likings in common: both were inclined to be *bon-vivants*, and were fond of a good story. Finlayson was a reputed adept in the use of the long-bow. No one could more cleverly cap an extraordinary tale by one still more extraordinary. The Earl, too, had ambitions in that direction, and was anxious to get the better of his friend. So he bent his wits to the invention of a tale that would make Finlayson confess himself vanquished. On the occasion of the writer's next visit to Talla, the Earl enquired if he had ever heard of the wonderful sailing cherry tree. Finlayson said he had not, and desired to be told about it. He was then gravely informed that a goose had swallowed a cherry stone, that the seed had germinated and grown inside the bird, and that the goose went paddling about the lake with a full-grown cherry tree springing from her mouth, "which tree," added the veracious Earl, "can be seen at the present time bearing a full crop of ripe cherries." The visitor was duly impressed with this marvel, and owned that it would be hard to beat. Then he asked his chuckling lordship if he had ever heard of the famous shot that was made by one of Cromwell's artillerymen, when they were in garrison in the Castle of Airth. "No," said the Earl, interested at once in what happened in the old house from which he derived his title, "how was it?" "The man fired his cannon in the direction of Stirling Castle, on the battlement of which was a trumpeter, with his instrument at his lips, in the act of blowing defiance to Cromwell and all his host. The ball went straight to this mark, and lodged in the mouth of the trumpet." "And was the man killed?" asked the unsuspecting Earl. "No, indeed," said Finlayson, "he simply drew in his breath, and blew out the ball with such force that it travelled all the way back to Airth and killed the artilleryman who had fired it."

It is a tall story in every point of view. Airth is a good many miles distant from Stirling. In this contest of wits, as it has come down to us, Finlayson is always called the Town Clerk of Stirling. But he could not have been Town Clerk at the time of the encounter. He did not become so till after the Earl's death in 1694; although he had previously been associated with the actual clerk in some special pieces of business. However, he was well known in Stirling and neighbourhood, then and afterwards, as Clerk Finlayson.

Quaint Mode of Fishing for Pike.

The Lake of Menteith abounds with pike which afford exciting sport to the angler with rod and line. If we are to believe an author who wrote a century ago, the farmers in the neighbourhood, when they wanted fish as relish to their usual fare, used to resort to a rather curious method of obtaining them—in something like wholesale quantities, so to speak. They employed for the purpose of the capture their farm-yard geese. The manner in which the fishing is described seems to indicate that it was a kind of holiday sport, or engaged in at set times and with the consent and combination of the dwellers around the lake. But it will be best to let the writer tell his own tale in his own words. "The manner of catching this fish here," he says, "is somewhat novel and diverting. On the islands a number of geese are collected from the farmers who occupy the surrounding banks of the lake. After baited lines of two or three feet in length are attached to the legs of these animals, they are driven into the water. Steering naturally homeward, in different directions, the bait is soon swallowed. A violent and often tedious struggle ensues; in which, however, the geese at length prevail, though often much exhausted before they reach the shore."[1]

It is to be inferred that the owners of the geese would claim the fish landed by their respective birds. After 1694, at any rate, there was no lord of the manor resident on the islands, who could organise such fishing tournaments or lay claim to the spoils. Yet the author speaks as if this method of catching pike was common, and still practised in his time. In fact, his language encourages the inference that he had himself been an eye-witness to such a scene as he describes. On the other hand, Mr. M'Gregor Stirling, whose "Notes on Inchmahome" was published just eighteen years later than M'Nayr's "Guide," and who was himself a native of the lake-shore, affirms that he had never seen—and, until he read M'Nayr's statement, never even heard of—this method of fishing. Other natives of the district, of whom he made enquiry, reckoned it "fabulous."

Mr. Stirling, however, afterwards had the fortune to meet with an old Glasgow lady, brought up in her girlhood at Lochend, who distinctly remembered a diversion of the kind, and had herself taken part in it. From her statement it is quite clear that about the middle or the earlier part of the eighteenth century a sport resembling that

[1] A Guide from Glasgow to some of the most remarkable Scenes in the Highlands of Scotland, &c., by James M'Nayr, Glasgow, 1797, p. 55.

described by M'Nayr was occasionally practised by the family at Lochend.[1] It seems, however, to have been nothing more than a "merry diversion," possibly devised merely as a good joke by the young folks at Lochend, and certainly practised purely for amusement. It never could have been a common method of fishing, or it would have been remembered among the "farmers of the surrounding banks," of whom M'Nayr speaks. He cannot himself have seen it in the form in which he describes the process. He may have heard some account of the merry doings at Lochend, and misunderstood or misrepresented them as the usual mode of pike fishing in the lake. The touches about the neighbouring farmers collecting their geese, and the birds making their way in different directions across the lake to their own homes—thus ensuring that the whole water was fished—are probably due to a lively imagination. This same quality of imagination is not absent from M'Gregor Stirling's own account of the sport as it was described to him by Mrs. Rowan—the lady who was his authority. His description of the pike-and-goose fight is quite Homeric. It deserves quotation.

"A line, with a baited hook, was tied to the leg of a goose, which, thus accoutred, was made to swim in water of a proper depth. A boat containing a party, male and female, lord and lady fair, escorted this formidable knight-errant. By and by he falls in with an adventure. A marauding pike, taking hold of the bait, puts his mettle to the test. A combat ensues, in which, by a display on the part of both the contending heroes of much strength

[1] Then the property of the Campbells ; now belonging to Cardross.

and agility, the sympathetic hopes and fears of the anxious on-lookers are alternately called into lively exercise, until, at length, the long-necked, loud-shouting, feather-cinctured, web-footed champion, vanquishing his wide-mouthed, sharp-toothed, far-darting, scale-armed foe, drags him a prisoner in triumph."[1]

ROYAL VISITORS TO THE LAKE AND NEIGHBOURHOOD.

The more important of the royal visits to the lake and district have been referred to and discussed at greater or less length in the course of the preceding narrative, but it may be advisable to sum up these here, and to add some others of which, as yet, no notice has been taken.

The statement that King Duncan II. was slain in the Castle of Menteith in 1094 has been shown to be erroneous. Another statement made by popular writers[2] that King Edgar, who reigned from 1098 to 1107, resided frequently at Inchmahome, has no authority whatever to vouch for it.

We are on more certain ground when we come to the time of King Robert the Bruce. Three visits of that monarch to the Priory of Inchmahome—in 1306, 1308, and 1310—have already been mentioned,[3] and it is not unlikely that he may have been there oftener. There is a local tradition current that he slept in Cardross, the manor-house of Inchmahome, on the night before the

[1] Stirling's Notes on Inchmahome, p. 68.
[2] Dun's Summer at the Lake of Menteith, p. 15; Marshall's Historic Scenes in Perthshire, 1880, p. 382; and others.
[3] See *supra*, chap. v. pp. 143-145.

Battle of Bannockburn.[1] If taken quite literally, the story is impossible. Bannockburn was fought on Monday, the 24th of June, 1314. The two nights preceding that day were spent by Bruce on the field of the battle, and previously to that, he had been with his army at the Torwood, awaiting the approach of the English. Some time earlier, however, a visit from the King was not impossible, as he seems to have been resident mostly, during the assembling of his army, in the neighbourhood of Stirling—living, it is believed, chiefly in the Castle of Clackmannan.[2] But there is no record of any such visit.

It is right to add that a most interesting relic of the Bruce has long been carefully preserved at Cardross. This is a mighty sword reputed to have belonged to the hero-king, and said to have been left by him at Cardross on the occasion of one of his visits to his friend the Prior of Inchmahome—although why he should either have forgotten his sword or left it as a present to the Prior is not clearly accounted for. There can be no doubt, however, either of the antiquity or of the formidable character of this weapon. The total length of it is 6 feet $2\frac{1}{4}$ inches, while the blade alone measures 4 feet $7\frac{1}{4}$ inches; and it is no less than ten lbs. in weight. It was certainly no ordinary man that could skilfully wield a weapon like this. Whether the sword was left by the King on one of his ascertained visits to the Priory previous to the battle of Bannockburn, or at some later period of his life,

---

[1] Dun, p. 127; Hunter's Woods, Forests, and Estates of Perthshire, 1883, p. 296.

[2] Sir Herbert Maxwell's Robert the Bruce, 1897, p. 193.

the tradition does not say. The Cardross where he died was, of course, not Cardross in Menteith, but the place of the same name in Dumbartonshire, on the shore of the Firth of Clyde.

David II., the son of Robert Bruce, was a benefactor of the Priory, but there is no distinct evidence to show that he ever visited the place. The story of his marrying Margaret Logy at Inchmahome has been shown to be a mistake. David's successor, Robert II., was certainly living at Inchmahome in 1358, but he was at that time High Steward; he had not yet reached the throne.

From the time of the forfeiture of the Albanies, the Castle of Doune, in Menteith, became a royal residence, occasionally occupied by the monarchs of the Stuart line from James the First onwards. Doune Castle, with the lordship of Menteith, formed part of the dowry of the queens of James the Second, James the Third, and James the Fourth successively. The Castle was conveniently situated for the royal huntsmen enjoying their sport in the forests alike of Glenfinglas and Menteith. Many a time, no doubt, the monks of Inchmahome and the dwellers on Talla saw the royal cavalcade passing along the lake shores on its way to the forests of Duchray and Lochcon. The Chamberlains' Accounts[1] include sums for the maintenance of the Castle and its officials in the time of James the First, but there is no evidence to show that he went a hunting in the neighbourhood. He had possibly too much of sterner work to do in reducing his turbulent nobles to

[1] Exchequer Rolls, vol. iv., pp. 279-280; Chamberlain Rolls, vol. iii., pp. 551-552.

order to leave him much time to spare for that amusement; and, indeed, Glenfinglas, at any rate, was not afforested in his time. But it is certain that he and his family occasionally sojourned in the Castle of Doune. That they were there with the infant Prince James in 1431 is attested by an entry in the Exchequer Rolls.[1] After this young prince had become King (James II.), and had reached the period of his vigorous manhood, we learn—on the same authority[2]—that he recreated himself with hunting in Menteith in the intervals of his struggles with the power of the Douglases. Indeed, it was he that afforested Glenfinglas in 1454, and built the Hunt Hall there in 1458.[3]

The erection of the burgh of barony of Port in favour of the Earl Malise, in 1466, proves that James the Third had experienced the hospitality of the Earl at that place, and expected often to be there again. John le Graham was made keeper of the forest, and the Earl would no doubt aid his son in looking after the royal convenience and comfort.

On a dark night in October, 1489, James the Fourth galloped past the lake on his ride from Dunblane to Talla Moss and Gartalunane. Even had it been broad day, and James had been disposed to halt, it is not likely that the old Earl could have had any desire for a visit from his young King at that time. He was too recently from the field of Sauchie, where he had backed, with all the

[1] Exchequer Rolls, vol. iv. p. 529.
[2] *Ibid*, vol v. pp. 595, 677; vol. vi. pp. 284, 640.   [3] *Ibid*, vol. v. p. 676.

forces of Menteith, his unfortunate sovereign, James the Third. That, however, may have been forgiven, as the men of Menteith had obeyed the muster for the siege of Dumbarton Castle in 1489. But the King did not stay to visit the Earl or his fortalice. He was hurrying on to take the enemy by surprise. Neither did he disturb him on the following day, as he returned to Stirling, apparently by way of Buchlyvie and Kippen. James the Fourth was certainly at Doune Castle in April, 1490,[1] but he did not on that occasion seemingly advance further up the vale of Menteith. He was, however, hunting in Menteith in July, 1492, and again in May, 1496.[2] After his death, Queen Margaret was frequently at her dower house of Doune.

King James the Fifth, like the others of his line, was a keen hunter, and probably enjoyed the chase in the forests of Menteith. But the only recorded instance of his having been on or in the immediate neighbourhood of the Priory lands is that visit of his to Arnprior—a place whose name bears witness to its early connection with Inchmahome—narrated by Buchanan of Auchmar,[3] and retold in his interesting style by Sir Walter Scott.[4]

"Once upon a time," says Scott, "when the Court was feasting in Stirling, the King sent for some venison from the neighbouring hills. The deer was killed, and put on horses' backs to be transported to Stirling. Unluckily, they had to pass the Castle gates of Arnpryor, belonging to

[1] Lord High Treasurer's Accounts, p. 133.   [2] *Ibid*, pp. 198, 200, 274.
[3] Buchanan's History of the Family of Buchanan, 1723, p. 60.
[4] Scott's Tales of a Grandfather, First Series, chap. xxvii.

the chief of the Buchanans, who chanced to have a considerable number of guests with him. It was late, and the company were rather short of victuals, though they had more than enough of liquor. The chief, seeing so much fat venison passing his very door, seized on it; and to the expostulations of the keepers, who told him that it belonged to King James, he answered insolently that if James was King in Scotland, he, Buchanan, was King in Kippen; being the name of the district in which the Castle of Arnpryor lay. On hearing what had happened, the King got on horseback, and rode instantly from Stirling to Buchanan's house, where he found a strong fierce-looking Highlander, with an axe on his shoulder, standing sentinel at the door. This grim warder refused the King admittance, saying that the laird of Arnpryor was at dinner, and would not be disturbed. 'Yet go up to the company, my good friend,' said the King, 'and tell him that the Goodman of Ballengeich is come to feast with the King of Kippen.' The porter went grumbling into the house, and told his master that there was a fellow with a red beard at the gate who called himself the Goodman of Ballengeich, who said he was come to dine with the King of Kippen. As soon as Buchanan heard these words, he knew that the King was come in person, and hastened down to kneel at James's feet, and to ask forgiveness for his insolent behaviour. But the King, who only meant to give him a fright, forgave him freely, and, going into his castle, feasted on his own venison, which Buchanan had intercepted. Buchanan of Arnpryor was ever afterwards called the King of Kippen."

Queen Mary resided occasionally at Doune Castle. The rooms she is said to have occupied when there, in the west tower of the Castle, still bear her name. Whether she ever revisited the peaceful Isle of Inchmahome, where she spent a brief period of her infancy, has not been ascertained.[1] Perhaps she had pretty well forgotten that early episode in her life. Had she stayed on the island so long as has been generally supposed, or enjoyed so much happiness there as imaginative writers have feigned, one might suppose that, in the less happy circumstances of her maturer life, she would have been tempted—at least when living in the neighbourhood—to revisit the scene of her childish felicity. But there is no indication that such was ever the case.

James the Sixth is said to have been frequently at Doune,[2] and his visit to Cardross is a matter of constant tradition. Whether this visit was paid before he ascended the throne of England, or on the occasion of his return to his native land in 1617, is not in any account definitely stated.

One recent writer affirms that Charles I. " took his poor dejeune " at Milling Farm—on what authority the present writer does not know.[3] But that Charles II. halted at Portend in February, 1651, is certain, and the letter he addressed from that place to William, seventh Earl of Menteith, is still extant.[4]

---

[1] For a full account of Mary's residence at Inchmahome, see chapter vi. pp. 170-176.
[2] Red Book of Menteith, vol. i. p. 481.
[3] Notes on the District of Menteith by R. B. Cunninghame Graham (1895), p. 4.
[4] *Supra*, chapter xi. p. 296.

No other royal personages found their way to Menteith, until Prince Charles Edward Stuart made his appearance in the neighbourhood in "the forty-five." There is a local tradition to the effect that he either stayed for a night, or, at any rate, halted for refreshment at the Ferry Inn of Cardross, on his way to visit Buchanan of Arnprior.[1] But this tradition finds no support in the authentic annals of the expedition. On the 12th of September, Prince Charles marched from Dunblane to Doune, where he was entertained at Newton House, and "pree'd the mou'" of Miss Robina (or Clementina) Edmondston. On the following day he crossed the Forth by the Ford of Frew (or Boquhan, as it is called in some of the records), below Kippen, and proceeded to Leckie House, where he remained for the night. Again, on his return from the raid into England, he crossed the river by the same ford, on the 1st of September, 1746, and rode straight to Drummond Castle, leaving his troops quartered in Doune, Dunblane, and the neighbouring villages. These were the only occasions on which he was in the neighbourhood, and on neither was there time or opportunity for a visit to Cardross and Arnprior.[2]

The most recent royal visitors to Menteith have been our present gracious Queen Victoria and her daughter, the Princess Beatrice. In the autumn of 1869, they spent a "quiet and cosy" fortnight at Invertrossachs—the ancient Drunky—lying on the north side of the Menteith Hills,

[1] Dun's Summer at the Lake of Menteith, pp. 110 and 128 ; Marshall's Historic Scenes in Perthshire, p. 389 ; and other writers.

[2] Blaikie's Itinerary of Prince Charles Edward Stuart (Scottish History Society), 1897, pp. 13 and 38.

above Loch Vennachar. During their stay the royal party twice visited the Lake. These were private visits, without ceremony or formality, and the royalties were not disturbed by crowds of curious sightseers. The first journey was made on the 2nd of September. After passing the little Loch of Rusky and Rednock Castle, they "came," says the Queen's Journal, "upon the Loch of Menteith (the only loch in Scotland which is ever called lake.) It reminds one very much of Loch Kinnord, near Ballater, and very low blue and pink hills rise in the distance." They drove down the eastern side of the lake, past the gate of Rednock House, and Her Majesty made special note of "the very fine large trees in the park."

The second visit was on the 8th of the same month, when the drive was along the north shore of the lake, on the way to Aberfoyle and Loch Ard—with the "intenser charms" of which region the Queen seems to have been much delighted. "Here"—after passing Aberfoyle—she says, "the splendid scenery begins. . . We came upon Lochard, and a lovelier picture could not be seen. Ben Lomond, blue and yellow, rose above the lower hills, which were pink and purple with heather, and an isthmus of green trees in front dividing it from the rest of the loch. . . Certainly one of the most lovely drives I can remember, along Loch Ard, a fine long loch, with trees of all kinds overhanging the road; heather making all pink; bracken, rocks, high hills of such fine shape, and trees growing up them as in Switzerland. . . Altogether the whole drive was lovely. . . This solitude, the romance and wild loveliness of everything here, the absence of hotels and beggars, the independent, simple people, who all speak Gaelic here, all make Scotland the proudest, finest country in the world. Then there is that beautiful heather, which you cannot see elsewhere. I prefer it greatly to Switzerland, magnificent and glorious as the scenery of that country is."[1]

With this royal appreciation of the scenery of Menteith, and of the humble dwellers therein, one may be well content to leave the subject.

[1] More Leaves from Our Life in the Highlands, pp. 122, 123.

NOTES AND CORRECTIONS.

Page 3, line 22—For *Killearn*, read *Aberfoyle*.

Page 9, *note*—For *Cosmographic*, read *Cosmographie*.

Page 29, line 3—For *tobair*, read *tiobair*.

Ibid, line 5—For *stone*, read *stones*.

Page 30, second line from foot—For *of*, read *to* Inchtalla.

Page 89—In opposition to the opinion generally held that some at least of the very aged trees on Inchmahome may have been planted by the inhabitants of the Priory, there is a statement by one of the M'Curtain family reported in Ramsay's "Scotland and Scotsmen in the Eighteenth Century," vol. ii. p. 128, *note*:—"John M'Courton, whose predecessors for four generations have been gardeners in the Isle of Menteith, says it is a tradition in their family that the first of them who came to the Earl of Menteith's service, soon after the Restoration, planted the whole trees that are now in the island—there being then only a few to the south of the Priory, which have long ago been cut down."

Page 141—Leny remained an independent parish for some time after the Reformation. From 1567 to 1585 it was supplied by a reader named Salomon Buchanane—possibly a member or connection of the family that had supplied so many of the pre-Reformation vicars. But, because of the insufficiency of its revenues for the support of a minister, the parish was suppressed in January, 1615, and united to those of Callander and Port. (Fasti Eccl. Scot.)

Page 156—The bailieship of Inchmahome held by John, Lord Drummond, in 1492, is found some years later in possession of Alexander Drummond of Carnock, by whom it was disponed, previous to 31st December, 1530, to James Erskine (of Little Sauchie). This fact is instructed by an entry in the Protocol Book of John Graham, where Erskine protests that a certain arrangement made between Drummond and Sir John Stirling of Keir should not prejudice his right and interest in the office

Z

Notes and Corrections.

of bailiary of Inchmahome—"and that because the said Alexander Drummond has disponed the said office of bailiary, with the profits of the same, to the said James Erskine." The protest was taken before witnesses in the Chapter of the place of the Friars Minors, situated within the burgh of Stirling, on the 31st December, 1530. The bailiary remained with Erskine of Little Sauchie till it was resigned in favour of John, Lord Erskine, in 1562 (see page 180).

Page 166—M'Gregor Stirling, in his edition of Nimmo's History of Stirlingshire, gives the date of the (second) Buchanan lease correctly as 1531. The 1581 of the Notes on Inchmahome may therefore have been a misprint merely, but it seems to have misled Sir William Fraser.

Page 168—The Autobiography of Buchanan here referred is the short tractate printed in his collected works under the heading, *Georgii Buchanani Vita ab ipso scripta biennio ante mortem*. George Chalmers (in his Life of Ruddiman) strenuously maintains that this *Vita* was not written by Buchanan himself, but by Peter Young, his coadjutor in the tutorship of the King. He admits, however, that Young obtained his information from Buchanan.

Page 170—The reading of the Protocol on this page is taken from the transcription of Sir William Fraser as printed in the Red Book. In the Manuscript Protocol Book—which was not available at the time of writing—the reading is found to be *apud ecclesias de Port et Dolare*—which makes the matter quite clear. Port was the parish of the young lady, and Dollar that of the Earl of Argyle.

Page 179—David Erskine, Commendator of Dryburgh and Inchmahome sat in the Parliament which met at Edinburgh, 1st August, 1560, and effected the Reformation settlement (Acts of Parliaments of Scotland, vol. ii. p. 525). In a Parliament of James VI. at Edinburgh, 28th August, 1571, he was appointed member of a Commission for treating with the Queen of England (vol. iii. p. 64). On 17th September, 1571, at Stirling, he was chosen to be of the Privy Council (*Ibid*, p. 69); and he was in the *sederunt* at Edinburgh, 24th December, 1572 (*Ibid*, p. 77).

Page 186—*Den Thomas M'Lellan*. On 22nd December, 1559, Sir Thomas Maknellan, Canon of Inchmahomok, as lawful heir of Sir William Litstar, Chaplain (who was also Town Clerk of Stirling), resigned an annual rent from a house in the burgh in favour of Agnes Nicoll, relict of William Forrester. (Ramsay's Protocol Book, 1556-63.)

Notes and Corrections. 357

Page 186—The statement that Robert Short dropped out of the list of members of the Convent in 1562 must now be altered. Among the *Laing Charters*—published since this portion of the text was printed—is one, dated at Stirling Castle, 25th July, 1573, in which Commendator David, with consent of the Convent of Inchmahome, granted to George Graham of Blaircessnoch and his heirs a tack for two terms of nineteen years each of the teind sheaves of Garturs Over and Nether, Blaircessnoch, Ballemannoch, Easter Dullatur, Nether Glenny, and others, for a yearly rent of £6 13s 4d. The tack is signed by the Commendator and by *Robert Schortus*, John Baxter, James Bradfut, and William Stirvling. Short was therefore alive in July, 1573. His name does not appear on the deed of 7th September of the same year. (Laing Charters, No. 881, p. 221.)

Page 191—The same collection contains another lease of the same subjects, granted apparently on the expiry of the former one by Commendator David to Jasper Graham of Blaircessnoch. It is signed by the Commendator alone, and is dated at Cardross, 6th November, 1610. That was after David had demitted, and the Priory had been given to Henry Erskine. It appears, therefore, that David continued not only to reside at Cardross, but to manage the estate of Inchmahome till his death, which took place six months after the date of this deed. (Laing Charters, No. 1591, p. 386.)

INDEX.

ABERDEEN, Robert Erskine, Dean of, 159-69.
   Breviary of, 132.
Aberfoyle, Forest, 10, 14.
   Skirmish at, 23-6.
   Patronage of Church and Settlement of Minister, 292.
   Fracas at the Bridge, 335-7.
Abirnethe, George of, Procurator of Prior John, 150.
Abthane, Lord of, 247.
Account for Beggar Earl's burial, 332.
Achray, Loch, 1, 16, 269, *note*.
Achmore, 269, *note*.
Adam, Prior, 141; Swears fealty to Edward I., 142.
Agreement between Menteiths and Drummonds, 324-6.
Airth, William, first Earl of, 299-307.
   William, second Earl of, 307-17.
   Castle of, garrisoned by Cromwell, 303.
   Earldom of, created, 299.
   Lands apprised, 302.
   Tower and Fortalice acquired by Earl of Strathern, 297.
   Salt-pans and coal-pits, 306.
Aisle of the Priory Church, 104.
Albanies, 2, 243-52.
   Duke Robert, 243; Governor of Scotland, 244; estimates of his character, 247.
   Duke Murdach, 247; Governor, 247; made prisoner, 248; place of his arrest, 250; execution, 252.
Akyr, *le*, 272.
Alan, Earl of Menteith, 143, 146, 226, 233-4; earldom of Fife entailed in his favour, 233; captured at Methven, 233.
Alexander, Earl of Menteith, captured at Dunbar, 232; swears fealty to Edward, 232; sons left in England as hostages, 232.

Alexander, second Graham Earl, 275-277.
Anderson's (Robert) Statements Regarding George Buchanan, 165-7.
Andrew, Prior, 157, 158, 177.
Approach to Vault, 116.
Ard, Loch, 1, 70, 354.
Ardenclericht, 180, 194.
Ardmach—see *Arnmauk*.
Ardoch, Camp and Chapel, 187.
Ardvoirlich, Stewart of, 318-22.
Argyle, Earl of, hereditary Justice General, 293.
   Archibald, Earl of, 170.
Arnbeg, 193.
Arnchly, 47, 141.
Arnevicar, 180, 194.
Arniclerycht, 157.
Arnmawk, 73.
   Traditional story, 52.
   Colonel Erskine in hiding at, 54, 194.
Arnprior, Mill of, 180, 194.
Arran and Knapdale, 261.
   Earl of, band with Earl of Menteith, 276.
Arrot of Arrot, George, 162.
Arthuile, Master William, 150.
Auchveity, Tradition of, 46.
Auchyle, Cliffs of, 15, 17.
Augustinians (Canons Regular), settlements in Scone, Cambuskenneth, Inchmahome, 133-4.
   Dress, 138-9.

BAD, Dene James, 158, 176, 177, 279.
Baleth, 269, *note*.
Balfour, George, 291.
Ballingrew, 180, 193, 194.
Ballintoun, 190.
Balloch (Bulloch), 227.
Balquhidder, Braes of, 16.
Banished Lords, the, 190.
Banks, Lands of, 156.
Bannock, Whummle the, 265.

Index.

Bannockburn, Sir John Menteith at, 260.
   Robert Bruce at, 34.
Barclay-Allardice claim to the earldoms, 333-4.
Bathok, Patrick, 180.
Baxter, Dene Alan, 180.
   Dene John, 180, 181, 186, 187, 189.
Bede, The Venerable, 58 and *note*.
Beggar Earl, the, 327-32.
Bell, John of Antermony, 37.
   Patrick, minister of Port, 34, 36.
   H. Glassford, on Queen Mary at Inchmahome, 143-5.
Bellenden, 9.
Bell-tower, 104.
Ben-dhu, Ben-dearg, 14, 15; Ben Arthur, Ben Chonzie, Ben Gullipen, Ben Ledi, Ben Lomond, Ben Venue, Ben Voirlich, 16.
Bishop of Glasgow, William, 136.
   Dunkeld, Galfred, 136.
   Dunblane, Clement, 136, *note*, 138.
Bishop, Mrs, claims earldom for her grandson, 353.
Blaircessnock, 180, 194.
Blairhoyle or Leitchtown, 65.
Blareboyane, 269, *note*.
Blaretuchane, 269, *note*.
Blareuscanys, 269, *note*.
Blind Harry's story of the Capture of Wallace, 257.
Bobfresle, 269, *note*.
Boece, Hector, 8, 11.
Bogle family, the, 331-2.
Band to support the claim of Bruce, 253.
Boquhapple, Chapel of, 141.
Borland, 179, 193, 194.
Borrow-banks, 155.
Bovento, 269, *note*.
Bowie, Marion, witch, 337.
Bradfute, Dene James, Sub-Prior, 158, 176, 177, 180, 181, 186, 187, 189, 190.
Bretagne, Sir John de, Guardian of Scotland, 256.
Bretches or Hoards, traces of at Talla, 207-8.
Brew-house of Talla, 211.
Brigend, 269, *note*.
Bright Sword, John with the, 274.
Brown, Dr John, on the Teith, 5; the Lake, 69; Queen Mary's Bower, 86; the Queen at Inchmahome, 173.

Bruce, Lord of Annandale, 253.
   Edward, Irish Expedition, 260.
   Dame Catherine, wife of last Earl of Menteith, 116, 314-7.
   King Robert, his visits to Inchmahome, 153-5, 344; his sword at Cardross, 345-6.
Buchan, David, Earl of, 195, 201.
Buchanan, George, of Buchanan, 287.
   Dene Gilbert, 154.
   Margaret, wife of Earl Alexander, 277.
   Robert, of Leny, 154.
   George, his account of Menteith, 10, 11; his connection with Cardross, 165-9; his house in Castle Wynd, Stirling, the Prior's Manse, 185-6.
Burgh, Richard de, Earl of Ulster, 253.
Burial-vault on Inchmahome, 111, 114-6.
Butler and the Witches, the story of the, 337-9.

Caledonian Forest, 9, 10.
Callander, 2.
Calquhollat, 156.
Cambuskenneth, resigned by Adam Erskine, 197.
Campbells of Argyle in alliance with Menteiths, 324.
Campbell, Sir Colin of Lundie, 291.
   Duncan of Glenorchy, 288.
   Gillespie and Colin, 326.
   Sir John of Glenorchy, 303, 307.
   Mary, wife of Earl John, 206.
Cardross—Estate and Mansion, 54.
   Mains of, 179, 180.
   Bailie of Barony, 157, 180, 193.
   Mill of, 180, 194.
   Lordship of, 192, 194, 197.
   Manor Place, 195.
   Residence of Commendators, 190.
   House—Enlarged by David Erskine, by Earl of Mar, 197; occupied by General Monck, 199, and by Royalist troops, 197, 200.
   Lord David, 198.
   Lord Henry, his persecutions, 199.
   David, fourth Lord, 201.
   Lady, 191.
Carrick, Earl of, 304.
Chapel-larach, 141.
Chapels dependent on Priory, 32, 47, 59, 141.
Chapter House, 107, 115.

Index. 361

Charles I. and Earl of Airth, 293-302; at Holyrood, 299; at Milling, 350.
Charles II. at Portend, 44, 350; acknowledges his father's debts to the Earl, 296.
Charles, Prince, in Menteith, 351.
Charter-chest at Talla, 292.
Cheese of Menteith, 10.
Choir of Church, 108; Monuments in, 121.
Christin, Prior, 145-9.
Churches belonging to Priory, 141.
Claimants of the Earldom, 333-4.
Clare, Sir Thomas de, 253.
Clement, Bishop of Dunblane, 136, *note*.
Clerkum, 194.
Cloisters, 111.
Cnoc-nan-bocan, 53.
Coldon, 43, 276.
Colkitto, 321.
Collatta, 156.
Collouth, 155.
Colman (Colmoc), 40, 74, 76, 130-2.
Commendators—Robert Erskine, 159-69.
  John Erskine, 169-78.
  David Erskine, 178-91.
  Henry Stewart, 189.
  Henry Erskine, 191-2.
Comrie, hills of, 16.
Comyn, Walter, Earl of Menteith, builds the Priory, 137-8; sketch of his career, 219-224.
  Regent, defeated at Stirling, 255.
Con, Loch, 5.
  Forest of, 269, *note*.
Conaeus, Georgius, his Life of Queen Mary, 174.
Conjurer, story of Earl of Mar and the, 195.
Conventual day, 139.
Countess of Airth, her unfortunate speculations, 303-6.
Countess Mary of Menteith, 325.
Covenant, signing of the National, 301.
Cragannet, Banks of, 177.
Cragingelt, Rev. John, 292.
Craguthy, Easter and Wester, 269, *note*.
Craig of Port, 17.
Crancafy, 269, *note*.
Cravaneculy, 269, *note*.
Craynes, Easter and Wester, 269, *note*.
Crichton, Lord, of Sanquhar, 287.
Cristisone, Dene Adam, 158, 176, 177.
Crockmelly, 20.
Cross at Port, 32.

Culdee Churches at Dunblane and Inchmahome, 133.
Culyngarth, 269, *note*.
Cup-marked stone at Milling, 47-8.
Cunningham-Bontine claims Earldom, 334.

Dangaud, J. M.—Childhood of Queen Mary, 172-3.
David II.—Grant to Priory, 148; marriage to Margaret Logy, 147, 346.
David, Lord Cardross, 198.
David, Prior, 153-7.
Deforcement of the Sheriff of Perth, 147.
Dog, Sir Thomas, Prior, 150; deposed, 151.
Domestic arrangements of last Earl of Menteith, 314.
Domestic crafts at Talla, 214.
Donald the Hammerer at Tobanareal, 27, 59.
Donaldson, Rev. James, minister of Port, 33, 35-6.
Doorway of the Priory, 103.
Dormitory, 118, 121.
Dougall, Andrew, reader at Port, 34.
Douglas, Earl of, tried for death of Rothesay, 241.
  Margaret, wife of Earl William, 287.
Doune Castle, 2, 346-8, 350.
Downans, 269, *note*.
Drinking on Sundays, 33-4.
Dromore, Colman, Bishop of, 132.
Drumannet, 269, *note*.
Drumboy, 269, *note*.
Drumlaen, 269, *note*.
Drummaniklocht, 157, 180, 194.
Drummond, Brice of Boquhapple, 324.
  John of Concraig, 238.
  John, 324-6.
  Sir John, monument, 126, 146.
  John, Lord, disputes with Prior, 155.
  Lord, at Tillymoss, 51.
  Sir Malcolm, 128; gift to the Priory, 145.
  Maurice, 325.
  Barony of (Drymen), 297.
Drummonds and Menteiths, feud, 323-6.
Drury, Sir William, letter to Lord Burghley, 178.
Dryburgh Abbey, 191, 192, 197, 200.
  Lady, 191, 194.
Drymen, House of, burned, 303.
Drysdail, Mr. Alexander, vicar of Lany, 181.

Index.

Duchray, Graham of, 65.
  Glencairn's Rising, 20, 23.
  Quarrel with Earl of Menteith, 335-7.
  Forest of, 271.
Dugall, Arthur, a Kippen Covenanter, 307.
Dumbarton, 195.
  Castle and Sheriffdom, 256, 258.
  Alleged Treachery of Menteith, 259.
Dun, Erskine of, 162, 164.
Dun, Michael, gives infeftment to Earl Alexander, 276.
Dunbar, Earl of, 253.
Duncan II., murder of, 11, 344.
Dupplin, battle of, 235.

EARLDOM of Menteith, divided between Stewart and Comyn, 225; confiscated by James I., 252; erected of new, 268.
Earls of Menteith—see Menteith.
Earls' Residences, 203; Stables, 45.
Earth-dogs—Earl of Menteith.'s, 99.
  Laird of Glenorchy's, 99, *note*.
Eas-gobhain, 5, 16.
Easter Isle, 116, *note*.
Edgar, King, 134, 344.
Edmonstone, John, M.A., 150.
  William and Archibald, 62.
  William of Duntreath, 150.
Edward I. of England, and Capture of Wallace, 263.
Eglinton, Hugh, Earl of, 287.
Elphinstone, Michael, 190.
  James and George, 291.
Eric, King of Norway—Marriage to Princess Margaret, 229.
Ernchome, 277.
Ernecomy, 269, *note*.
Ernetly, 269, *note*.
Erngobil, 279.
Ernoml, 269, *note*.
Erskines of Cardross, 201.
Erskine, Admiral, 57.
  David, Commendator, 62, 178-191.
  Henry, Commendator, 191-192.
  Fiar of Cardross, 198.
  Henry David, of Cardross, 201.
  Hon. John (the Black Colonel), 57, 201.
  John of Dun, 162, 164.
  John, Commendator, 165, 169-176; Master of E.
  Lord E., Earl of Mar, Regent, 169-170; receives pension from Inchmahome and Dryburgh, 180.

Erskine, John, D.D., of Carnock, 201.
  John of Carnock obtains Cardross, 201.
  James of Little Sauchy, Bailie of Cardross, 180.
  James, first Erskine of Cardross, 201.
  Lord, Queen Mary's keeper, 171.
  Robert, Rector of Glenbervy, Commendator of Inchmahome, Dean of Aberdeen, 159-169.
  Robert, Master of Erskine, identified by Fraser with the Commendator, 160.
  Thomas, Commendator of Dryburgh, 169 and *note*.
  Sir Thomas of Halton, 161, 162, 163.

FAIR, St. Michael's, 32.
Ferguson, Rev. John, minister of Port, 37.
Ferries to Inchmahome and Inchtalla, 30.
Feuds—Grahams and Leckies, 287-8.
  Menteiths and Drummonds, 323-6.
Fiar of Cardross, 198.
Fife, Earldom of, 133, 240.
Finlayson, James, Town Clerk of Stirling, 339-40.
Fintry Hills, 16.
Forbes, Rev. Arthur, minister of Port, 37.
Forester, Duncan, 153.
  William—teinds of Row, 151.
Forests, Royal, in Aberfoyle and Glenfinglas, 9, 31.
Forrester, Lord, 304.
Fraser, Sir Symon, 256.
Frisefieware, 269, *note*.
Furnishings of House of Talla, 309.

GALBRAITH, Thomas, 51.
Galfrid, Bishop of Dunkeld, 136.
Galloway, Earl of, 304.
  Expedition of Wallace to, 254.
Gallows Hill, 45.
Garbh-uisge, 5.
Garden, 194.
Gardens of the Monastery and of the Earls, 77, 78.
Garlies, Lord, 304, 307.
Garquhat, 269, *note*.
Gartalunane, 51, 347.
Gartavertyne, 189.
Gartincaber, 190.
Gartinhagel, 269, *note*.
Gartladerland, Gartladernick, Gartcledeny, 167, 194, *note*.

Index. 363

Gartmore, 278.
Gartmulne, 269, *note*.
Gartnerthynach, 269, *note*.
Gartur, 54.
  Over and Nether, 180, 194.
Gateside Ferry, 31, 44.
Gateway of the Burial Place, 117.
Gilchrist, Earl, 217.
Glasgow, William, Bishop of, 136.
Glassachoile-Cheese, 314.
Glassart and Milton—Woods cut down, 303.
Glassel, 289, *note*.
Glasswerde, Lands of, 269, *note*.
Glenbervy, Rector of — *vide* Robert Erskine.
Glencairn, Earl of, his Rising, 20.
Glenfinglas, Forest of, 10, 31, 271.
Glenny, Skirmish at, 22.
  The Pass and its Traditions, 26.
Glenorchy's Earth-dogs, 99, *note*.
Goodie, Gudy, Guidi—Loch and Water, 58.
  Ward of, 180, 194.
  Bede's Pictish town, 58.
Goose with the cherry tree, 340.
Goose and pike fight, 343.
Graham, Rev. Dr., of Aberfoyle, 3, 5, 75.
Grahams of Duchray—Alexander, 7, 118.
  John, his quarrel with the Earl of Airth, 335-7.
  Thomas, younger of, 335.
Graham, Alexander, son of Earl Malise, 273.
  Anne, wife of Sir Mungo Murray, 307.
  Archibald, 307.
  Charles, 307.
  Christian, wife of Sir W. Livingstone, 278 and *note*.
  Christian, wife of Sir John Blackadder, 289.
  George, of Rednock, 62; tutor of Menteith, 288.
  Euphame, 275.
  Helen, daughter of Sir James, 306, 308-12.
  Sir James, Governor of Dundalk, 306; negotiations for marriage of his daughter and succession to the earldom, 310-12.
  Jean, 307.
  Sir John, of Gartmore, 116, 328.
  Sir John, Earl of Menteith, 235-7.

Graham, John with the Bright Sword, 272-5.
  John of Claverhouse—Compliments Earl of Airth, 308; proposes to marry Helen Graham, 310; correspondence with the Earl, 312.
  Margaret, 170.
  Margaret, married to Earl of Argyle, 278.
  Margaret, wife of Lord Garlies, 307.
  Mary, wife of Sir John Campbell of Glenorchy, 307.
  Nicol, 329.
  Patrick, son of Earl Malise, 273.
  Patrick, son of seventh Earl, 307.
  Robert, vicar of Drummond, 160.
  Robert, son of seventh Earl, 307.
  Robert of Gartmore, 278.
  Walter, son of Earl Alexander, 165.
  Walter of Gartur, 277.
  Walter of Gallangad, 328.
  Walter of Glenny, 302.
  William of Gartmore, 328.
  William, the Beggar Earl, 327-32.
Grahams of the Borders, 274.
  Feud with the Leckies, 287.
  Earls of Menteith—*vide* Menteith.
Gray, Lady Agnes, wife of William, seventh Earl, 291.
Gregor, Robbers of Clan, 277, *note*.
Grey, Lord, 176.

HALDANE, John of Gleneagles—Transactions with Teinds of Leny and Kilmadock, 153, 154, 155.
  Margaret, widow of Commendator David, 191.
  of Gleneagles, 261.
Haliburton, Ralph de, engaged in search for Wallace, 257.
Hall of Talla, 209-11.
Hammerer, Donald the, incursion into Menteith and fight with the Grahams, 27, 59, 281-4.
Hardie, Elspet, witch, 337.
Hastings, Sir Edmund, obtains Comyn portion of Earldom, 225.
  Sir John, obtains Stewart part of Earldom, 227.
Henderson, Rev. Thomas, minister of Port, 35.
Henry III. of England, 8.
Henry, Abbot of Cambuskenneth, factor for Prior of Inchmahome, 154.

Index.

Henry the Minstrel—Wallace and Menteith, 263 *et seqq.*
Hewes, Anna, wife of last Earl—her divorce, 314.
High House of Talla, 205-8.
Hills of Menteith, 14 *et seqq.*
Hilltown of Cardross, 167, 194.
Hoardings or Bretèches, traces of, at Talla, 207-8.
Hodge, James of Gladsmuir—Mary, 328.
Holyrood, meeting of Peers in 1744, 327-8.
Hornahic, 180, 194.
Horseman's Rock, 22.
Hume, Sir Patrick of Argaty, 61.
   David, 62, 187.
Hutchison, Robert of Carlowrie—report on trees on Inchmahome, 90.
Hutton, Canon John, 158, 165, 176, 177.

INCH-CUAN, Dog Isle, 99, 100.
Inchere, 260, *note.*
Inchie, Chapel at, 59, 141.
Inchmahome — origin, meaning, and various forms of name, 74-6.
   Description of Island, 77-92.
   Priory, site and description, 101-129.
   Writ of foundation of Monastery, 136.
Inchmurdach, 148.
Insche, 209, *note.*
Inventories, furnishings of Talla House, 209 *et seqq.*
   Earl William's (seventh Earl), Charters, 292.
Irving, Dr. David, statement regarding George Buchanan at Cardross, 166.
Isabella, Countess of Menteith, marriage to Sir John Russell and subsequent history, 222.
   the younger, wife of Sir John Comyn, 224.
Isle of my Rest—a misinterpretation, 75.

JAMES I., 2; prisoner, 244; negotiations for release, 246; coronation, 249; arrests and executes the Albanies, 249-50; death, 252; at Doune, 347.
James II., 347.
James III.—Makes Port a burgh of barony, 31, 270, 347.
James IV., at Tillymoss, 51, 347; at Doune, 348.

James V., story of the King of Kippen, 348-9.
James VI., letter about terriers, 99; coronation, 286; Earl of Mar's marriage, 196; visit to Cardross, 197, 350.
Jebb, Samuel—his History of Queen Mary, 174.
Jonet, Lady, wife of Earl Malise, 271; her husband's gift, 272.
John, Prior, and his rival, Thomas, 149-50.
Johnston, Rev. J. J., minister of Port, 39.
Justiciar of Menteith, appointment of, 293.

KATHERINE, Lady, her bequests, 214.
Katrine, Loch, 1, 16.
Keir, Laird of, 303.
Keith, Lady May, wife of Lord Kilpont, 317.
Keps, 194.
Kidd, Colonel, at Glenny, 23.
Kilbryde, John of, 274; house, 206; house sold, 302.
Kilmadock, 2.
   Parish of, 190, 155.
   Church and chapels, 141, 195.
   Teinds, 154.
Kilpont, Lord—burial place, 111, 115; thanked by Charles I., 302; death, 306, 317-22.
Kincardine, 2.
Kinloch, John—tenement, 182.
Kinross, Malcolm—tenement in Castle Wynd, Stirling, 182.
Kippen, 2.
   James IV. at, 51.
   Church of, 123.
   Drums of, 193.
   King of, 348-9.
Kirktoun of Aberfoyle, 277.
Kitchen—of the Monastery, 118; of Talla, 208.

LADARDR, 260, *note.*
Lanark (Lanrick), 190.
Langside, battle of, 236.
Langtoft, story of the capture of Wallace, 256.
Largs, battle of, 228.
Lauder, Sir Robert, 261.
Law-tree at Port of Menteith, 32.
Leckies—feud with the Grahams, 287-3.

Index. 365

Lennox, Earldom of, given to Sir John Menteith, 258.
Leny, Teinds of, 154.
   Kirklands of, 194.
   Kirk of, 195.
Lenchris, Church of, 152.
Linlithgow, Earl of, 297, 305.
Livingston, William, and the Countess of Airth, 306.
Lochcon, Forest of, 269, *note*.
Logy, Sir John, 148.
   Margaret, married to David II., 147.
Lonanys, 269, *note*.
Lord of Menteith—Walter Stewart, 240.

MACANRER, Loch, tradition regarding, 46.
Macaulay of Erngabil and Gartmore, 279.
M'Corranestoun, 190.
M'Curtains, hereditary gardeners, 78.
M'Gibbon of Blairhoyle, 65.
M'Gregor, brother of Gilderoy, captured, 301.
M'Kessons in Rednock, 61.
Mackie, Charles—Queen Mary at Inchmahome, 174.
Maclellan, Dene Thomas, 158, 176, 177, 180, 181.
M'Nayr's Guide—mode of fishing, 342-3.
M'Queen's Pass, 21.
Maiden of Norway, 229.
Maistertoun, Elizabeth, lease to, 157.
Major, John—Intimacy of Wallace and Menteith, 263.
Malcolm, Parson of Insula Macholem, 133.
Malcolm, Earl of Lennox, 144.
Malise, Earl of Stratherne, 143.
Manse of the Priors in Stirling, 195.
Maolpeder, Macpender, 11.
Mar, John, Earl of, marriage and family, 195-6.
   Thomas, Earl of, 238.
Marduffy, lands of, 269, *note*.
Margaret, Princess—Marriage and coronation, 228-9.
   Lady, her four marriages, 237-9.
Mariota, second wife of Earl Malise, 272.
Marriage Contract of last Earl, 316.
Martyrologies of Aberdeen and Augus, 132.

Mary, daughter of Earl Maurice and wife of Walter Stewart—marriage, 224; death, 230; monument, 123, 132, 231.
Mary of Lorraine, Queen Dowager of James V., 159.
Mary, Countess of Menteith, marries Sir John Graham, 235.
Masar, le, 213, 272.
Matilda, wife of Earl Alexander, 123.
Maurice, Prior, receives Robert Bruce at Inchmahome, 143.
Maurice, senior and junior — Earls, 217-9.
Meikleour Writs, 177, 181.
Memorial of Scottish Nobles to Pope, 261.
Menteith—District, earldom, stewartry, 1-3, 13.
   Derivation, meaning, and varied forms of the name, 6-8.
   References by early writers, 9-18.
   Hills and their traditions, 13-29.
   Vale of, 16.
   Huntings in, 9, 10.
   Lake of, 67-100.
   Lands of later earldom of, 268-9.
   Residences of Earls of, 216.
   Mormaers, 216.
Menteith Earls—early Earls: Gilchrist, 217.
   Muretach, 217.
   Maurices, 217-9.
   Walter Comyn, 219-24.
   Walter Stewart, 224-31.
   Alexander, 231-3.
   Alan, 233-4.
   Murdach, 234-5.
   Sir John Graham, 235-7.
   Countess Mary, 237-9.
   Robert Stewart—Earl of Fife, Duke of Albany, 237-47.
   Murdach, Duke of Albany, 247-53.
   Graham Earls—Malise, 268-75.
   Alexander, 275-7.
   William, 278-84.
   John, 284-6.
   William, 286-8.
   John, 288-9.
   William, Earl of Stratheru, Earl of Airth, 290-307.
   William, Earl of Airth, 307-17.
Menteith, Alexander, of Rusky, 324-325.
   Alexander in Polmont Mill, 176.

366 Index.

Menteith, Agnes, co-heiress of Rusky, 261.
   Maister David, 156.
   Elizabeth, co-heiress of Rusky, 262.
   John of Menteith, 60.
   John in Rednock, 61.
   Sir John, 253-67.
   James, 61.
   Malcolm, of Rusky, 324-5.
   Dene Patrick, 156.
   Walter, son of Sir John, 146.
   Walter, of Rusky, 325.
   William, Master of Menteith, 166.
   William, of Rusky, 325.
   Lord of (Robert Stewart), 240-1.
   Menteiths of Rednock, 18, 60.
   Menteiths and Drummonds, 323-6.
Mercer, Laurence of Meiklecour, 177.
Mercurius Politicus, extracts from, 24, 25.
Meyners, Sir Alexander, 255.
Michael, Fair of St., 32, 45, 128.
Milling, Fair, 32, 45.
   Cup-marked stone, 47-8.
Milton of Aberfoyle, lands of, 277.
Monachedin, Mondynes, 12 and *note*.
Mondhui, lands of, wadset, 302.
Mont, Dene John, 158, 176, 177.
Montrose, Earl, 293.
   Marquis, 311 *et seqq.*
Monuments in Choir of Church—Earl Walter and Lady, 123.
   Sir John Drummond, 126.
   Others, 128-9.
Monybrachys, 269 *note*.
Moray—Sir John, 238.
   Walter of, 325.
Moss, birthplace of Buchanan, 165.
Mowbray, Sir John, sent to take Wallace, 256.
   Margaret, wife of William, Master and Earl of Menteith, 165, 277-8.
Murdach, Earl, 234-5.
Murdochstoun, 190.
Muretach, Earl, 217.
Muriella, wife of Duke of Albany, 242.
Murray, Sir Mungo, 199, 307.
Muschett, Alexander, messenger-at-arms, 335.
My Lord's Chamber, 211.

NAPIER of Merchiston, 262.
Neven, Duncan, schoolmaster of Dunblane, 190.

Neville's Cross, battle of, 236.
Newcastle, truce of, 261.
Newton of Doune, 180.
Nobles, Scottish, in the War of Independence, 264.
Nomenclature, local, 2.
Nunnery, 118.
Nuns' Walk and Nuns' Hill, 78, 81.

OCHTERTYRE, 3.
   Ramsay, John of, 355.
Ogilvy, Sir James, of Ernby, 152.
Oliphant, Allan, 180.

PARLIAMENT, riding the, 309.
Peace Stone, 47.
Peblis, Dene Adam, 158, 176, 177.
Pensions and promises of Charles I., 294-7.
Perth, Sheriff of, representatives deforced by Prior, 147.
   Earl of, 297.
Piper's House and Strand, 45.
Plate of Earl William claimed by Keir, 213.
Polder, West and East, 194.
Pollox, John de, confiscated, 145.
Popes—Gregory IX., 136.
   Gregory X., 142.
   Paul III., 169, *note*.
   Paul IV., 178.
   Clement VI., 238.
   Innocent VI., 238-9.
Port of Menteith, 2, 30.
   Made a burgh, 31, 270.
   Church, 32, 39, 170, 195.
   Kirk Session Records, 33-4.
   Ministers from Reformation, 34-9.
   Lands of, 40, 43, 141, 269 *notes*.
   Kirklands, 194.
Portend, 30, 40; Charles II. at, 43; burn, 19.
Princess Margaret, marriage and coronation of, 228-9.
Princess Beatrice in Menteith, 352-3.
Pringle, Dene Duncan, 158, 177.
Priors of Inchmahome—Adam, 141.
   Maurice, 142-5.
   Christin, 145-9.
   John, 149.
   Thomas Dog (Doig), 149-50.
   Alexander Ruch (Rough), 151-3.
   David, 153-7.
   Andrew, 157-8.
   Disputes regarding Priorate, 150-1.

Index.   867

Priors' Chamber, 116.
Priors' Manse in Stirling, 181-6.
Priors' Meadow, 40, 194.
Priory—Valuation by Bagimont's Roll, 142.
   Church described, 103-29.
   Marriage of Earl of Argyle at, 170.

QUEEN, Mary, of Scots—Memorials at Inchmahome, 82-9; residence there, 170-6; bed-chamber at the Monastery, 116; chamber at Doune Castle, 350; demission, 286.
   Mary of Lorraine, 159; at Doune, 350.
   Victoria—visit to Menteith, 352-3.

RAMSAY, Robert, minister of Port, 36.
   Robert, notary, Stirling, 182.
Randolph, Earl of Moray, 261.
Read, Colonel, at Aberfoyle and Glenny, 245.
Rednock—Castle, 59; estate, 60-5.
Refectory of Monastery, 121.
Robert II., 147, 346.
Robert III., 243, 244.
Robertson, Rev. Dr., of Callander—Derivation of Teith, 3.
   Colonel, 4.
Rose with the Cragmuk, 269, *note*.
Rosneath, 325.
Rothesay, Duke of, 243-4.
Row—Wester, 180; teinds of, 151, 197.
Ruch, Sir Alexander, Prior, 151-3.
   David, Procurator for Prior, 151.
   John, Vicar of Garioch, 152.
Ruskie, 251, 257.
   Loch, 18.
   Castle, 18, 19.
   Fight at Tar, 61, 66, 265, 324.
Russell, Sir John, husband of Countess Isabella, 223-4.

SACRISTY of Church, 107.
St. Andrews, 259.
   Bishop of, 261.
St. Colman (Colmock), 74, 76, 128, 130.
St. Michael, effigy on monument, 128.
Savnach, 269, *note*.
Schaughill, 269, *note*.
Schort, Dene Robert, 180, 181.
Scot, Sir John, of Scotstarvet—True Relation, 298.
Scott, Sir Walter, 4, 28, 257, 265, 281, 319, 348.

Scott, Sir William, of Ancrum, claims earldom, 383.
Seal of the Priory, 131, *note*.
Session Records, lost and recovered, 33, 37.
Seton, James, of Tullibody, 186.
   Marion, widow of Earl John, 286.
Seytoun, Rev. James, minister of Port, 35.
Shirgarton, 193.
Short, Jack, Wallace's man, 256.
Silverplate, Earl of Airth's, 302.
Sinclair, William, of the Banks, 177.
   William, of the Camp, 187.
Somerset, Duke of, 176.
Spittals, 155.
Spittaltoun, 156.
Stables, Earl's, 45.
Stair, Master of—Letter to Earl of Airth, 312.
Stewarts of Appin, 281-4.
Stewart Earls—*vide* Menteith.
Stewart, Alexander, son of Duke Murdach, 249, 250.
   Andro, lease to, 157.
   Henry, Commendator, 189.
   Isabella, daughter of Duke of Albany, 252.
   James, son of Duke Murdach, 249, 250.
   James, of Ardvoirlich—death of Lord Kilpont, 316-22.
   Lady Mary, Countess of Mar, 195.
   Prince Charles Edward in Menteith, 351.
   Robert, the High Steward, 147.
   Walter, son of Duke Murdach, 249, 250.
   Sir William, of Dalswinton, 275.
Stirling—Town, 195; Prior's manse in, 181-6.
   Elizabeth, 187.
   Robert, minister of Port, 37.
   William, minister of Port, 35.
   William, reader, 34.
   Dene William, Canon of Inchmahome, 180, 186, 187, 189, 190.
   Rev. W. Macgregor, minister of Port, 38; his works, 38; his interpretation of Inchmahome, 75, 77; reference to his Notes, *passim*.
Strathern, Earldom of, 297, 298.
Strickland, Miss, on Queen Mary at Inchmahome, 173.

Index

TALLA, the Island, 92-6.
    The buildings on, 202-13.
    Household arrangements at, in time of last Earl, 314-16.
Tar of Rusky, 61, 66, 261, 265, 267, 324.
Teith, the river and the name, 3-5.
Tereochane, 269, *note*.
Thaich, district, 56.
Thirds, the Commendator's, 187-8.
Thom and Lanarkine, 146.
Thomson, Canon James, 158, 165, 177.
Tibbermuir, Battle of, 318.
Tilly Moss (Talla), battle, 51, 347.
Tobanareal, Tipardnerheil, name and site, 28.
    Cairn at, 29.
    Earl William's death at, 27.
    Legendary and historical accounts of the fight, 279-84.
Tom-a-mhoid, 57.
Trees on Inchmahome, 89.
Trumpeter of Stirling, story of the, 340.
Tulliallan, Lord, 304.
Turnberry Castle, 253.
Turner, Rev. Dr., minister of Port, 30.
Tyeper's path, 27.

UAM-VAR, 16.
Ulster, Earl of, 259.

VAULT, the, 111, 114-5.
Vennachar, 1, 16.
Visitors, royal, 344-53.

WALLACE—Expedition into Galloway, 254; capture, 256-8.
Wardrobe of Talla, 211; of last Earl, 213.
Wat Dog's town, 155.
Wat Smith's town, 155.
Wemyss, Earl of, 309.
Whummle the bannock, 265.
Will of last Earl, 215.
Wishart, chaplain of Montrose—Account of Kilpont's death, 319-20.
    John, correspondent of Earl of Airth, 301.
Witches in Menteith, 337-9.
Wylie, William, minister of Port, 39.

YLE, 92.
Youngar, Dene John, 176, 177.
Youngman, Canon John, 158, 165, 170, 177, 278.

www.ingramcontent.com/pod-product-compliance
Lightning Source LLC
Chambersburg PA
CBHW020741020526
44115CB00030B/732